Film Studies in China 2

Film Studies in China 2

Selected Writings from *Contemporary Cinema*

Bristol, UK / Chicago, USA

First published in the UK in 2020 by
Intellect, The Mill, Parnall Road, Fishponds, Bristol, BS16 3JG, UK

First published in the USA in 2020 by
Intellect, The University of Chicago Press, 1427 E. 60th Street,
Chicago, IL 60637, USA

Copyright © 2020 Intellect Ltd

All rights reserved. No part of this publication may be reproduced, stored in a retrieval system, or transmitted, in any form or by any means, electronic, mechanical, photocopying, recording, or otherwise, without written permission.

A catalogue record for this book is available from the British Library.

Copy editor: MPS Technologies
Cover designer: Aleksandra Szumlas
Production manager: Jessica Lovett
Typesetting: Contentra Technologies
Translated by: Chase Coulson Christensen

Print ISBN 9781789381627
ePDF ISBN 9781789381634
ePUB ISBN 9781789381641

Printed and bound by Short Run Press.

To find out about all our publications, please visit
www.intellectbooks.com.
There, you can subscribe to our e-newsletter,
browse or download our current catalogue,
and buy any titles that are in print.

Contents

SECTION I: INDUSTRY	1

1. On Chinese Film Industrial Trade Structure and Its Internationalized Strategic Path 2
   张宏/Zhang Hong

2. On the Differentiation Strategies of Four Internet Film Production Companies 13
   胡黎红/Hu Lihong 胡慧/Hu Hui

3. From the Golden Age of the Market to the Golden Age of Creativity —2016 A Memo to Chinese Filmmakers 27
   尹鸿/Yin Hong 梁君健/Liang Junjian

4. The Analysis and Strategy of Chinese Rural Film Market Development 49
   张小丽/Zhang Xiaoli

SECTION II: CULTURE AND AESTHETICS	67

5. The Internationalization Strategy of Chinese Cinema: Theory and Practice 68
   饶曙光/Rao Shuguang

6. Seven Visions: Rooted in the Traditional, Steeped in the Nouvelle —A Study of Zheng DaSheng and his Films 81
   万传法/Wan ChuanFa

7. A Kaleidoscopic View of Wang Han-lun's Celebrity Image 101
   岳莹/Yue Ying

8. The Impact of Hong Kong Cinema on Mainland Cinema after the Return of Hong Kong　116
赵卫防/Zhao Weifang

9. The Celebrity Face: Contemporary Celebrity Culture – Body Obsession and Physical Fetishism　134
陈晓云/Chen Xiaoyun

10. Significance in Survival: On the Auteurial Visions in Lu Chuan's Films　146
皇甫宜川/Huangfu Yichuan

Section III: History　165

11. Revisiting 1920s: Reflections on the Nationalism in Early Chinese Films　166
秦喜清/Qin XiQing

12. The Optimistic Tradition in Early Chinese Films: A Perspective of Intellectual History　185
安燕/An Yan

Section IV: Interviews　205

13. Interview with Director Guo Ke: Whispers through a Crinkle in Time　206

14. Interview with Director Mei Feng: The Aesthetic Compass of Classic Films　222

15. Interview with Director Lu Yang: What Matters Is What You Do with the Truth　241

Notes on Contributors　261

SECTION I

INDUSTRY

1. On Chinese Film Industrial Trade Structure and Its Internationalized Strategic Path

张宏/Zhang Hong

Part 1: Domestic Film Trade Conditions

In the summer of 2017, the Chinese film market was gripped in *Wolf Warriors 2* mania. The film smashed Chinese box office records and went on to gross a record-setting CNY¥5.6 billion. Yet, contrary to the Chinese film industry analysts' lofty expectations, the film's first-quarter North American box office receipts practically flatlined, a striking contrast that has been striking at the soul and tugging at the heartstrings of the Chinese populace ever since. As a result, the chilly reception for Chinese films abroad has once again cast a spell over nearly everyone in Chinese showbusiness.

With the development of the 'Belt and Road' initiative, Chinese films 'going out to the world' is undoubtedly an extremely effective means to promote cultural understanding between China and her foreign neighbours in the global village, and even convey a foreign-friendly image of China and export her cultural soft power. The thing is, it is an indisputable fact that there is a massive annual trade deficit in China's film industry. This chapter will attempt to analyse the domestic film trade structure through classic international trade theory. On this basis, it proposes that China take the path of internationalization to develop its domestic film industry by enhancing its competitiveness internationally and strengthening its cultural soft power.

At that time, the deputy director of the Film Bureau of China's State Administration of Press, Publication, Radio, Film and Television, Mr Luan GuoZhi, summarized China's film exports as 'three more and three less', meaning, a high number of films were being made, but few made it 'outside' the country. Chinese films were being played at a great number of international charity events, but few were being let into commercial theatres abroad. Chinese films were being shown at numerous Chinese theatre chains, but fewer were being played at foreign art theatres, and far fewer at mainstream cinemas in any country other than China.[1] Starting with recent statistics, we can do a bit of snooping around to gain some insight into how Chinese film exports have really been doing.

Chinese Films 'Hot on the Mainland, Cold in Other Lands'

In examining the big picture of the Chinese film market, we are shown that domestically produced films have been heating up year by year, both in terms of glowing word-of-mouth and sizzling box office performance – becoming a superpower in the film market. Yet when these films, which are highly acclaimed and wildly popular in their homeland, have gone abroad, they have met with an icy reception. This 'hot-at-home, cold-abroad' phenomenon shows no signs of letting up.

Case in point, Chinese films fizzled out in North America, the world's largest film market, in the first half of 2017. One of the biggest bombs of the year was the wildly popular *Journey to the West – The Demons Strike Back*, – an adaptation of the famous Chinese classic – which hit North American theatres on 3rd February and grossed a paltry $880,000 US dollars (about ¥5.81 million CNY). Yet box office receipts in China for the same film totalled ¥1.656 billion CNY (2017 Biannual China Film Report). The comparison of domestic and foreign box office receipts of the remaining films in the top five is shown in Table 1.

Film	Box Office (USD Millions)	Chinese Box Office (CNY Billions)	North American Ranking
Journey to the West – Demons Strike Back	8.803	1.656	7602
The Devotion of Suspect X	6.864	4.00	7916
Battle of Memories	5.945	2.9	8095
Duckweed	4.715	10.49	8383
Kung Fu Yoga	3.626	17.53	8713

Table 1: Top Five Chinese Films at the North American Box Office (First Half of 2017). Source: 2017 Biannual China Film Report.

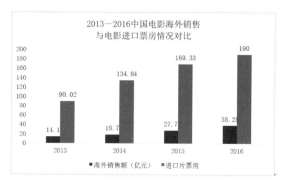

Table 2: Source: The State Administration of Press, Publication, Radio, Film and Television (SAPPRFT).

A long-standing trade deficit of the Chinese film industry is steadily increasing. The Chinese market has been inundated recently with an influx of import titles boasting a cast of strapping stars and starlets dripping sex-appeal, top-notch production values and state-of-the-art effects technology that have reaped huge box office. *The Fast and the Furious 8* is a perfect example. On its first day of the screening, the film broke the record for the mainland single-day box office champion with a massive box office take of ¥386 million CNY. Finally, it became the most popular imported film in 2017 with a box office take of ¥2.6 billion CNY. Even the Indian film *Dangal* simply waltzed in and earned nearly ¥1.3 billion CNY at the box office.

It can be seen from the chart that most foreign films entering the country often rake in the cash and have not hit the 'hot-in, cold-out', wall like their Chinese counterparts. For the purposes of this essay, a list has been compiled of overseas box-office performance for domestic films as well as box-office market performance for films imported into China over the past four years (as seen in Table 2).

Table 2 shows clearly that the overseas grosses of Chinese films are much lower than the box office of imported films, and this gap has been expanding year by year. Grosses of Chinese films in other territories can be understood as 'out' and the box office is understood as 'in', thus showing a serious trade imbalance.

As can be seen from Table 3, domestic and overseas grosses for Chinese films have exhibited varying degrees of growth, but the ratio between overseas grosses and domestic box office is relatively low, hovering between 10% and 14%. It is clear from the data that the exportability of domestically produced films in recent years has been weak and has shown no strong signs of improvement. The largest market for domestically produced movies is still Mainland China.

In this era of global economic integration, every industry is concerned about domestic and international markets, and the film industry is no exception. But it is not simply the film industry's push for profits that drives it to foreign lands

Year	Overseas Grosses (Billions CNY)	Domestic Grosses (Billions CNY)	Overseas Grosses/ Domestic Box Office
2013	1.41	12.76	11%
2014	1.87	15.70	12%
2015	2.77	27.13	10%
2016	3.82	26.66	14%

Table 3: Box-office performance of Chinese and foreign films from 2013 to 2016.

like this, but also its value as a vessel carrying Chinese cultural messages out to the thronging waves of humanity beyond her shores. So, taking full advantage of the current momentum and combing the appropriate international political and cultural environment to better enable Chinese films to 'go out' beyond her shores is an important issue for the Chinese film industry.

Part 2: Chinese Film Industry Trade Structure Analysis

Film exports, in a sense, belong in the domain of international trade. It is apparent from the above analysis that the successful export of Chinese film products is no simple matter, as it possesses no unique competitive advantage to set it apart within the fiercely competitive international matrix, meaning that the value-added of the industry cannot be recovered from the diversified market. It is this very issue that has prompted the author to frame the Chinese film industry through the lens of international trade theory and industrial economics to analyse the reasons why China's film trade has experienced such a state of imbalance.

The Law of Comparative Advantage and Chinese Film Productivity

The theory of absolute advantage proposed by Adam Smith, the pioneer of free trade theory, laid the foundation for international trade and explained the rationality of the division of labour and international trade between countries with different production advantages. There are many parallels between British scholar David Ricardo's theory of comparative advantage and the Adam Smith's theory of absolute advantage, but unlike Smith's theory, it analyses the relationship between the opportunity cost of different industries and international trade. According to the theory of comparative advantage, a country should focus on producing goods with lower opportunity cost for export, in exchange for products with higher opportunity cost. In theory, an international trade model setup in this manner means that a country can achieve optimal resource allocation and industrial structure. In this sense, trade conditions in the Chinese film industry and its industrial structure just goes to show that the opportunity cost in China's film industry is fairly high and naturally lacks international competitiveness.

Breaking it down into layman's terms, what underlies opportunity cost is the question of how much production resources to invest. Meaning, when China produces a movie of the same quality as Hollywood, the amount of resources used and invested are much greater than the resources used by Hollywood to make the same film. Therefore, in theory, the current trade structure of film reflects how competitive the Chinese film industry is in relation to the foreign film industry. In this case, exporting other products in exchange for film imports actually makes a whole lot of sense.

Factor Endowment Theory and International Film Trade

Being that comparative advantage is a form of 'static' economic analysis, it can help provide a theoretical basis for the current state of international competitiveness of the film industry, but it also has certain inherent limitations. To make up for the limitations of this theory, Swedish economists Eli Heckscher and Bertil Ohlin developed Factor Endowment Theory. The two scholars explained the difference in production costs from the differences in the relative production factor endowments, which led to disparities in industrial trade structure. According to this theory, a certain country becomes a film powerhouse because the said country is more endowed with resources suitable for the film industry, and it uses these endowment resources intensively to raise its international competitiveness. If any country's film production factors are relatively scarce, its film industry would not have a cost advantage in international trade. The difficulty in exporting filmed entertainment products from China is precisely due to the scarcity of some factor endowments used in film production and export.

The quality of their filmed entertainment products is closely related to the resources invested. Undoubtedly, the film industry is a capital, technology, and talent-intensive industry, as only people can effectively drive capital and technology to bring quality movies and a corresponding competitiveness to the table. Obviously monetary and material elements are not scarce in the Chinese film industry.

First of all, from the perspective of capitalization, Chinese film companies have no problem finding financing for their projects. Social capital (SOCAP) has accumulated in the film industry through the stock market and banking systems, and diversified investment entities have provided sufficient funds for industrial development. For example, when a large number of Internet companies such as Baidu, Alibaba, Tencent and other giants began injecting the film industry with capitalization, large-scale entertainment companies such as China Film and Huahai

Times also entered the capital market through getting listed on the Chinese stock exchange, as well as other methods to finance their own films and even distribute them in overseas markets.

Second, from the perspective of materials, being the oldest continuous civilization with five thousand years of history, China has accumulated a wealth of creative materials that are fodder for the film industry. The country's profound cultural heritage can be transformed into a competitive advantage, but in the actual production process, the material element is not transformed into a competitive advantage with the support of capital. For example, some traditional or modern cultural elements have been used by screenwriters from outside China in films such as *Kung Fu Panda* and *Mulan* and secured advantages when they were in turn entered back into the Chinese film market to compete with its own domestic films. These examples show that China is still unsuccessful in transforming its traditional culture and content endowment resources into product competitiveness.

Next is the technical perspective. China has actually been doing post-production work on foreign-animated films for quite a while now, and it is certainly no wimp in its technical abilities. Moreover, personal interviews were conducted with special effects houses in-country and this author has concluded that their effects equipment is capable of producing ultra-modern special effects. In terms of equipment, Chinese post-production houses are not inferior to Hollywood, or even incapable of living up to Hollywood standards. That said, domestically produced films with high production values have been criticized by viewers for the quality of their visual narrative, even though they were produced through the latest powerful technologies such as 3D and IMAX. The reason for this is that Chinese filmmakers tend not to pay attention to fusing technology and content, making China like a meek little baby that is trying to run before it learns to walk. Unfortunately, the prevailing ethic in Chinese filmmaking is apparently, *l'technologie pour l'technologie*, as opposed to *L'technologie pour l'art* – using technology as a tool to serve and enhance the story. It is just not possible to bring a quality viewing experience by simply flexing special effects muscle, while breaking from the context of the story. And a special effects bonanza is no longer what the viewers would consider to be a quality viewing experience, no matter how you slice it.

Based on the above analysis, the most critical factor in the film industry is talent, and the Chinese film industry is lacking in talent resource endowment. The talent factor is the all-important element in film production. In the international market, materials, capital and technology can flow quickly and easily between countries through the mechanism of free trade, but the flow of talent always lags far behind. Talent is not quantitative, it is qualitative. It is skilled labour in the strictest economic sense. In the process of film production and exports, a shortcoming in quality talent causes a lack of endogenous motivation in film production, making it impossible to convert sufficient materials, capital and technical elements into a highly acceptable and internationally competitive quality. Not only in terms of creativity, but also the creative process, China is in desperate need of a group of talent who measure up to international standards and are well versed in the fields of film management, marketing, financing and law.

Cross-Industry Trade Is the Main Form of China's Film Trade

It can be concluded through a situational analysis of the current trade model used in China's film industry that it has no comparative advantage, on account of the nature of the global market, and consequently it is exporting other industrial products of which it has a comparative advantage, in exchange for others, including filmed entertainment products. In the domain of international trade, this is actually what is referred to as inter-industry trade. Nowadays, it is necessary to export domestically produced films out beyond the borders of one's own nation to obtain higher box office returns. The fact of the matter is that this requires intra-industry trade between the Chinese and international film industries. Yet, the good sense of international economics tells us that intra-industry trade is largely a trade model used between developed economies, or between those with close industrial economic developmental standards. Plus, the state will most certainly implement an import quota system to control the strong impact of foreign films on the Chinese film industry due to the fact that the Chinese film industry quite possibly lacks a comparative advantage. Protectionism, however, is an ad-hoc measure at best. The industry just plain needs to grow up. After all, Chinese film must enter the international market at some point to face the cream of other countries' great creative minds, vis-à-vis. The ultimate goal of protectionism is to bide time and gather steam in order to gain a competitive advantage down the road.

State protection of the film industry actually recognizes that the industry is still in its infancy stage; and asking the film industry to leave the nest would require a rapid maturation process, not only necessitating the recognition of the prevailing structural weaknesses outlined above, but also a rational and effective plan for industrial development, as well as an ace internationalization strategy.

Part 3: Internationalized Strategic Plans in the Works

As mentioned above, transforming the Chinese film industry from an international inter-industry trade to intra-industry trade model is a prerequisite to gain a comparative advantage going forward, which is something worth waiting for, though there is still such a long way to go before it materializes. From an exhaustive survey of the Chinese film industry, it is quite apparent that everyone from the relevant national authorities, to agencies, to film and television companies of all sizes, are all working tirelessly to help Chinese films get seen abroad.

Nevertheless, in getting to know the current prospects of Chinese movies going out beyond the borders of the Middle Kingdom, this author has found that, in addition to a few various achievements, Chinese films go out of their own way and amuse themselves and have not fully realized what commercial profitability actually is. There are two main ways of exporting Chinese movies at present. One is, of course to get it into the various international film festivals. However, the influence and promotion that can be gained through the film festival are limited and are not very commercially viable. Two, China utilizes public relations methods as a vehicle to get Chinese films into overseas film festivals to promote the country's image. The problem then lies in the fact that these film festivals are generally organized by Chinese, and the majority of the audience is Chinese.

These two ways of getting seen outside China are universal. Regardless of whether a country's film industry is developed or not, it will use methods just like this to get its films 'out there' and fight for public recognition. However, this has amounted to not much more than a dead end for China's film industry. Because, to start with they have not been able to gather much momentum that way. And second, Chinese films are regarded as something akin to art film. From the perspective of foreign film themes, commercial films that espouse national ideologies and values are the ones that the most effectively gain influence. Without the wheels of the commercial machine spinning in their favour, it is difficult for Chinese films to truly realize the advantages of intra-industry trade. Therefore, marketing models such as the film festivals circuit may still have some future viability, but cannot be the focal point of promotion, nor relied too heavily.

Therefore, looking at the film industry in its entirely, bringing international competitiveness up to par is the only way to achieve intra-film trade, and is a long-term strategy that must be implemented after the film industry develops to a certain point. The road of Chinese film internationalization must be paved with effectively enhanced competitiveness, and partnerships formed with all links of the industrial chain that will enable Chinese films to enjoy international brand recognition status. To cut out a reasonable internationalization path from the weeds and overgrowth, the internationalization strategy has been divided into two segments, namely macro-government policies and micro-enterprise strategies; long-term value orientation and short-term content creation.

Macro-Government Policy Support and Micro-Business Strategy

At the macro-level, to improve export Chinese films to the international market, the Chinese state has introduced policies to prop up the film-and-television industry. First, it has relaxed market access thresholds and supported various cultural enterprises to engage in the export of cultural products and services. Second, it has adopted financial support policies, subsidizing the export of film-and-television products, and has implemented incentives. Furthermore, it is providing financial support, and has set up special funds for national cultural development, including funds for supporting the development of cultural product exports. Finally, it has emphasized the training talent to work in the film-and-television industry, in the hopes of building a talent pool to help develop cultural product exports.

The state is perfectly justified in implementing such policies and standing by them for the long-term is definitely the way to go. That said, the effectiveness of such policies once they are implemented has been largely fallen flat. The reason for this is mainly due to the lack of a dedicated institution to promote the implementation of the policies and then to convert the resulting kinetic energy produced by them into actual international competitiveness. In addition, the state should stipulate that the entry standards for the entertainment industry cannot be lowered, which can lower the threshold for firms entering the market, thereby incentivizing them to use every method at their disposal to develop effective internationalization strategies that can help make the push for quality Chinese films to gain the acceptance of international audiences and gradually build positive word of mouth.

Beyond that, the present array of Chinese and foreign co-productions are also an effective means of internationalizing Chinese film. Collaboration like this can reap a whole host of other benefits, such as boosting the political, economic and cultural relations between China and the country that participates in the co-production. Thus far, China has inked film co-production contracts with more than ten nations including Canada, Britain, South Korea and France. Furthermore, co-produced films are treated as a regular domestic film release in China and not restricted by the foreign film quota system. Agreements such as this are very effective in promoting and popularizing Chinese movies on the Western front, which is one of the important paths for the internationalization of Chinese film.

Consequently, the government and the film industry should continue with Chinese and foreign co-productions over the long-term, but not be short-sighted in the process. They should not only consider the market value of a single film, but also focus their attention on the talent endowment accumulation effect that goes hand-in-hand with a long-term co-production strategy. Learning and improvement happen gradually during the co-production process as a result of the knowledge spillovers that will spread throughout the entire industry chain. For example, even considering the model of exporting capital only from China, China's human resources will gradually be integrated into the whole process of production and international marketing, and finally achieve total change from partial change.

At the micro-level, if companies want to create an internationally competitive film, the most important thing is to turn their gaze straight to the outside world. If a company wants to realize the commercial value of a film investment, it must take into consideration its market niche right from the outset of planning and pre-production to make it a product that is keyed into global tastes and idiosyncrasies, which will be shown to global audiences and rewarded on a global scale. Or if the product is better suited to a certain International market, perhaps Europe and Asia, this should be accurately assessed in order to reap the rewards to a greatly expanded marketplace. Due to market differences, a whole host of issues, from audience demand, to product positioning, to marketing strategies must be taken into account individually and addressed on a case-by-case basis.

Building on this foundation, companies can laser focus on the appropriate promotional channels and expand overseas resources. The most direct way is to distribute capital overseas and control the target market with hands-on involvement in their investment during the actual production stage. They should also attack the overseas distribution issue from every angle by controlling channels, mergers and acquisitions, and opening subsidiaries. For example, the Wan-da Company acquired film companies such as North American AMC and American Legend Film to gain direct overseas production experience and expand overseas distribution channels. Huayi Brothers and STX collaborated in-depth by jointly investing in, filming and distributing no less than eighteen productions cooperatively.

Long-Term Value Guidance and Short-Term Content Creation

In addition to macro policy support and micro-enterprise strategies, Chinese cinema must achieve a long-term value-oriented strategy in order to achieve an employable internationalization strategy. In contrast, many resources that enable foreign film-and-television programming played in China are non-profit subtitling group or fan-sites that introduce and present the material to Chinese audiences. Perhaps this could be a potential path for Chinese cinema to be internationalized. Cultural organizations abroad, like Chinese cultural embassies and overseas Chinese cultural centres, can encourage Chinese film fans in their respective areas to form clubs, or for foreign Sinophiles enamoured with Chinese cinema to form voluntary independent organizations whose purpose is to introduce quality Chinese film content to the world on a grand scale through foreign media channels such as the Internet, thereby getting viewers abroad in the habit of watching Chinese films, thus building recognition of Chinese cinematic values and ideologies. After a long period of subtle exposure, the audience will become naturally curious about the cinema of China and more likely to consume internationalized Chinese films when they are finally commercialized abroad.

Besides building up long-term viewing habits, Chinese film companies and filmmakers can utilize the singular channel known as the Internet to take advantage of the network effect created by it, with which to get fans with the same viewing habits in different regions onto the same bandwagon, grouping them all into one massive internationalized market. And through a thorough analysis of the particular proclivities and propensities of these fetishistic film fans, content can thereby be created with captivating cinematographic and quality effects standards, precisely targeted at this potentially sizeable demographic.

In conclusion, the Chinese film internationalization strategy requires short- and long-term cooperation. Film producers and researchers must truly understand this international market trends, so they can break out of the traditional mode of thinking and formulate a pragmatic internationalization strategy. This will enable Chinese films to be seen by a wide international audience.

Acknowledgement

Liu DongMei, Cao Xue and Wang YiMing EMBA have contributed greatly to the writing of this chapter. Wang YiMing contributed to the statistics and text of the first part. Liu DongMei contributed to the discussion of the trade model and the film industry in the second part. Cao Xue contributed to the specific recommendations in the third part about the film industry internationalization strategy.

NOTE
1. See http://yule.sohu.com/20130905/n385943768.shtml.

2. On the Differentiation Strategies of Four Internet Film Production Companies

胡黎红/Hu Lihong 胡慧/Hu Hui

In 2015, politician Li Keqiang presented the 'Internet Plus' action plan in the government work report, which subsequently triggered waves of innovation and transformations in a whole host of industries. In the rapidly growing film industry, the most significant change is the level of its involvement with the Internet. A contingent of dominant large-scale Internet-based film companies has emerged. These companies ambitiously staked their claim to segments of territory in the film industry, thereby pushing the competitive landscape of the Chinese film industry into a new phase.

Renowned business guru Michael Porter noted in his book *Competitive Strategy* that differentiation is one of the three basic strategies for companies to gain advantages in the fiercely competitive market landscape. In this sense, creating products and creating industries is creating differentiation (Porter 2003: 10–15). In this regard, Internet companies that have developed in the wake of the wave of commercialization know this all too well. Therefore, when Internet companies enter the film industry and 'fuse Internet with movie', they are consciously positioning, incubating, modelling, and consolidating differentiated advantages as the key to winning competitive opportunities and with which to establish their own brands. Alibaba Pictures, Tencent Pictures, iQiyi Motion Pictures and LeVision Pictures (LEVP), which are backed by Internet giants such as Baidu-Alibaba-Tencent (BAT) and Leshi Internet Information and Technology Corporation, have grown like weeds in just two short years to become the leaders of a new breed of film company. Since they began collectively blitzing the film-and-television industry in 2014, these four companies have sought out differentiation strategies from different levels and different links, with which to seek competitive advantages, such as strategic architecture, business model, content structure, platform creation and service. Through the power of innovation and novelty, they have blazed a highly unique developmental trail.

Part 1: *Strategic Architecture and Business Models*

Like a chess championship, elite players always look at the big picture and seek out emerging patterns. These four companies, each with its own mighty capital strength and far-reaching resource advantages, began competing on the levels of strategic architecture and business models when they first threw their hats into the new 'Internet + Film' ecosystem that was under construction.

It should be noted that there is no commonality and consistency among any of these companies in terms of strategic objectives and evolutionary paths. The most prominent commonality is that the Internet is the basis for the transformation and integration of the traditional film industry, by means of financing, production, distribution and marketing, derivatives development, copyright management and other links in the value chain that ultimately cover the film, video, game, animation markets and both extend and power-load their overall influence in the chain. However, differences in each company's respective first-mover advantages, core resources, and business structure, as well as the diversity in their unique strategic goals and promotional paths, has given rise to highly differentiated business models.

The company with the strongest financial position and the greatest reach is Alibaba. With its mighty capitalization and capital operations, Alibaba has been striving to create a 'making it easy to do business everywhere' image for itself. Through an intoxicating cocktail of measures and actions, such as mergers and acquisitions, share purchasing, equity interest, and Internet finance, Alibaba Pictures has been able to quickly carve out its own expansive territory within the film industry. It all started with the establishment of Alibaba Pictures through the acquisition of 'ChinaVision Media', and then the purchase of sizeable shares of major production companies like Huayi Brothers and Beijing Enlight Media, and then forging alliances on the domestic front with legendary Internet colossuses such as video streaming sites like Youku and Tudou, and strategic partnerships with the giants of the industry. Alibaba Pictures has quickly established a supercharged business model powered by four major components: content development and production, Internet, entertainment and e-commerce and overseas business through the acquisition of a number of companies throughout the supply chain – starting from facilitating franchise incubation, to content development and production, distribution and marketing, and finally derivative product development.

In contrast to Alibaba Pictures' ability to find breakthroughs by aggregating resources, Tencent Pictures implemented its 'pan entertainment' strategy by creating Tencent's own self-contained video ecosystem and its own content resources. The makeup of its value chain mainly starts from the upstream content construction and includes strong interactive platform support and a large number of consumer groups. Hinging on intellectual property rights and founded on four major business platforms: Tencent Games, Tencent Comic, China Literature (AKA: Tencent Literature), Tencent Pictures Plus +, and its game, animation, literature, and film departments are integrated into a single, massive 'pan-entertainment' business platform. In 2015, Tencent proposed the 'pan-entertainment' strategy that relies on Tencent's video playback platform, media channels and diverse social platforms to further strengthen the integration and sharing of internal resources such as games, animation, literature, film and television and derivatives markets, founding a cross-domain, multi-platform business development and operating model.

As both an industry leader and a benchmark in the field of online video, iQiyi has a developed, highly integrated Internet operating platform, which is endowed with a massive stockpile of videos, precise positioning, targeted user matching, and most importantly, an uber-professional and supremely original production team. It has an extensive and rabid fan base who has contributed to the success of its original programming. For example, the Internet variety show, *I'm Off to School* the online drama, *U Can You BB* and *Two Idiots*, proves unequivocally that iQiyi's in-house production + independent broadcast strategy has fully matured as a business model. Having gained ground with these resources, it has centred itself around product incubation and collaborative development , making streaming content the link to pivot into the film industry.It gradually integrates film and television production, online games, derivatives development, online sales and online copyright management which thereby develops a complete value chain.

LeTV was originally a video site, and initially positioned itself as more of a copyright operator but has gradually transitioned from a video-streaming website to a film-and-television production company. From a copyright operator doing film distribution to an investor, and finally to an independent film production company, LeTV has constructed a complete value chain that ranges from planning to production to distribution to marketing and service in just a few short years. At the same time, the LeTV video platform has gradually begun exploring a successful 'Dramacasts + Spectaction' operating model, which has brought a boost to LeTV's traffic and the influence of it as a platform. It is based on the full integration of LeTV and Le.com video websites and has set up a four-in-one business model of 'platform + content + cloud + application'. What enabled LeTV's developmental boost was its core business model: the internet integrates the various links in the film industry chain – from production, to editing, storage, the distribution and playback of content, and finally to the consumer's cloud experience. These have created a higher level of engagement and a greater transformative effect, thus more effectively opening up and enhancing competitiveness along the entire value chain. It creates a basis for the grand scale of LeTV's film production, marketing and financial operations on the Internet.The essence of = LeTV's model is not only a vertically integrated value chain of film company constituents, but also an open cross-domain and cross-industry 'LeEco', ecosystem model. It includes Le Vidi, Le Vision Pictures, LeTV, LeTV Mobile and LeTV Finance. With the full spectrum of development and the integration of finance, it went from a vertical ecosystem to an open ecosystem, gaining powerful competitiveness from its LeEco rebranding, which is open and has a stronger 'transformative effect'.

Part 2: Content-Product Strategies

Whether it is a good ol' fashioned film company or a new-fangled Internet film company, strong content production capacity is the source of development, and a core element in a differentiation strategy. The difference between the two is that the latter replaces the former's work thinking with product thinking, and the way to realize the product value is no longer the release in the single market, but a linked development throughout the whole industry chain. At present, the production experience of these four Internet film companies is not comparable to traditional film companies such as Huayi Brothers and Bona Film. However, obtaining and optimizing a large number of intellectual property resources through different channels was their most important content advantage.

Alibaba Group, which started from e-commerce, has a comparative lack of film and televisiongenes, so Alibaba Pictures has had to compensate for its shortcomings in the interim, mainly through forging partnerships. One of its strategies is to enter production and the production process upstream via capital intervention, such as participating in the film project such as *Breakup Buddies* and signing strategic cooperative agreements with directors such as Wong Karwai, Peter Chan and Stephen Chow to obtain their future projects. Priorities are investment rights and extensive collaboration with film production companies. Among Alibaba Pictures' stable of partnerships, there are traditional film production companies such as Huayi Brothers, as well as many emerging companies such as China Television Shengdian and Confucian Film. The second strategy is to introduce the source of film and television content by purchasing or investing in franchises. For example, it purchased popular franchises such as *The Heroic Age* and *Candle in the Tomb* to start the adaptation of movies and TV series, and worked with Sina Literature, Taji Literature, Changjiang Media and other literary websites to gradually innovate them. At the strategic launch conference in June 2016, Alibaba Pictures officially announced the production of seventeen (17) films, including developed franchises such as *Legend of the Antique Saber 2* and *The Legend of Zu 2*, as well as those developed from new franchises, *Double World*, *Thirty Years of Surprises*, *No Other Love*.[1] It is also worth mentioning about Alibaba Pictures' cross-border cooperative strategy. Through a strategic agreement with Hollywood Lionsgate, participating in the production of *Mission Impossible 5*, and selling a series of Hollywood mainstream derivatives on its own business platform, Alibaba Pictures has begun accumulating experience in the international production world.

Compared with the industry startup-like power of Alibaba Pictures, Tencent Pictures undoubtedly has the gene it needs to compete for supremacy, in the form of greater originality and richer content resources. Therefore, its content offerings are mainly based on its own resources such as games, literature, animation, online video, QQ music and so on. Tencent's acquisition of Shanda Literature and its rabid reading group has given Tencent's online literature a 50%+ market share, providing a large number of literary IP adaptation resources for Tencent's display in the film field. Tencent used its own literature, animation and games to incubate and generate high-quality literary, animation and game franchises, and then create spectacular film productions through their successful adaptations, which is the most powerful aspect of Tencent's content holdings. At the same time, Tencent Pictures has also begun experimenting with star-driven franchises with market development potential. The first project it managed to corral was author Guo JingMing's *L.O.R.D: Legend of Ravaging Dynasties*. In addition to the efficient use of its own pool of franchise to achieve integration with film content, Tencent has also adopted a shareholding, joint investment and other means to accelerate the development of its content and accumulate greater production experience. In that vein, its related initiatives include a capital investment in Lemon Productions, purchasing a stake in Huayi Brothers and securing the movie rights to online games and literary works – co-producing *Dragon Blade*, *Zhong Kui: Snow Girl and the Dark Crystal*, *Black & White: The Dawn of Justice*, and others.

IQiyi Film, whose genesis is in a video-streaming website, has firmly zeroed in on its main strategy of parlaying content advantages into a winning hand by creating 'independently broadcast, self-produced' video content. Through years of intensive development and by progressing through measured and thoughtful steps, iQiyi has accumulated a wealth of original resources in the Internet variety show and drama genres. Many of its quirky home-grown dramas have garnered a large fan base and the platform itself has become something of a star vehicle. The combination of content, platform and talent has created competitive capital for iQiyi with which to refine and develop 'Internet franchises' and create iconic products. Based on the concept of coordinated franchise development, right from the get-go, many of iQiyi's video programs are developed with sequels, spinoffs or follow-ups in mind that can extend and add value. In 2016, iQiyi developed a literary copyright library through Baidu, bringing many popular literary franchises under one stable, enabling the service's content resources to continue to grow, thereby taking the lead in the film industry in securing material and transferring copyrights.

Of these four companies, Le.com has shot way out ahead in the film production industry, and its experience and professionalism far outclass the other three. Based in its copyright management and self-produced content, LeTV has positioned itself with two huge advantages in terms of content production and product development. First and foremost, it possesses the largest and most comprehensive content library. Capitalizing on a lengthy but steady advance along the Internet franchise film rights battlefront, Le.com has not only weaponized the largest library of films and videos from China but has also taken control of an extensive library of officially licensed films and shows from abroad. With this massive storehouse of copyrighted entertainment products along with the LeTV brand's extensive repository of self-produced entertainment, LeEco has a clear diversification advantage in the content world that allows it to innovate upon the Internet to film content conversion model. Second, demographic categorization. Having the most complete content literally supercharges LeTV to consistently provide a wholly new product experience to its users; and having a user-traffic advantage and demographic categorization feature has further separated it from the pack. Starting from these advantages, LeTV has emphasized the 'user demographics' and 'multi-channelled distribution' in its franchise development. Through demographically separated content production, online categorization + offline social-marketing, the primary strategy is the accurate segmentation of targeted push notification delivery based on user demographics, with which it can develop its content advantage to the fullest. In addition, LeEco is also on the cutting edge within the grand scheme of the global matrix, with its established subsidiaries in Los Angeles and Silicon Valley. It has also formed cooperative strategic partnerships with American companies to develop entertainment products for the Chinese and American audiences. In 2016 alone, LeTV invested in the film *The Great Wall*, as well as nine other Hollywood co-productions ('Why do LeTV and Wanda Cinemas all want to break into Hollywood?'). Predictably, an increasing number of films co-produced with American production companies will come out of the woodwork in the years to come.

Part 3: Platform Strategies

Platform strategies are a new operational strategy that is representative of the Internet era's burgeoning industrial model, which play an integral role in the growth of Internet Media enterprises (Shangbin and Shanshan 2016). As long-established senior Internet firm, BAT and LeTV have the power of their own respective comprehensive platforms in the palm of their hand. After getting into the film business, in connection with disadvantages like limited content exposure to the audiences in traditional film industry, each of these companies has invested in a series of new financing platforms, content creation and a broadcasting platform, a social networking platform, an online ticketing platform, an end-user platform, with which to throw a portal to a brand-new world wide-open.

As an e-commerce giant who made a big splash in showbusiness, the edge that Alibaba's existing e-commerce platform gives the company is as plain as the chin on Alibaba's smiling face. Capitalizing on its massive userbase of its e-commerce platform and its commercial data stores, Alibaba was the first to develop and roll out an equity crowdfunding platform, AliFund, 'YuLe Bao', which not only created a new film financing channel, but also transformed the traditional film production model by way of attracting user-participation in the film production process, along with getting double duty from the subsequent sales and promotion with only a fraction of the effort. At the same time, the e-commerce platform leaves plenty of space open for the merchandising after production wraps. The Alibaba Pictures flagship store on T-Mall primarily sells film derivative products that effectively helps Alibaba pictures better tap into and merchandise its derivative products. With respect to online ticketing platforms, Alibaba's existing products, Cat's-Eye Movie and Taobao, have gone from financing to production to ticket sales, distribution and promotion. Alibaba Pictures platforms have singlehandedly created a closed-loop supply chain in the film industry.

Tencent, which developed from the creation of a social networking site, first found its advantage by piggy-backing its platform on top of the massive social networking site it had set up. The two giants of the social networking world, QQ and WeChat, alone have Tencent sitting pretty in an enviable position that is difficult for other companies like it to topple, due to the sheer size of its substantial userbase. Entering the mobile-Internet era, Tencent developed and released mobile user platforms like QQ and 'MyApp', and its advantages in social networking and instant communication became all the more obvious. Second, Tencent has continued to flex its muscle in its three well-integrated professional content production platforms, Tencent Games, Tencent Comic, Tencent Literature, which have each respectively evolved the entertainment workshop, the blackbody workshop and the dream movie workshop, which is responsible for adapting game, manga and literature franchises into film. Meanwhile, Tencent pictures also jointly set up an entertainment production matrix. With the QQ and WeChat platforms functioning as connectors, Tencent linked content, users and service, forming a loop through the versatility of mobile payment liquidity. In addition, Tencent rapidly build its own online ticketing platform by bringing two major online ticketing entities, Gewara and WePiao under its banner.

IQiyi doesn't hold a candle to e-commerce goliath Alibaba in terms of the sheer size and scale of its platform. In the mobile terminal and interactive platform sphere, its professionalism and coverage is a second-class citizen next to Tencent, the Hercules of the industry. It is, however, a highly refined video platform that is closely linked to the film and television industry, and its muscles are built up to do the heavy lifting of film and TV broadcasts, promotion and sales via its world-class video delivery platform. After formally merging with PP Stream, the 'iQiyi/PPS Audio-Video' service was introduced, which was like a steroid boost to the size and operational capacity of the iQiyi video platform. Besides that, iQiyi has also launched an e-commerce platform called "iQiyi Mall" that relied heavily on sales of derivative and peripheral products from popular films and TV shows, achieving a crossover and conversion between e-commerce and showbusiness by making the platform all the more well-integrated. Beyond that, iQiyi has joined forces with a plethora of professional content producers, such as Huace Film and TV, CG Power, to launch the 'Fen'gan Tongwei' entertainment ecosystem project, which specifically opened up a 'featured' channel to highlight the ordering setup, further enhancing iQiyi's influence.

The advantages of the LeTV platform are embodied in Le.com. There are three commercial platforms under LeEco: LeMall, the LeTV official flagship store and the LeEco official flagship store. Through these e-commerce platforms, the LeTV network has collected a massive number of daily users, which has helped LeTV win over an army of fanboys. Meanwhile, LeCloud is built on a steady stream of consumer information which provides flawless data support for the development of film productions through the processing and application of big data. Second, as a multi-functional platform for broadcasting, publicity marketing and interaction, the LeTV video site under the LeTV banner has developed nicely. This has afforded Le Vision Pictures an avenue from which it has gained tremendous content support and commercial performance. Third, in the development and application of a smart user platform, LeTV embodies its unique and forward-looking strategic vision. It has not only developed and launched LeTV Television, Le Mobile Phones, Le Set-top Boxes and other smart applications and built a smart operating platform, but has also integrated the three platforms through a UR System to merge multiple terminals, thus furthering its competitive advantage.

Part 4: Service Strategy

The film industry addresses the audience, while the service of Internet film companies addresses both the audience and the user. In one respect, the overlap between the two groups has bought more business opportunities and space for differentiation between companies. In another respect, the audience demands a more diverse, personalized and refined Internet experience in the information age, which his made perception, attentiveness and precision that much more difficult to provide. It can be argued that he who yokes more user loyalty through effective service strategies shall occupy a greater space in the heart and mind of the consumer, and by this outstrip the competition.

From this point of view, the setup of each of these platforms is to improve and strengthen its service capacity. Case in point, Alibaba Pictures has fully capitalized on the effective service it provides for their platform along a whole series of links that range from user access to purchasing to after-sales service to fully develop effective service. First of all, the content development process makes use of the world's largest and most powerful e-commerce platform. Through an exhaustive analysis of its massive data stores, the demands and habits of mainstream movie-goers can be analysed, thereby allowing films that correspond to the vote of public opinion to be made. AliFund, which was launched as an equity crowdsourcing platform, is not necessarily set up to do financing but aims to address the user-participation question at the source by enhancing user-interactivity, attracting public participation in the investment process and giving film fans freedom of choice.

Second, in terms of promotion and marketing links, Alibaba provides audiences with services like choosing seats, movie recommendations and online video streaming, all under the banner of its two online ticketing platforms, Taobao and TMall.

Third, the construction of user terminals at cinemas, through Alibaba's acquisition of Guangdong YKSE (Yueke Software), a generation of smart cinemas has been set up that empower audiences with new services such as automatic ticket checking, no-questions asked refunds and easy ticket changing all with a simple scan.

Finally, in the development and sales of derivatives, Alibaba makes full use of Taobao's high traffic to zero in on user demand for derivative products in real time; and with this valuable information in hand, various factories are contacted to help develop derivative products that audiences prefer.

Tencent has fused film with social networking in an attempt to bring a social aspect to filmgoing. The WeChat instant messaging app not only provides online ticketing services, but also a wealth of video and peripheral services. More importantly, through the openness of the WeChat public Account, WeChat Pay and Shake and Scan, it can seamlessly connect online with offline. The 'My App' application developed by Tencent is designed with the smart, smart phone user in mind, and covers users' diverse needs like app downloading, management, collection and sharing along with social entertainment. Through micro-integration and micro-innovations brought about by regularly upgraded versions, My-App has scaled the heights of the industry by providing the ultimate in 'experimental distribution' services that can match users to the content and products they need with the greatest of ease.

As China's largest video content provider, iQiyi has focused the core of its services on producing and distributing high-quality, personalized and diverse content. As a result, iQiyi has tightly linked its video-streaming site with PPS Video and Baidu data, originating 'the green lens' feature that converts every user operation to source code, and creates a 'snapshot' of each user with the assistance of big data, instantly taking into account things like theme, genre and style to automatically create a dynamic formula that is used to make real-time suggestions in line with consumer psychology and consumption characteristics. Based on the location and time zone of the individual user, content is chosen, thereby creating a personalized user preference system with which to cater recommendations for the main page.

The company with the most distinctive service strategy is Le.com. User demand and experiences have always been a top priority, one which was highly emphasized even in the very genesis of the company's business model. Its differentiation primarily takes the following three forms: First, it emphasizes the 'last mile' in its service. It has astutely and firmly grasped consumption psychology and viewing habits in the multiscreen and mobile eras. It takes the concerted efforts of the diversified platforms of Le.com, LeTV, Le Set-Top Box and Le Smart phones to provide the oomph necessary to cover every possible consumption scenario. LeTV video streaming and Le set-top boxes can deliver a one-stop download, management and upgrade platform that can create a convenient and all-encompassing user experience. Second is its emphasis on audience categorization. CEO Zhang Zhao put it best when he said, 'In the Internet era, the biggest business is truly understanding users, to focus hard enough and care deep enough to capture their hearts and change their minds' ('When we talk about movies'). Through the strategic combination of marketing based on the consumer's psyche along with focused push notifications, LeTV strive to satisfy users' differentiated needs and preferences, with the goal in mind of segmented mapping of content on the platform.

Part 5: Issues and Reflections on Competitive Differentiation

Undoubtedly, a wide variety of novel ideas aimed at innovation and differentiation infuses power, vitality and imagination into the development of the film industry and creates limitless possibilities for market actors in the industry. Undeniably, in the game of differentiation however, there are some nagging issues left for us to reflect upon.

As mentioned earlier, in terms of strategic architecture and business model, although the four companies have their own characteristics and an entry and pivot point, along with an overall business structure, their ultimate goal is to find direction within the grand scheme of the industry chain. Of course, the pursuit of overall distribution and competitive balance can optimize the allocation of resources and reduce operational risks, but real excellence often occurs only when there is a total imbalance. In order to achieve excellence, it is necessary to have choice. Michael Porter once pointed out that the bigger the market is, the higher the threshold of product specialization and the higher the requirement of firm specialization. Therefore, any company that implements competitive differentiation should make some choices when positioning its advantages. Only by doing something and not doing something else can real differentiation be found. When more and more Internet film companies compete for success, and when they are facing global market instead of the national market, will it be possible for them to rise to the top in the industry, or to strengthen their advantages and rise to the top of the heap. It all takes time for things to play out, and to know which company has the more ingenious ideas, and whose decisions are more logical.

Second, in terms of content strategy, although each of these four companies has its own emphasis, there is a consistency among them, in that they all rely on big data and are trying to scoop up the rights to the popular franchises. The contribution of big data and franchises to innovating business models, expanding product resources and increasing production experience is tremendous and obvious, but at the end of the day it can be a double-edged sword, which is something that cannot go unheeded. Big data logic and franchise operation models are closely related to mass systems, the fan economy, repeat readings, multidevelopments and other business routines, which sometimes drive forward a competitive differentiation that requires innovation, but may actually lead to the opposite, which may even become the root of new misconceptions and traps that ensnare market participants.

Even in light of the fact that there are many successful cases in film production under the guidance of big data and franchises, such as *The Monkey King: The Hero Is Back*, *Old Boy: The Way of The Dragon*, *The Ghouls*, and others, in the past two years, the silver screen has the image of franchise films, soft films rife of Internet flair and popcorn movies with commercial appeal, burned right into it from an endlessly recycled loop of the same old content. And then there are the increasingly prominent issues of overwrought entertainment and overimagined productions. It also sounds an alarm to policymakers who call themselves franchise-savvy yet lack rational judgement and foresight of big data. As Wang ChangTian, president of Enlight Media once quipped,

> Making movies is not really about your professional background, how much money you have, or even big data. But it is all about your smarts, concentration, judgment, past experience and attitude. So what it boils down to is this, in this

industry, small companies still can become big companies overnight, and big companies may become to small companies in the blink of an eye. China's film industry still needs to adhere.

If there is not a solid effort to upgrade and re-innovate content creation, if the content production and quality cannot match the energy of platform and pipeline themselves, then no matter how powerful a platform it is, nothing can make up for a shortage in quality content production.

Third, in terms of the platform layout, even though the architecture, look and feel, and features are somewhat different, the development and operation of some new platforms are still in the initial stages, breakthroughs still need to happen in the way of competitive differentiation. For example, online ticketing platforms; although the number of online ticket buyers on all platforms is increasing at near light-speed, according to the survey statistics, online ticket buyers and mainstream movie-watching groups at the cinema chains are still highly coincident. In other words, despite the fact that these platforms show strong guiding ability, their role in attracting and cultivating new movie-watching groups has yet to come into full play.

In the next round of the game, how to get out from under price wars and undercutting in the industry, how to dream up and buoy up movie-watching incentives, how to meet the demands of segmented film-audiences, how to develop a new crop of filmgoers, and how to effectively develop and expand in the current market is not only the questions that mark the direction for these companies to move, but also highlights the challenges they face.

Finally, on the service level. Though the four companies have gone all out to emphasize user experience and spared no expense in building service pipelines and platforms for this purpose, it remains to be seen whether the heavenly vision depicted by these companies can come down to Earth, as factors outside of their control, such as the technical threshold and increasing numbers of medium-sized competitors getting in on the action and fighting for their share of the pie will inevitably cloud their future to some appreciable degree. Any differentiation advantage cannot be truly established without two links in the chain being established: First, companies should identify and develop their own unique advantages. Second, they need to somehow get consumers to perceive, identify and accept the differentiation. Only the services that are fully experienced, developed and valued can successfully occupy the minds of consumers and ensure long-term profitability. For this reason, while getting a view of the big picture, the major Internet film companies should better position themselves and put their plans into action in stages, which does call for a certain level of wisdom, foresight and vision.

Besides competing on the above four levels, as it stands now, none of them have seemed to show that they value talent in a way that matches their strategic architecture and plan of attack. Talent is the most vital and long-term factor in the development of any company. And it is for this reason that the differentiated talent training plans, training mechanism and human resources management can best reflect the strategic vision and strategic deployment model of a company. For the foreseeable future, the team will undoubtedly be the true force that brings forth the innovation and development of the film industry.

Therefore, how to guide and motivate individuals to realize their dreams, and how to stimulate their internal creativity, and ultimately achieve the greatest fit between personal vision and corporate strategic objectives, is a subject that any company must put right smack-dab in the middle of its sights when seeking a core competitiveness advantage.

Just as a pyramid will eventually collapse with a hollow foundation, no matter what differentiation strategy is sought and on what level it is launched, ultimately it all comes down to the foundation of the company in building their brand, which will eventually be distilled down to brand differentiation.

To create a unique and non-replicable brand, efforts must be made from the full value content of the firm, from the systematic operation of internal and external factors and from the combination of hard and soft assets.

Wu XiaoBo, a well-known financial and economic writer who was once named the annual 'Chinese Youth Leader' by *Southern People Weekly*, once said that the left hand is the content and the right hand is the connection, then values should be the middle. Only by expanding the strategic profit model from the coordinated development of the left, the middle and the right, giving full impetus to the sweeping development of intellectual property, can truly high level of competitive differentiation and a broader development space for firms be realized.

REFERENCES

Anon. (n.d), 'China's film industry still needs to adhere to "Content is King" in the Internet age', *China Economic Net*, http://www.ce.cn/culture/gd/201603/21/t20160321_9652429.shtml. Accessed 1 January 2018.

Anon. (n.d), 'When we talk about movies, we talk about the Internet', *CEIBS Business Review*, http://www.haokoo.com/startup/2083351.html. Accessed 1 January 2018.

Porter, Michael (2003), *Competitive Advantage* (trans. C. Xiaoyue), Beijing: Huaxia Publishing House.

Shangbin, Lv and Shanshan, Dai (2016), 'Platform strategy and instruction in the internet plus era', *Shandong Social Sciences*, 4, pp. 13–18.

Wang Xinxi (2016), 'Why do LeTV and Wanda Cinemas all want to break into Hollywood?', Business Sohu.com, http://business.sohu.com/20160125/n435699815.shtml. Accessed 1 January 2018.

NOTE

1. Zhang Qiang, CEO of Alibaba Pictures: Changing Films with Internet Thinking and Technology, Ent.people.com.cn, Zhang Qiang, CEO of Ali Pictures: Moving Movies with Internet Thinking and Technology.

3. From the Golden Age of the Market to the Golden Age of Creativity — 2016 A Memo to Chinese Filmmakers

尹鸿/Yin Hong 梁君健/Liang Junjian

After 14 consecutive years of high-speed development, 2016 marked the year that the Chinese film market finally entered a 'growth fatigue period' and a 'creative change era'. Reliance on the dividend created by reform, the distribution channel advantage facilitated by the Internet and the capital created by the profit motive have begun to give way to focus on quality and on the more-and-better avenues created by cinematic excellence that seems to symbolize the new norm in Chinese cinematic development. Judging by the creative landscape, the era of reliance on big event movies, beautiful faces, sex appeal and dazzling special effects – the 'Sex + violence + gimmicks' formula – sweeping the market seems to have passed. This year many franchise films, and even 'Super IP' event movies, though technically advanced and visually stunning, have underwhelmed audiences, as these films fail to tell a bankable story with compelling characters, emotional truth and market effectiveness. Plus, the formulaic romantic-comedy built on the 'love + laughs' model that has been such a guaranteed hit over the past few years was also given the cold shoulder by the movie-going audience. Banking on over-the-top hype and marketing gimmicks to sell a ho-hum movie seems no longer able to sell tickets by 'manipulating' the audience's emotions. Any element other than quality is having a greatly reduced impact on the film market, as a better-quality film production is now necessary to get the big thumbs up from the audience (Hong 2017).

This year, Chinese cinema revealed no explosive growth or surprise hits. Discourse was bandied about the mainstream value in *Operation Mekong* and the commerciality offset by an environmental protectionist theme of *The Mermaid*, then there was the Asian action aesthetics of *The Monkey King 2*, the black humour and cultural connotations of *Mr. Donkey*, the circular composition and realism of *I am not Madame Bovary*, and even Ang Lee's 3D technological extravaganza shot at 4K resolution with a jaw-dropping 120 frame rate just served to subvert the aesthetics of the cinematic experience with his technically innovative, the contribution of Song of Phoenix to Chinese art films. Obviously, all this means that the focus of Chinese film is shifting from the market to the creator. Everyone from the audience to the media, from the industry to the government management has realized one thing: if development is top priority, then quality is the lifeblood of development. This is also the basic consensus reached by the forty-five filmmakers at the Changchun International Film Festival in the 'Second Chinese Film New Force' forum (Hongsen 2016).

Of course, due to the fact that the inertia of the market and capital goes on, and the exploration of creativity and aesthetics takes time. So, judging from what we see happening, creative films coming out of Mainland China in 2016 were numerous, but excellent quality films were scarce. There weren't many films released in 2016 that were a legitimate poster child for that must-see movie that has something for everyone. However, it should be said that quite a few remarkable movies have come out this year. Filmmakers from the Mainland, Hong Kong and Taiwan have very notably recognized the excellence of the Mainland film this year. Most of the top prizes of the 53rd Taiwan Film Golden Horse Awards in 2016 went to Mainland films, with the best dramas award going to *The Summer is Gone*. The best director award went to Feng XiaoGang for *I am not Madame Bovary*. The best actor and best actress awards went to Fan Wei for *Mr. No Problem* and to Zhou DongYu and Ma SiChun respectively for the film *Soulmate*. In addition, *Crosscurrent*, *Candle in the Tomb* and *Detective Chinatown* won technical awards, such as best cinematography, best sound effects, best visual effects and best production design. In addition, films like *Cock and Bull*, *The Wasted Times*, *Kaili Blues*, *Big Fish and Begonia* and the co-productions *The Great Wall*, *Born in China* that came out this year are those with that must-not-miss-out movie significance. Compared with the ambiguity and chaos of past years, the quiet and calm 2016 seems more diverse and more serene, more like the transformation of the Chinese film from the golden age of the market to the golden age of the creator.

Part 1: The Rise of Mainstream Newtopia-Themed Films

If the Chinese Dream is a foundation for an epoch, then letting every Chinese citizen live free and safe, and with dignity and conviction should be the essence of this dream. The previous crop of Chinese films was markedly polarized into two extremes in terms of the values expressed therein. One extreme is the 'main-line' film that espouses upright Christ-like morality and anti-individualist values, while the other extreme is the commercial film, which openly espouses mammonist, utilitarianist and sensationalist values. In 2016, Chinese filmmakers took to more consciously conveying the value system of the Pretopia that is based on respect for the life, freedom and dignity for the common man. An increasing number of films are expressing respect for freedom and equal rights, preservation of fairness, social justice, and love and sacrifice out of one's own free will. The best candidate to represent this type of film in 2016 is definitely *Operation Mekong*.

As a film based on real events, *Operation Mekong* did not attempt to accurately re-create actual events, nor did it adopt the, 'Godlike, Daring, Quixotic' hero narrative of the typical 'main-line' film, but attempted to boldly remake the genre by highlighting the legendary quality of the events with tension, drama and action, as well as successfully infusing the modern reverse patriotic value of 'the nation loves its people' into the traditional patriotic value of 'the people love their nation' (Hong 2016a). The film evoked an enthusiastic response from the market and great word of mouth, being that it managed to hit a level of creativity and high production values expected in commercial films. The story interlaces many intricate elements together into a tightly woven fabric, creating a seamless and compelling plot. It tells of Gao-Gang, the captain of a special forces team whose members each have varying elite skills and unique personalities. The portrayal of the character of Xin Wu, the undercover agent, represents a radical breakthrough. His dual nature that vacillates between 'human' and 'demon' deepens the emotional appeal of the character. Though these features seemingly embody all the conventions and stereotypes of the police action movie genre, for a Chinese made film to successfully integrate characters, subplots, details, action and story so perfectly and do it in such a beautiful homage to the action adventure genre makes this film one in a million. It is because of the perfect understanding and consistent execution of the rhythms and pulses of the genre that make this film a fine example of homebrewed Chinese cinematic excellence.

In addition to the high degree with which it fulfilled the expectations of the genre, the success of *Operation Mekong* hits the modern interpretation of mainstream values at a much deeper level. In recent years, commercial films have often been strongly denounced for their deviation from wholesome values. some films tout the 'Gilded Flawless Swashbuckler' and 'Billion-heiress Fashionista Maiden ethic as the gold-standard of success in life. They hype fame and fortune, power and supremacy. They ballyhoo individualism, self-interest and hedonism. They work to subvert integrity, innocence, faith, dignity and other positive values. *Operation Mekong* gives a positive portrayal of a group of fearless, loyal, self-sacrificing anti-drug police officers devoted to their mission. In the film, Gao Gang and company are on a cross-border enforcement mission because thirteen Chinese seamen were killed, and drugs smuggled across the Golden Triangle hurt their loved ones and ordinary people alike. Therefore, what their heroic actions represent is more than just an abstract idea of a country, but a concrete idea of citizenry. In the film, the nation becomes a community of citizens made up of ordinary folk. The leading man's heroism is not only related to the abstract notion of honour, but moreover the safety and dignity of every citizen, even to themselves. The murder of the loved ones and comrades-in-arms is related to sacrifice. So, heroism and patriotism in the film are associated with each person's individual identity as well as their national identity, and the audience feels that the power that a nation imbues in every one of its heroes is palpable to every member of the audience.

The success of *Operation Mekong* shows that the main-line ideology of a nation should never be a lone voice preaching from the pulpit in an 'I-say-you-follow' manner, nor should it be indoctrinated into the people with no respect to their own spiritual needs. The true main-line (ideology) should be closely related to the people's own values. It is the value system and sentiment in which everyone can willingly share and share-alike. In this film, patriotism is not just the people-love-the-country sermonized ideology emphasized in the past, but one that emphasizes that the country that loves the people. Only when the country loves every citizen will the citizens feel pride and esteem for their country; to love and safeguard, to honour and cherish their country. In fact, quite a few Mainstream Hollywood's hits also express similar patriotic values, be it *Saving Private Ryan*, or the recent *Argo*, *Captain Phillips*, *Bridge of Spies* and *Sully*, and Mainland films such as *Bodyguards and Assassins* and *Assembly* have also done this successfully. And it is under the context of these new values that Chinese cinema has gradually improved. *Operation Mekong* Action has a new interpretation of the patriotism theme and the main-line values that are on par with the modern national concept and humanistic values.

Speaking from the perspective of sociocultural laws, only those values that are recognized commonly as shared values could ever truly be considered the main-line, and the new value system in Chinese movies should likewise be built upon the rock of these shared values. Fidelity, purity, integrity, respect, freedom, equality, perseverance and sacrifice; these are and have always been the common values that serve as a spiritual basis for human kind to understand each other, support each other and encourage each other. If we break away from these shared values and fanatically preach anger out of individual need or simply the desire to vent our emotions, we will divorce ourselves from the culturally edifying properties of film. On surveying China's 2016 film landscape, we found that a large number of commercial films have returned to shared values in different ways, expressing a new set of values that have become the new norm. For example, the treatment of money and affection in romances such as *The Mermaid*, *Finding Mr. Right 2*, the promotion of the power of justice and friendship in *Cold War 2* and *Chongqing Hot Pot*, and even *Mr. Donkey*, *I am not Madame Bovary* and other films that reflectcommon values. We have also seen environmental protectionist and the entrepreneurial spirit themes popping up in a great many films, which pointedly express the shared values of freedom and equality. Only when Chinese films can gain audience recognition ,achieve high level of production quality, express mainstream values, we can have a real mainstream cinema, and only then can a popular culture that brings spiritual edification and cultural influence on ordinary audiences. And with this subtle influence provide a spiritual and emotional home that can be shared by everyone at a time on confusion when values are being torn asunder.

Part 2: Categorizations and Upgrades

Heading into 2016, 'franchise' is still a fifty-cent word inevitably bandied about in the financial and creative practices of the Chinese film industry. In a broad sense, a media franchise is all the creative texts and stories that can be spun-off into intellectual properties (the rights to film adaptations of literature and dramas can be put into this big basket for nearly a hundred years), and in a narrower and more accurate sense, a media franchise is primarily the Internet properties disseminated via the vehicle of the Internet, such as online literature, games, animation, Internet celebrities, videos and so forth. IP is not only about the creative texts that appear on the Internet, but also the crowd experience that forms in the process of Internet communication, the crowd emotion formed in the user sharing process and the shared-crowd emotion formed in the user interaction. Users, emotion and shared-emotion are three aspects of the wisdom of the crowd on the Internet. The unparalleled accessibility and attention it brings to media franchises reaches far beyond traditional literary and artistic creation methods. Therefore, adapting Internet properties with their own established patterns of dissemination has become an important model for creating film and television products.

This year, Chinese cinematic offerings were only the touched-on adaptations of traditional Chinese mythological fiction and other literary works, such as *The Monkey King 2*, and *The Legend of the Gods*, but also the adaptation of *Operation Mekong* based on actual events. Then there is *Happy Dad and Son*, *Masters in the Forbidden City* and other TV programs adapted from animated series or documentaries that have an established audience, as well as *Soulmate* adapted from Annie Baby's eponymous novel, and *I am not Madame Bovary*, adapted from Liu ZhenYun's eponymous novel, as well as *Someone to Talk To* and other traditional literary adaptations. These adaptations are mainly based on the thematic expression of the work itself or the accurate capture of the realities of life, as well as the long-established national cultural memory, rather than the original Internet influence and possible adaptations of fan crowdsourced resources. This year's real Internet properties were taken mainly spun-off from online literature, such as *Time Raiders*, *L.O.R.D. – Legend of Ravaging Dynasties*, *Belonged to You*, *See You Tomorrow* and a large number of youth romances, as well as Sino-Xenic co-productions based on video games such as *World of Warcraft*.

Big multimedia franchises have been an unstoppable force over the past several years, and have mowed down the competition, but in 2016 they have suddenly hit a wall. The zero-growth rate at the summer box office has become a major obstacle in the franchise's story arc. The summer movie season is targeted at young people, and this demographic is greatly influenced by Internet culture and constitutes the core fanbase for Internet properties. Consequently, from 2015 'franchise year one', the summer movie season has become a time for media franchises to gather in the market in droves. In 2016 most of them were adapted from online literature, such as *Time Raiders*, *Sweet Sixteen*, *A Smile is Beautiful*, *Never Gone* and *L.O.R.D. – Lord of Ravaging Dynasties*, which swarmed the summer film market hoping to cash in on name-recognition in conjunction with sultry sex-symbols cast to bring the franchise's rabid fanbase flocking to a theatre near them. But in the end, with the exception of *L.O.R.D. – Lord of Ravaging Dynasties*, which took in a little over one-billion CNY, other major franchise films failed to impress in terms of word of mouth and box-office receipts, and even withered on the vine. The audience and the market alike have become cold and detached towards franchise movies, and when the current market boom flatlines, only those that live up to the standards of business logic and artistic convention will have a shot at seeping into the collective consciousness of Chinese cinema.

From a thematic perspective, youth and fantasy are the two main categories of popular online literature and are likewise the two main types spun-off into franchise films. According to statistics, from 2009 to 2015, twenty-three online novels were adapted into films, and teen movies with romantic elements accounted for nearly 90% (Xiaomin 2016). However, this year's teen films have become far less able to resonate with the audience and the market, and the entire genre is in a state of decline. Many films only focus on the characteristics of the media franchise itself. They fail to analyse the characteristics of the fanbase, not breaking down the 'affective state of the crowd' attached to the franchise. They cannot extrapolate a set of genre rules or story styles that meet fan demand. More importantly, the creative models used are nothing but bad carbon copies. The narratives are pretentious, the characters are robotic, the imagery is formulaic, and the storylines are bogged down in newfangled conventionality. They lack the sharp wit of human expression or the profound novelty of artistic insight. Plus, many of these projects are actually just slapped together for a quick buck. On the other hand, some films based on literary adaptations reflect real artistic concepts and human emotions like serenity, delicacy and exploration. For example, *Soulmate*, *What's in the Darkness* and *The Summer Is Gone*, which break new ground in the realm of youth-themed art films.

Just as film adaptations of novels and stage plays are one of the important ways of creating movies, in the Internet age, spinning off Internet properties has brought with it a treasure trove of resources for film creation. Of course, any adaptation is a new art form of re-creation, but whether it can accurately capture the core values or crowdsourcing experience of the Internet property, and whether it can adapt the Internet property into a film that conforms to cinematic communication standards with proper cinematic visual expressiveness. That coupled with the ability to produce afresh and unconventional adaptation, one that gives that 'familiar sense of unfamiliarity'. This is the basic prerequisite for a successful adaptation of an Internet property. The wealth of creative experiences that have emerged and lessons learned through the long process of adapting literature have worked together to steel and refine the practice, while studies and classic texts now provide the basis for judgement and evaluation of the quality of these adaptations. As a new and unknown, there is a lack of the requisite analysis and research on the art and science of the proper adaptation, regardless of whether it is the producers or researchers doing the work. But the adaptation in and of itself does not necessarily guarantee a successful film even though it is the right thing to do. These IP holdings have value, but it has to be adapted into a successful movie before the value can be fully realized. At the end of the day, the owners of any property that is adapted quick and slipshod manner just to get it to the market under the he-who-hesitates-is-lost banner will just end up drinking the Kool-Aid. How to transform the Internet text into a successful film script still poses a difficult question for the adapter to address, and the answer is, more creative methods are needed.

Part 3: The Opportunities and Challenges Facing Technical Aesthetics

Besides the theme of young love, in 2016, films with the made-in-China label adapted from Internet properties also turned their attention towards the fantasy genre, with its intriguing themes and imaginative worlds that reflect the aesthetic tastes of Internet users and trends in today's online literature. The thing is, fantasy is inextricably linked to the technological side of filmmaking. The Chinese film industry may have been calling for domestically produced fantasy and sci-fi films, saying that the appeal is universal, but the problem is the investment is astronomical, and the industrial process requirements for the entire film industry are off in outer space. Only the big franchise films provide the crowd emotion and audience size, but that in and of itself is not enough. It also requires the support of a fairly well-rounded and well-integrated industrial system. This year the fantasy film genre in China has entered a time of development opportunity. One side of the equation is the Internet property adaptation boom happening in China that has strong demand from the younger generation of viewers, and the fact that the current mainland box office is strong enough to allow any medium-scale fantasy film to recover its cost. The other side of the equation is the cumulative experience Chinese film producers have in putting the technical aesthetics of the fantasy genre on celluloid, and coupled with the formation of a global film industry support system, fantasy film production in China has entered a period of rapid development. 2015's, *Monster Hunt* – a made-in-China fantasy film – with its high-box-office numbers proved that fantasy is a mainstream and bankable genre in China. 2016's *The Mermaid* has once again proven the bankability of the genre with a record ¥3 billion plus in domestic box-office receipts. Fantasy movies have a huge audience. *The Monkey King 2*, *Time Raiders* and *The Great Wall* have all, in rapid succession, shown the new explorations in the technical aesthetics of Chinese cinema to the world.

Journey to the West is a household fantasy story in China, then presenting that storythrough film technology is a big test for fantasy film creators. This year *The Monkey King 2* breathed new life into an ancient story by creating a 'fantasy world' that embodied a relatively high level of mastery over technology and aesthetics. If the traditional 'three-battle' story is to illustrate right, wrong and justice by The Monkey King's victory over the White Bone Demon, then this film tells the story of human salvation with the monk Tang Seng's sacrifice of his own life as an allegory for human salvation. In that sense, *The Monkey King 2* has the cultural confidence to reinterpret the traditional classics. Standing on the shoulders of the classics and with the help of new film technology, the cultural and aesthetic of a new era is embodied in world of the gods and Bodhisattvas flying overhead. The film's 3D stereoscopy, the action sequences, the richness of the spectacle and even the realistic rendering of the scenes serve to exhibit the high level of technical attainment that Chinese cinema has realized. It can even be compared with Hollywood productions of the same vein, reflecting the technology that Chinese films have the power to hold their own in the global grapple for cinematic supremacy. The drama, suspense and pacing of the film may be a bit uneven, especially the lack of proper act turns or story drivers, as well as believable psychological and emotional motivations for the characters, but the 'cultural awareness' of classical culture expressed in the film definitely provides vital inspiration for the 'creative transformation' of traditional culture and the improvement of Chinese fantasy films from technology to aesthetics (Hong 2016c).

Chinese animated films, which are striving to make the move from just-for-kids to for-all-ages and for-the-whole-family, have also contributed mightily to the exploration of the fantasy genre and technical aesthetics. If we say that we have seen many traces of imitation and copycatism in *Monkey King: Hero Is Back*, then in 2016, the Chinese animation, 2016 is the year that *Big Fish and Begonia* – a film meant to be the poster child for Chinese animation – learned all the tricks in Hollywood's creative book and made a concerted effort to fuse them together with Chinese culture. This fusion highlighted new accomplishments in Chinese cinema by imagining a fully realized fantasy world. The opening titles of *Big Fish and Begonia* bring to mind images from the classic Chinese Taoist text, *The Zhuangzi*. The old woman's opening monologue serve to set the scene and draw parallels between the universe, the sky and the sea that draw the viewer into the world, and later a subsequent coming-of-age ceremony make for a systematic visual presentation. Moreover, the film is not content to just lay out the broad strokes of the world it creates, but as the story develops, it continually sketches in new details and dabs vivid new colours. The extraordinarily imaginative world unfolds languidly before our eyes, like the opening of a picture scroll, slowly unveiling each new stanza and graphic that brings the audience new surprises and delights. The shortcomings of the film however lie in the relative simplicity of the story and the nonsensical emotional transitions of the characters. *Big Fish and Begonia* lacked emotional punch for some viewers who felt it failed to strike an emotional chord. However, the outstanding production values and imaginative story are still enough to make it a masterpiece of Chinese animation and a true standout in the crop of 2016 films. The philosophical overtones conveyed in the film's message about the circle of life and the endless cycles of the universe provide superb cultural references that can be used to transform Chinese cinema.

The tomb raiding theme has been adapted into three films in just a single year, contributing nearly 2.4 billion CNY to the Chinese box office, which is the other major fantasy themed Internet properties in the film market besides *Journey to the West*. This was a year when *Time Raiders* put valuable 'Orientalized' creativity to good use in film technology and visual design. Director Daniel Lee's name is synonymous with art design and special effects, and this film contains more than 2,600 separate special effects shots. The welcome hall sequence is a combination of visual wonder, local symbols and narrative power, peppered with references to history and culture, and showing off some pretty potent technological advances in terms of the quality of the visuals. Yet the technical wizardry and aesthetic artistry alone do not have a prayer of carrying the film alone. One problem is that the clues and characters are so poorly conceived and fleshed-out, badly besmirching the pristinely polished imagery of the fantasy world. Another problem is the inconsistency in the film due to the excessive commercial influence in the storytelling and visual style. These two issues come to a head in the part leading up to the climax; namely, the Snake Empress Tomb sequence in its tedious entirety. It went on for a full half-an-hour and was simply a smorgasbord of mind-numbing discombobulation. The fates of the characters and the completion of the missions were nonsensical and predictable. The carefully crafted visuals and logical narrative structure of first hour-and-a half were ruined by the snake pit in the Snake Empress Tomb sequence. The film turned to lengthy battle sequences and wondrous spectacle that only served to distract the audience from the lack of dramatic tension and catharsis that quality storytelling would otherwise bring.

Time Raiders continues the original online novel's characterizations, although different characters have seemingly been given unique personality traits and special skills. The crisis caused by the out-of-the-blue tasks getting in the way of character development did not allow for proper attention to be placed upon the inner conflict or struggles of characters. Most of the time, the characters were not faced with challenging ethical dilemmas to overcome their worst fears and vices, and as a result, the inner lives of the characters were short on emotional truth and inner characterization regardless of whether it is was in a scene of enemy becoming an ally, or a special emotional connection being made with a stranger. These narrative shortcomings are not unrelated to the lack of clear values expressed in the film. When a fantasy world has poorly integrated aesthetics and values, any attempt for visual technology to spackle over the carbuncles becomes a case of misappropriated energy. *Time Raiders* attempts to circumvent these inherent flaws prevalent in Chinese fantasy films. And even *The Great Wall*, an East-West collaboration directed by the great Zhang YiMou, had trouble breaking out of this quagmire. *League of Gods* and *L.O.R.D – Lord of Ravaging Dynasties* are even shakier in terms of the integrity of their respective artistic visions. Let us not mince words here. When the storytelling, character portrayals and emotional colourings in Chinese fantasy films all miss the mark, the remaining showmanship can only be called in-your-face technological showboating. And this only serves to diminish dramatic anticipation.

Technical aesthetics is an important tradition in world cinema. Following in Georges Méliès' footsteps, film auteurs have followed suit and are committed to creating new visual experiences through film technology. The emergence of computer technology has greatly strengthened the tradition of technical aesthetics. In addition to science fiction films, fantasy films, mythological films, action fantasy films, animated fantasy films and even animal fantasy films are emerging, forming a mainstream aesthetical trend. The technical aesthetic in film is most apparent on the transnational stage. Although Hollywood has crafted many a technically proficient drama, such as *Lincoln* and *Argo*, the degree to which they are globalized does not hold a candle to the likes of franchise mega-giants, *Star

Wars, *Harry Potter*, *The Lord of the Rings*, *Transformers*, *The Avengers* and other films steeped in the astounding technical wizardry popular with young people around the world these days. An emphasis on technical aesthetics is an unavoidable challenge for Chinese cinema and the filmmakers who work in it. The aesthetics behind technology involves aspects of microaesthetic image design, and, to an even greater extent, fantasy world design that conveys a macroaesthetic concept through a specially designed fictional world complete with narratives and values. One that is heavy on production values, light on artistry; heavy on eye-candy, light on acting; heavy on spectacle, light on emotionality; heavy on archetypes, light on characterizations; heavy on setups, light on details. In other words, the emphasis is on technology but not on aesthetics. It is vacuous, loud and flashy. It is the tell-tale signs, a 'symptom' showing that Chinese fantasy films have apparently become infected with the international pandemic known as 'Hollywood summer popcorn movie syndrome'. Unfortunately, a mild case of this may just provide the necessary vaccine to strengthen Chinese cinema for the next leg of the journey to proficiency in technical aesthetics. Be that as it may, it is nevertheless expected that Chinese-style fantasy films will create a fully realized imaginary world that reflects an orientalist worldview, outlook and aesthetics, which will aid in the transformation of traditional Chinese culture by means of creative transformation of traditional Chinese culture. For the globalized Chinese and for the world!

Part 4: Trade-offs between Hard and Soft

In the past ten years of industrial reform, China's conventional commercial films may be visually resplendent, but they can largely be categorized into two categories under two labels, soft and hard. The soft type consists of two genres, 'comedies + romances'. While the 'hard' type consists of the 'martial arts + police dramas'. The former is dominated by mainland films, while the latter is represented by Hong Kong cinema. In 2016, there were still a good deal of important commercial films made fitting within these categories that took up the lion's share of the Chinese film market. That said, in 2016 there was no clear soft-type box-office underdog, like *Breakup Buddies*, or *Goodbye Mr. Loser* in 2015. And there was apparently a resurgence of hard-style martial arts and cop films. Not only did this year bring us powerful Hong-Kong cop thrillers like *Cold War 2*, *Three* and *Line Walker*, but it also saw mainland films *Operation Mekong* and *Chongqing Hot Pot* moving towards the same hard-type narrative style, and visual and sound design. Even for fantasy films, *The Great Wall*, *The Mermaid* and *Time Raiders* exhibited a hard-style by their prominent use of fight scenes.

One of the few standout romantic comedies this year was Stephen Chow's, *The Mermaid*, which set the Spring Festival film season on fire, blazing its way into the Chinese box office record books. The film tells the story of a group of mermaids that sends alluring mermaid Shan to seduce and assassinate real-estate development tycoon, Liu Xuan, due to his water reclamation project that is threatening the mermaids' living space. But owing to a set of odd coincidences the two of them end up falling in love. The film carries the torch of Stephen Chow's signature hyperbolic style known for its exaggerated and farcical comedic elements. Although no longer considered fresh and hip to the young crowd, it nevertheless made its powerful appeal to the young crowd. The film not only makes a statement about the destruction of the ecological environment by the supremacy of money and commercial interests, but also with great imagination satisfies the spiritual needs of a young generation desperate to transcend worldly desires. This romantic comedy was specially made to be suitable for all ages, and with big points scored for its environmentalist, it is all the more perfect for the Spring Festival movie season. More importantly, the central motifs of the film are of conspiracy and salvation. There are chase scenes, and fight scenes that are action threads weaving the plot together with the love and comedy interspersed throughout, like an embellishment. Like the previous year's *Monster Hunt*, Action + Romance + Comedy seems to be a new trend in popular commercial movies, which brings us to Zhang YiMou's film, *The Great Wall*. Besides deviating from artistry, two of the important commercial elements, love and comedy, went noticeably missing from the film, ultimately dividing audiences.

Finding Mr. Right 2 is another long-awaited soft-type romance. In terms of the screenwriting, the film utilizes a challenging parallel plot structure with narrative patterns that work well with its thematic development. It imbues the love story with life and rhythm and provides an in-depth exploration of the emotional underpinnings of the relationship. That said, the complexity of the film impacts the crispness of the narrative rhythm. While at the same time, the love story mainly unfolds while the two are getting to know each other before they actually meet. It plays out underscored by a rhythm that is out-of-step with the current Chinese moviegoer's habit of acceptance, which led directly to the film's relatively poor word-of-mouth compared to the first film praised as fresh and inspired. However, *Finding Mr. Right 2* still shows us a serious love story that has a rightful place in China's modern film annals. *I Belonged to You* and *See You Tomorrow*, films with high audience expectations, were largely panned. Meanwhile, heavily hyped *MBA Partners* and *When Larry Met Mary* should have made a killing, but instead got killed at the box office. The stories of these films lack punch, and the artistry is often uninspired. Even the affective logic of the characters is obviously porous

– that coupled with the lack of genuine narrative and character-driven affection and sentiment just vastly reduced the artistic and commercial value of these projects.

Compared with the feeble and fizzling soft-type rom-com genre, the hard-type commercial film, bolstered by visceral cop flicks and chop-socky martial arts movies, is on the rise. The high-octane action and excitement of the genre gives it an edge with audiences. *The Cold War 2* continues the brutal infighting of the first film, and *Line Walker*, adapted from the popular TV series, injects new blood into the genre in terms of narrative and style. *Cold War 2* not only carries its predecessor's portrayal of the dirty power-jockeying that takes place in government agencies such as the police and the ICAC, but also further develops the narrative through a number of new characters. It gives a detailed insider look at the power struggles that exist in politics from law enforcement to legislation and extends them to the highest authority in the land – the SAR itself – which is very rare in the history of Hong Kong police films. Faced with a complex and sordid web of interdepartmental and interpersonal relationships, the story makes for a high-intensity audiovisual experience, and a high-octane thrill ride that promotes positive values such as justice, law and family, while at the same time entertaining action enthusiasts and the average moviegoer alike. *Line Walker* organically fuses the two narratives of 'brotherhood and loyalty' with 'undercover agent and hidden identity' in the Hong Kong action film and police drama genres. The former establishes the structure and emotional value of the relationship between the characters, while the latter provides the dramatic turns and narrative power. In addition, buddy cops Francis Ng and Charmaine Sheh partnership almost perfectly re-creates the action comedy stylings in the early Hong Kong police films. In short, though the same Infernal Affairs-esque quantum leaps have not been made in recent Hong Kong action cinema, the plot setups, characterizations, visual style, scene creation and pacing were very solid. Most well-founded of all were the individualist and legalist themes. It seems the ideas of fairness and justice have struck a cross-cultural and ageless chord for the Mainland audience.

Several other hard-style type films also have their own characteristics. *Chongqing Hot Pot* is also a hard-type film that hits commercial aesthetic standards right on the head. It not only propagates the basic values of justice, friendship, affection and dignity, but also in an instant grips the audience in a bold action-packed adventure and a unique visual experience. Although the film is too overburdened by overwrought fight scenes, which hurts the characterizations and emotional details of the film, the storytelling is nonetheless strong and stylish. *Ip Man 3* uses a familiar recipe to continue the tale of Ye Wen's life in Hong Kong. The story spends a great deal of its ink on life quality and family values. This sequel seems determined to make the value of kinship its greatest common denominator, as opposed to the nationalism in the first two. However, much of what happens in the film seems intrinsically and extrinsically motivations inorganic and unmotivated. The narrative was really loose and lax. What is undergone by the protagonist played out like a level-boss fight in a video game, which lowered the film's artistic merit.

After the popularity of the 'rom-com' began to wane, the hard-type film revival indicated demand for different types of movies, and just goes to show that, as filmgoers grow savvier, they will expect a more cinematic experience. They will want stronger narratives, more elaborately staged scenes, more well-fleshed out characters and more intense action, which are the key differences between the cinema experience and TV or online video experience. Consequently, the soft-type of film should definitely amp up the intensity of the story and the emotion, so that it can offer an extraordinary, remarkable and potent experience. The hard-type film needs exactly the opposite. Besides intensity and action, it is necessary to add more human feelings and a sense of karma. Contemporary soft-type movies in China are too gentle and lack strength, while hard-type movies are too stylish and lack conscience. Putting softness into the hard and hardness into the soft is a pressing issue that must be addressed in commercial film production. In this connection, *Lost in Thailand* was an example of a successful soft-type movie from 2012, while this year *Operation Mekong* is an example of a fairly successful hard-type movie.

Part 5: Audience Fragmentation and Stylized Films

The new normal of Chinese cinema is the new normal for moviegoers. Due to the rapid expansion of the film market, a large number of inexperienced 'new audiences' lacking film savvy have become a blip on the film consumer demographic radar over the past few years. Especially the 'Internet generation', which has been epitomized with recent Chinese slang like, 'Small-town youthy', 'internet feely', 'zany' and 'levelled-up'. But as this audience becomes more experienced, audience standards will soar, and as a result viewing habits will diversify. This will in turn work to improve Chinese film stylings. Looking back on 2016, there were fewer bona-fide blockbusters or sleeper hits, but audiences became increasingly fragmented and their interests became increasingly diverse. Fourth-generation director Wu TianMing made a traditional documentary film, *Song of the Phoenix* with plenty of marketing steam powering it, and after an extended run at the box-office, it took in ¥70 million CNY. The serene and languid romantic drama, *Soulmate* broke the ¥100 million CNY box-office threshold. Small-scale expressionist art films such as *Kaili Blues*, *Crosscurrent* and *Tharlo* carved out their own market niche. After Lu Chuan's nature documentary *Born in China* grossed nearly

¥80 million CNY at the box office, year-end documentaries *Masters in the Forbidden City* and *This is Life* also attracted widespread attention. *Mr. Donkey* followed in Jiang Wen's footsteps with *Let the Bullets Fly*, creating another Chinese-style historical allegorical film with cultural and artistic depth.

In 2016, Feng XiaoGang's, *I am not Madame Bovary* is an important milestone in Chinese realism. In world cinema, the three main aesthetic traditions are drama, spectacle and realism. Beginning with the Lumiere brothers there has been a long history of realism in filmmaking. Although movies are becoming more and more entertaining, realist cinema is still an important part of the world's film culture. In recent years, there has been a large number of films based on real people and real events across the world. Although these styles vary widely, they all reflect the spirit of cinematic realism by focusing on reality and history. *Lincoln, Dallas Buyers Clubs, Captain Phillips, Snowden, Spotlight, Sully, Hacksaw Ridge* and other Hollywood movies all reflect the return of a realist aesthetic. Movies in developing countries place more emphasis on realist aesthetics. Due to myriad convoluted reasons, in the practice of film production in China, the realist movement has basically been either all talk and no action, or mostly talk and little action. It does not correspond well with the true realities of China's transitional period when things were shaken up numerous times. *I am not Madame Bovary* not only reflects a conscious aesthetic standard in terms of shot selection and the stylistic conveyance, but also gives us a glimpse of the more private side of Chinese society. With restraint and tact, it shows the relationship between the government and the people within a complex social context of an ecological dilemma that reflects a long-lost realist creative attitude.

Although it is easy in comedy to go the way of simplified instead of real characters, the realism in *I am not Madame Bovary* is that there are no cartoonish characters, and no dramatic and moral drama conflicts. A cat and mouse relationship forms between a weak and corrupt petitioner and a spotlessly rationalized administrative system. Li XueLian is desperate, officials are helpless and everyone is blameless, yet no one is empowered to break free from the chaos and mutual destruction. The film vividly presents a vicious cycle involving the officials and the people caught up in 'other people's Hell', and the sense of real life is in a mirror image reflected back at us. This feeling is so close to some of our current real-life experiences that we have to read into the film from various angles, which reflects not only the intrigue of drama but also the power of realism (Hong 2016b). Before the film was officially released, there were many concerns and rumours about film censorship. The finished film ultimately shows how much confidence in art our society and film administration departments really have. From ancient times till today, true realism should reveal and reflect social contradictions and issues, and at the same time express the ideals and aspirations of social progress in this reality. This film is a mirror of real life. It puts the absurdities of life in our face so we can plainly see that, if life is a total disaster, then each and every one of us had a hand in it. And at the end of the day the answer to the question of what force it was that caused society to go to Hell is a riddle wrapped up in a mystery wrapped up in an enigma.

I am not Madame Bovary is comical, but the comedy is not through exaggeration, but through observational humour. It encapsulates all the things we are used to in life and splashes them on the screen before us. It is a window that that points our attention right at them. As Lu Xun once said, 'Comedy rips a hole in the wall of life and lets us peep through at everything meaningless inside, and at the same time shows us everything meaningless *in life* right there on the other side' (Xun 1980). In this sense, this is Feng XiaoGang's most unique comedy. It is the chemistry between Feng XiaoGang and the original author Liu ZhenYun that has produced a newfangled comedy aesthetic – one that is deadpan and foreboding, spiced with the flavour of Chekhov's *The Seagull* and *The Cherry Orchard*. 'The more objective the impression is, the deeper a chord it strikes'. This 'realism of daily life' has taken Feng XiaoGang's comedy to a new level (Hui 2013). Though Feng XiaoGang seems to hem and haw and pussyfoot around, leaving much of his message unsaid, there is still much to be said about the visuals, performances, rhythm and information intensiveness of the film. The reflective ending might actually be criticized as overly conceptual, but as a mirror for society, ordinary people and officials alike can look at themselves truthfully, which is the significance of realism that cannot be underestimated. Acknowledging the merry-go-round is the first step towards getting off the merry-go-round.

Besides *I am not Madame Bovary*, another film loosely based on the *Happy Twist* stage play is *Mr. Donkey* – and it is definitely its own animal. It shows how sad, pathetic, miserable, wretched and ill-fated the educated in China are. And it pulls this off by featuring a rural educational experiment for the enlightened in an unenlightened place without a modern political system – an area where officials were, more-often-than-not, roughnecks and gangsters, and the intellectuals simply nothing in front of them. It is a case of the petty fools taking over so the intellectuals have to run for cover. Though during the Republican Era, foreign nations stared straight at 'China's predicament', and did nothing but stand there glassy-eyed and stone-faced, unwilling or unable to be a lifeline the intelligentsia needed. The film has very few characters in it and a scant few scenes. Though the story took place during the Republican Era, the coda of the film 'deliberately' hinted at a happy ending for the intellectuals in Yan'an. Nevertheless, it depicts the intertwined fates of modern Chinese intellectuals, which was not and will not be them knocking on heaven's door, but rather them staring at the gates of Hell. Although the narrative of this film is somewhat convoluted, and the individual characters poorly fleshed-out, the film itself is concise and powerful, and its meaning profound. The sheer depth of its cultural satire and artistic expressiveness is rare in Chinese movies these days, which also goes to show how the artistry and profundity of the stage just runs circles around film in many aspects.

It should be duly noted that there was room for creativity and a market niche for more stylized films in 2016, though that does not mean that the movie audience is sophisticated enough, nor does it mean that Chinese art films and stylized cinema have reached a high enough standard. Some filmmakers and producers claiming to be auteurs grumble that art films are not given proper screen time at theatres, or groan about the lowly state of audience tastes. However, art films are not synonymous with good movies. Conceptually speaking, many are not creative or penetrating, and the finished product is often rough, oldfangled, amateurish and poorly acted. These so-called 'filmmakers' are nothing more than two-bit hucksters swindling the audience in the grand name of *cinéma d'art*. There are also some art films that lack excellence or are not a true communal experience, while others lack visual and aural impact, with lacklustre cinematography and sound design. Filmgoers certainly do not have to spend their hard-earned money or fight traffic to go to the theatre to watch a movie. A more economical way to experience these films might be on TV or online without any significant picture or sound loss as compared with their theatrical counterparts. So, for the likes of these so-called 'art films', the theatre doors will most likely remain perpetually closed. And this does not only go for art films, but if any movie is to be consumed, it must have that irreplaceable 'cinematic' factor that sets it apart from TV, Internet or Blu-ray. Now, the question of whether a movie will be given a theatrical release is directly related to its quality, and whether or not it gives the 'cinematic' experience that makes it fit for theatrical viewing. Only those art films with truly extraordinary content, sensory impact and communality can carve out a niche for audiences in the theatre.

Part 6: The East-West Co-productions in Cross-Border Film Production

The sheer size of the Chinese film market and the strong desire Chinese filmmakers have for their films to go international have led to the development of cross-border film production and international film production in the past few years. This development has not only caused an exponential rise in the number of co-productions, but also expanded the collaborative methods and dynamics. This year, Chinese filmmakers have been working in the spirit of cooperation with cultural neighbours like South Korea, as well as with European countries to produce art films. They also have even been collaborating with the Hollywood mega-giants, to make the small-market film, *Born in China*, as well as mega-budget movies like *The Great Wall*, and even in sequels to Hollywood's popular summer movies such as *Now You See Me*, *Jason Bourne* and *The Avengers*.

Over the past few years, Sino-Korean co-productions have been a major bright spot in the Chinese film market with both *Miss Granny* and *A Wedding Invitation* performing very well at the box office. However, with declining interest in soft-type commercial films in the Chinese film market, these Chinese-Korean co-productions created banking on the strength of their comedy and romance did not have many highlights to speak of in 2016. Sino-French co-produced art films have attracted attention. *Wolf Totem* and *The Nightingale* artistically express contemporary Chinese themes from an international perspective, which does have a certain value. But culturally speaking, for the Chinese audience watching these films conceived and produced in an exotic land is like French chefs from far off whipping up dishes of *escargot* and tête de veau and serving them to you with a side of *Rémoulade* sauce. They are bewildering. Staggering. And dizzying as trying to make out the petals of a flower through a thick fog while bobbing up and down on a raft. In a word, they are foreign. Inscrutable. Impenetrable. How can these films possibly connect with the viewer if the meaning is muddled and indistinct? That said, collaborations between the Chinese and American film industries seem to be more market-oriented and commercial. *The Expendables 2*, *Looper* and *Iron Man 3* are hard-type commercial films jointly invested in by Chinese and American studios, but the acting and plot had certain Chinese elements to them (Wei 2013). The importance of Chinese actors and Chinese elements in films such as *Transformers 4* has grown stronger (Yiping 2015). Some well-known Hollywood directors have also begun to explore partnerships with Chinese film studios. Judging from the films released in 2016, *Kung Fu Panda 3* and *Warcraft*, which are dominated by the US but fully engaged in the creation and distribution of opinions, have had fantastic box-office numbers and word of mouth, while Zhang Yimou's 'Hollywood-style movie, *The Great Wall* is a symbol for Sino-Xenic joint filmmaking effort with its star-studded cast, jaw-dropping budget and made-in-Hollywood attitude.

As a Hollywood-style commercial film, the frame of reference for *The Great Wall* should be *Transformers*, *The Avengers* and *Warcraft*, not *Red Sorghum*, *Raise the Red Lantern*, and not even Zhang Yimou's previous commercial films, *Hero* or *House of Flying Daggers*. With Hollywood stars Matt Damon and Pedro Pascal attached and ready to make *Hualiwood* gold, and it certainly did deliver a Hollywood-style opening, and even in later scenes it was even easy to see Hollywood in it as long as Damon and Pascal were on screen with their little jokes and witticisms. However, the moment they spurred their steeds bravely on to the foot of the Great Wall, greeted by the wave after wave and row upon row of officers and men on the wall with banners waving in the wind, it declared in no uncertain terms that this was a bona-fide Zhang Yimou movie. The Oriental magic he imbued into all those grand 'Impressions' gala outdoor musicals and the Olympic ceremonies were a feast for the eyes. *The Great Wall* is richly imaginative and diverse, with scores of disparate elements coming together in its sumptuous production design. This is something that is rare in world cinema. Of course, this spectacle greatly enhances the enjoyment of the film, and creates an unparalleled and singular viewing experience. But from the perspective of film art, getting back to the standards of technical aesthetics, these dazzling scenes and imagery are the exaggeration of showmanship, which does not match well with the plot, the story, the scene, the characters and the emotions of the audience. The thousands of people on horseback on the edge of the city wall, the gorgeously ornate costumes, the ceremony-like arrangement and the colourful military uniforms no different from stage costumes looked awkward and out of place. Then, of course, there were the female soldiers wearing giant hoops and holding bayonet rifles standing at high above the scene in a bungee-like manner. Beginning with the making of *Hero* to the opening and closing ceremonies of the director, almost all of Zhang Yimou's artistic concepts are arguably steeped in Hollywood fare.

While expressing his own aesthetic ideas with the help of Hollywood's industrial prowess, but Zhang Yimou also expects to use the Hollywood story model to convey Chinese values, and finally use the power of the market to return the iconic symbol of the Great Wall to the centre of the world. The Chinese people are also looking forward to breaking new ground economically through these new co-ventures. The film clearly imagined China as the centre of the world and showed that vision crystal clear to the Chinese audience, satisfying their 'I-developed-long-before-you' affective identification as the emotional scars of the great Chinese empire later pushed around at smoking gunpoint by foreign powers for ages after the Opium War have yet to heal. At the same time, the film also shows a foreign white man like William Garin going from mercenary to soldier, much like we saw the American artist John Miller in the film, *The Flowers of War* who rescued female students and fell in love with the sex worker Yu Mo. Despite all the Oriental magic, the real saviour here is the western Cowboy. So, this film fulfilled the Chinese fantasies of western praise for Oriental culture and the desire to save the West. Behind this, of course is a little goodwill gesture by the Oriental market and the embrace of it by the western audience. Zhang Yimou's desire to explore Chinese and western culture in his films is pretty much out in the open. But whether his desire to have the best of both worlds can be turned into reality depends on whether he follows the basic rules of film art.

Therefore, the dissociation, vacillation and concentration of values is obvious throughout the film. This is also where Zhang Yimou, who is steeped in China's national conditions, and ordinary Hollywood movies differ. Most Hollywood commercial productions are simple, direct and universal in their values. Freedom, dignity, justice, righteousness, love and martyrdom are common. In, *The Great Wall*, the question of why the soldiers marched forward to battle, to war, to slaughter, ready to embrace death with arms wide open, and what spirit it was that allowed them to conquer Garin and his band of 'foreign mercenaries' was not fully answered in the film. In the film, 'trust' seems to be the key to the interaction between the two East and West heroes, which is the 'signal' that turns enemies into allies and allows them to help each other in time of need. But regardless of whether it is the story development or plot design, 'trust' does not present a specific meaning in the film, including in the change of the relationship of the characters. 'Trust' has emotional appeal in Oriental culture and is a core value. And has drifted away from the collectivist consciousness of Chinese culture. If Tao Tieh represents the aggressors, then they are fighting to defend their lives and humanity, not an abstract construct like a country, or to defend a petty little emperor who lives in Peking. However, due to the complexity of information in the film, this potential theme is very vague and weak, never really seeing the light of day (Hong 2016d).

It should be said that whether it is from the size of investment or the massive scale of the film, *The Great Wall* is big enough to be magnificent. In this sense, it has set a precedent for Mainland directors to helm Hollywood's big commercial films, and its significance in the industry goes without saying. However, there are a number of questions for Chinese directors throwing their hat into the global cultural arena to answer. In the process of a co-production, how to convey the shared values of the East and West without pandering to both sides. How to use the expressive story rather than just playing the visual spectacle card. How to combine large production scale with creative refinement, and how to use creativity to transform cultural inertia. It should be said that for Chinese films that have just set foot on the road of international co-production, there is still a long journey ahead.

Conclusion

The supply side reform of Chinese film gradually deepened in 2016. The artistic quality and cultural influence of film have become the basic standards for the film industry and film production. Of course, in the process of development, new problems will continue to emerge. For example, the overall cultural aesthetic sensibilities of film viewers is still skewed. The film industry is far too eager for quick success due to external capital, and the unfairness brought about by the lack of supervision and oversight of the film market. Competitiveness has emerged, and the film creators' cultural consciousness and ethical responsibility are still insufficient. There is a lack of any true masterworks. In the world of filmmaking, the main three hidden concerns are low levels of systemization, lack of branding and market homogeneity. However, all of these issues actually stem from development, and reform. They can only be solved through more thorough development and more sweeping reforms.

As the audience matures, people's demands for film art will also rise. Movies are not just a business, people still need aesthetics. Actors should not simply cash in on their good looks or sex appeal, people still need interesting characters. Movies are just for entertainment, people still need to be moved. A movie is not just a plot, people need more details. Movies are not just spectacle, people need movies to strike a chord and resonate to the heart. Films cannot just be mindless action; people need their minds to be moved to action. In other words, the audience is not in the beginning stages of really knowing how to choose and judge the film. There are three surefire signs of a 'quality movie'. Mainstream value, including mainstream ideological value, ethical value and emotional value. Cinematic intensity is the reason people are willing to spend time and money to go to the theatre, which includes the novelty of the theme and story. The extreme sense of degree, plot and character, the irreplaceability of a sensory impact and an infectious quality. Superior craftsmanship, the ability to create perfection of film production, and the overall integrity of the finished film. Without mainstream value, there will be no real sense of resonance between thought and emotion. Without cinema intensity, there can be no real power to engage and captivate the viewer. Without the spirit of craftsmanship, there will be no satisfaction in the actual viewing. Regardless of whether Chinese films are mainstream commercial films or stylized art films, measures must be taken to improve in terms of emotional resonance, dynamic power and audience satisfaction. Chinese filmgoers not only want to watch movies, but more importantly, they want to watch quality movies.

Of course, we should also see that the film industry is one of the organic components of contemporary China. The problems in the film industry are inextricably linked with the challenges facing China's current society and economy. Chinese film cannot exist without social context, and it must be synchronized with the overall progress of society. In fact, our expectations of the film should be consistent with the expectations of society as a whole. The higher the social value consensus, the stronger the people's moral needs; the higher the audience's aesthetic appreciation, the greater the openness and tolerance of social culture, and the better the film will become. The skin is not attached to the hair, and the film is rooted in the soil of the times; therefore, how good China is, how good Chinese movies can be. In this sense, the future of Chinese film is both bright and the journey down the long and winding road will be tortuous.

REFERENCES

Hong, Yin (2016a), 'Building the mainstream popular film', *Chinese Literature and Art Criticism*, 11.

—— (2016b), '"I am not Madame Bovary": Not a circle, that is a mirror', *China Film*, 20 November.

—— (2016c), '"Subdue the white-skeleton demon": The traditional "creative transformation" and the "real imagination" of the world', *China Film News*, 17 February.

—— (2016d), 'The Great Wall: The skin of Hollywood and the heart of Zhang Yimou', *Beijing Youth Daily*, 23 December.

—— (2017), 'New normal', *People's Daily*, 3 January.

Hongsen, Zhang (2016), 'Focus on quality and a win-win future – Speech at the 2nd China Film New Power Forum', *Contemporary Film*, 11.

Hui, Chen (2013), 'The artistic features of Chekhov's drama', *Hubei Social Sciences*, 11.

Wei, Feng (2013), 'Industrial game and cultural dispersion effect of Sino-US co-productions', *Contemporary Film*, 1.

Xiaomin, Liu (2016), 'The film conversion of story and the cross-media conversion of fans – Commenting on Internet IP adaptation of domestic films', *China Film Market*, 5.

Xun, Lu (1980), 'Re-discussion of Leifeng *Pagoda*'s collapse', *The Complete Works of Lu Xun Grave*, Beijing: People's Literature Publishing House.

Yiping, Cao (2015), 'Dynamic power 2.0 – Sino-US co-production and selective reconstruction of Hollywood business genes', *Film Art*, 3.

4. The Analysis and Strategy of Chinese Rural Film Market Development

张小丽/Zhang Xiaoli

Part 1: Rural Film Market Development during the 12th Five-Year Plan Period

Circumstances

During the '12th Five-Year Plan' period, the Rural Film-Screening Project continued along its developmental lines of the 'Enterprise management, market operators, government purchasing, and public welfare' concept, satisfying the demand for 'Proactive administration, smooth operations, regulated management, and peasant satisfaction', by adhering to a people-centred approach. Grounded in the fight for peasant satisfaction, it afforded rural audiences the opportunity to view quality films and putting that population segment on equal footing in the public sphere.

Infrastructure Development Project

After five years of development, equal attention has been placed on public-welfare screenings and commercial screenings, gradually creating a near-flawless rural film-screening system. By the end of 2015, two-hundred fifty-two (252) digital cinema outlets had been established in rural areas. More than 50,000 mobile projection teams in rural areas and 44,056 sets of projection equipment were in actual operation at 212 ground satellite receiving stations.

Screenings

At the end of the 12th Five-Year Plan period, 45.9201 million screenings had been ordered, with an average of more than 9.18 million per annum, of which, 30.836

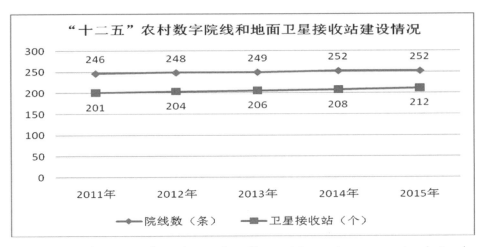

Figure 1: Digital cinema outlet and ground satellite receiving station construction during the 12th Five-Year Plan.

million were public-welfare film screenings, averaging 6.1673 million showings per annum. Also, 15,523,700 showings of non-welfare screenings (commercial) were ordered, averaging 3,147,000 showings per year. With respect to viewing trends, non-welfare showings has increased year-over-year, from 16.33% in 2011 to 49.14% in 2015 (see Table 1).

There were two reasons for the yearly decrease in public-welfare showings. First, urbanization in China has reduced the number of administrative villages. Second, an increasing number of commercial films have entered the rural market in the country.

Year	Total screenings (10,000)	Public-welfare screenings public-domain (10,000)	Percentage of welfare screenings	Non-public-welfare screenings (10,000)	Percentage of commercial film showings
2011	870.47	772.35	88.73%	142.12	16.33%
2012	911.16	709.25	77.84%	201.91	22.16%
2013	906.14	563.23	62.16%	342.91	37.84%
2014	927.03	541.83	58.45%	385.2	41.55%
2015	977.21	496.98	50.86%	480.23	49.14%
Total	4592.01	3083.64	–	1552.37	–

Table 1: Proportion of public-domain film screenings to non-public domain film in the 12th Five-Year Plan period. Source: China Film Market Report, published by the China Film Distribution Association, China Film Market Report, 2011–2016 Annual Report.

Film Distribution

On the film trading platform of the Digital Film Program Management Center of the State Administration of Press, Publication, Radio, Film and Television of the People's Republic of China, 3518 films were available at the end of the 12th Five-Year Plan, an increase of 1904 films over the initial period, of which, 1545 were public-welfare films and 1973 non-public-welfare films. The number of copyright holders involved increased from 119 in 2011 to 251, with a total increase of 132 over a five-year period.

Year	Available (films)	Public welfare (films)	Non-public welfare (films)	Copyright holders (firms)
2011	1614	871	743	119
2012	2320	1047	1273	156
2013	3132	1233	1899	196
2014	3262	1446	1816	231
2015	3518	1545	1973	251

Table 2: Film distribution in the rural film market over the 12th Five-Year Plan.
Sources: 2011–2016 Annual Report of the China Film Market Report, published by China Film Distribution and Exhibition Association and China Film Press; National Press, Publication, Radio, Film and Television, Digital Film Program Management Center website.

The Rural Film Public Service System

The central and local governments spent in excess of ¥1.5 billion CNY per year to subsidize the rural film project in order to ensure its sustainable development. By the end of the 11th Five-Year Plan, the rural film project infrastructure had been gradually seen to completion. New ideas for reform and development were put forward, including the cultivation of business entities, film supply, commercial projection facilities and improvements to viewing conditions and service.

Financing Mechanism

The Rural Film-Screening Project was implemented in 2006 and was incorporated into the public cultural system in 2007. The financing mechanism was initially established in 2008. In 2009, a functional transfer was competed at high speed. In

2010, the digital display system was fully realized. The notice, 'On quality work in Rural Film Project (Guo Ban Fa [2007] No. 38)' proposed a new idea for reform of the project and the, 'Enterprise management, market operation, government procurement services' plan came online. Instructions for the Implementation of the Rural Digital Film Distribution and Projection Project (2007) clarified how rural film exhibition and distribution should work. These two documents directly promoted the establishment of rural digital cinema operators in cities and counties and formed a rural digital film exhibition network with an ordering system and on-demand digital film service platform at its core.

Directives for Promoting the Prosperity and Development of the Film Industry (State Measures [2010] 9) of the General Office of the State Council put forward their goal for establishing and improving the public-welfare film system via 'Enterprise management, market operations, government procurement and public welfare'. On the same day, the notice, 'On promoting the sustainable and healthy development of Rural Film Projects' issued by the State Administration of Radio, Film and Television (Guangfa [2010] 7), proposed that the healthy and sustainable development of the Rural Film-Screening Project should be grounded in ensuring the realization of the goal to increase public-welfare cultural services through film-screenings every month in villages falling at the end of the 11th Five-Year Plan. Both these two plans emphasize 'sustainable development', for a public-welfare platform under market operation. Enterprises need to strengthen the 'self-mobilization' mechanism to power its own development.

During the course of the 12th Five-Year Plan, the public cultural and financing system was vast improved and perfected. The Provisional Measures for the Preservation of Special Funds for Local Rural Cultural Construction with Central Subsidies (Finance and Education No. 25, 2013) stipulated that the standard subsidy for each film showing in rural areas be set at ¥200 RMB. With its more developed economy, the standard subsidy for the eastern region was set at a significantly higher rate. In some areas, the subsidy for each showing was as much as ¥600 RMB, a policy put in place to raise the skill level of projectionists and to guarantee their stable employment.

Film Distribution System

The basic genres include narrative films, opera films, documentaries, educational films, art films, of which the number of narrative films account for approximately 80 per cent. The full spectrum of genres runs the gamut from romance, comedy, war, action, mystery, to children's movies, costume films, adventure pictures, sports flicks and biopics, all the way to inspirational, musical, disaster, animation, thriller, suspense, horror and so forth.

In order to meet the diverse demands of the audience, an initial competitive mechanism was introduced into the film distribution industry, which was exclusively adopted by the original China New Rural Digital Film Screening Co., Ltd. (hereinafter referred to as the 'China New Rural Film') and subsequently went under the joint control of 'China New Rural Film', and the 'Digital Film Program Management Center'. Huaxia Film Distribution Co., Ltd, Jiuzhou Tongying, Jiuzhou Yida, The Beijing Jiuzhou Dinghe Cultural Communication Co. Ltd, the Beijing Degao Culture Development Co., Ltd, the Beijing Scientific and Educational Film Studio, the Shanghai Animation Film Studio, the Shangdong New Rural Digital Cinema Network and other companies make additional contributions to the distribution nexus.

'China New Rural Film' was approved by the Film Bureau of the State Administration of Radio, Film and Television in June 2006. As the only specialized rural digital film distribution company in China, it is entrusted by the General Administration to purchase copyrighted films and distribute them in rural areas on behalf of the state. The total number of films released annually by means of either agency, outright purchase or sub-payment takes up a sizeable portion of the aggregate. By the end of 2015, the company had purchased the exhibition rights to 1558 copyrighted films and distributed them for public-welfare showings, accounting for about 45 per cent of the total number of films available for purchase.

Digital Cinema Ordering System in Rural Areas

Digital cinema chains in rural areas are responsible for ordering, supplying and supervising film showings via local film management stations. During the 12th Five-Year Plan period, there were over 100,000 film orders from cinema operators for a modest annual increase of between 10 and 16. Jiangsu New Hope, Shandong New Countryside, Jiangxi Xinrong, Gansu Feitian, Fujian Zhongxing, Chongqing Huimin, Liaoning Province Xinxing, Guangxi Bagui, Anhui Xin'an and other rural cinema operators ordered a consistent number of films, topping the list nationwide. At the beginning of the establishment of Rural Cinema Operator system, only Jiangxi Province had established provincial cinema operators, while Jiangsu and other provinces integrated resources and established provincial cinema chains out of developmental needs. Zhejiang New Rural Digital Cinemas was one of Zhejiang Province's outstanding operators of the rural film system reform pilot project in 2014, which established itself as such by integrating provincial resources. In 2015, this mobile cinema operator ranked seventh in the country, ordering more than 1300 films, and ranking third in the country.

Technical Support System

The National Digital Film Service Platform for Rural Areas

The exhibition platform is the core of the rural public film service system. The library of films on the platform are (0.8K) files projected via a mobile station with data, production, authorization, distribution, management and other technical services, and grounded in satellite and Internet technology, the platform works as a fast and convenient e-commerce delivery system with online film selection, ordering, payment and authorization, all the while providing fair, equitable and public services, open-source data and comprehensive operational support. Technical oversight for the digital film mobile projection services is rendered through a decoder card information return system independently developed by the digital centre and the wireless positioning (GPS/GPRS) monitoring system for the mobile digital film projection supervision service platform.

Projection Equipment Authentication System

Mobile projection equipment authentication information is recorded and put into use only after being examined and approved by the state-recognized inspection and certification agencies.

Equipment Integration Service System

Having been authorized by the State Administration of Press, Publication, Radio and Television, the China Film Equipment Company is responsible for training programs for government financed equipment along with its integration and organization, and after-sales service. Local equipment is mostly managed, trained and maintained by the local rural digital cinema operators.

Part 2: Characteristics of Rural Film Market Development

Providing rural audiences with the opportunity to see quality films is the operational goal of the rural film exhibition project. But what classifies a film as a 'quality' one? In terms of tangible factors, at least four conditions must be satisfied: (1) quality film content; (2) good projection equipment quality; (3) good audio and visual quality; (4) a quality viewing environment. In terms of intangible factors: good service competency and high-level service topped the list. Therefore, great efforts were made in the 'service supply' and many reform attempts were made to the supply-side structure throughout the country.

Genre Diversity, Content-Richness and the Manifestation of Diversified Genre Characteristics

New films are being released online at an ever more rapid pace, and the time-gap between the city and the countryside is ever shrinking. For example there were 483 new films available for purchase in the year 2015, of which 122 were produced (including 32 films with a box office return of over ¥100 million Yuan) and 198 were produced in 2014. Individual attempts at simultaneous releases in both urban and rural areas were made, like the film *The Hundred Regiments Offense* was released simultaneously on 28 August 2015, in urban and rural areas.

The film went on to gross more than ¥410 million CNY at the urban box office and was heavily ordered in the countryside. 165,483 film showings were ordered for the rural public-welfare market that year, ranking it first in the country. The public-welfare market is divided into seven CNY each, and the copyright income of the film is ¥1.16 million CNY.

Ordering trends showed that war movies were the preferred genre for rural audiences. From 2011 to 2015, all the top movies ordered were war movies. For example, orders began for director Feng Xiaoning's, *Hands Up* (1, 2) on 1 January 2007 and again on 31 January 2011. As of 23 June 2017, the total number of orders was 538.3 million and 47.02 million for the two respective ordering periods, and the total number of orders holding steady at second and third.[1]

Year	Welfare film (Feature)	Orders (Screenings)	Total (Screenings)	Ranking	Start of ordering
2011	Hands Up 2	330907	470184	3	1/31/2011
2012	Bloody Yan Men Guan	182256	269446	13	10/12/2011
2013	The Bloodbath at High Noon	107937	205019	37	1/30/2013
2014	82 Warriors	137580	338753	6	6/25/2013
2015	The Hundred Regiments Offensive	165483	296731	10	8/28/2011

Table 3: Public-welfare film annual rankings during the 12th Five-Year Plan period.
Source: China Film Market Report 2011–2016 Annual Report.

Analysis of viewing preferences has shown that opera films are becoming increasingly popular with rural audiences. The regional characteristics of opera films are highly palpable. He'nan opera is generally well-liked in Northern China and in a handful of cities near He'nan, such as Changzhi, Linfen and Jincheng, while in neighbouring areas to the north of Jinzhong, Shanxi opera is preferred. Zhejiang, by way of government customization, concentrates on ordering and creating a number of excellent opera films with the characteristics of Zhejiang local traditional culture. Peasant-themed films have also attracted much attention, such as *The Good Match* and *On the Way*.

Some areas have begun self-producing films locally that reflect the lives of ordinary people. These 'self-made films' are appreciated in their respective areas for their regional flair. Hubei has either produced or co-produced a host of films like *The Blood Stained Xiangjiang River* and others that focus on real life, tout the main-line and spread positive energy. The Huangmei Opera film *Love Beyond Eternity* and the feature film *I Have a Dream* were made specifically for the rural film market.

To better understand audience demand, Shandong Province solicited mass-audience opinion gathered by projection technicians at symposiums and used this information in the production of a variety of genre films, distributing them in rural markets. Good examples would be the educational film, *A Sensible Diet and Good Health*; the documentary film *Our Rural Civilization*; the feature film *Cheery Little Yangtun*; as well as the opera film *Merriment in the Maisonette of Felicity* (Lv Opera). In addition, Henan Province enters showtimes for educational films into the government work report. Kaifeng Peanuts became a best-selling brand as a result of the promotion it received from being featured in science and technology films.

Through efforts on all fronts, rural films have completely outgrown the outmoded and stodgy conventions of the past. The main reasons are as follows: (a) Linking an accounting method with film revenues and screenings attracted the attention of the copyright holders to the rural film market. For every ¥10 RMB made from public-welfare screenings, producers divvy up ¥7 Yuan. (b) When commercial films enter the rural market, copyright owners can obtain extended income from their intellectual property in the rural market through agency agreements, outright sales and profit-sharing. (c) Rural audience demand for quality films is strong.

'Film on Demand'

'Film on demand' is based on the needs of the audience. This 'many times in small amounts' format has increased the movie-going audience's selectivity. In 2015, there were 47,496 orders for production in rural cinemas (National Press, Publication, Radio, Film and Television, *Digital Film Program Management Center* website). The average number of films per order was 205, essentially breaking the audience's twice once-or-twice-a-year viewing habit.

Screenings

In connection with the general decline in the number of visitors, Shandong Province in 2013 proposed the 'regular screenings' pilot project for Anqiu. Through the practical application of policies and actions seen in the pilot project, this project has summarized the essence of 'seven norms' used in the regular welfare film screenings from seven aspects: rural cinema operators, management service stations, projection operators, projection facilities, projection programs, pre-screening advertising, screening scene and operation process, and forms a set of implementation methods for standardized screening of welfare film screenings, and the repeatable and reproducible work methods. Practice has shown that standardized regular screenings achieve four things: first, the number of people watching the film increases several times over or even tenfold. Case in point, Anqiu in Shandong; since September 2013, the number of people watching the film has exceeded 4.7 million. The second is to improve the quality of projection. Third, pre-screening advertising has improved the audience's awareness. Fourth, advertising revenues have increased substantially. Take Anqiu for instance, from September 2013 to June 2016, more than 2.4 million leaflets were sent out, and more than 50,000 announcements were posted.

Rural Cinemas

In improving viewing conditions, the excellent local characteristics of each area are explored during the construction of fixed screening locations, and the public-welfare screening rooms have been moving from exterior to interior fixed locations, which is a typical practice that has recently emerged. Anji County in Huzhou regards the construction of rural cinemas as a major welfare project that will improve the happiness index of the peasants. It has invested more than ¥13 million RMB into the construction of 35 theatres in rural areas. The number of indoor screenings has reached 86%, and the county has created a 'smart card' system for its public film service. The combination of public welfare and market has gradually instilled in the local residents the habit of paying for viewings.

In Chengdu, 'tea garden' movie screening locations have their fair share of local flair. The unique climatic conditions and tea culture that has been cultivated in the city for thousands of years have been brought into the tea gardens big and small, in and around city. Chengdu Jinsha Rural Digital Cinema and a tea garden have partnered to use the existing venues for indoor screenings. The pilot work began at the Cultural Station of Jinma Town, Dujiangyan. The system works in the following manner: public screenings of welfare movies are shown regularly, and the local rural residents are free to watch the films issued by the local government. Commercial screenings are held on weekends and holidays, so long as they are enjoyed in the tea garden, where the screening devices are set up and partitioned according to contractual stipulations.

In 2014–16, Ningxia built indoor screening facilities in all eligible administrative villages, gradually realizing the four transformations that brought the rural peasants from 'watching films outdoors to watching films indoors' and 'watching films for half a year to watching films for the whole year' from 'watching films while standing to watching films while sitting' and 'from watching others enjoy film, to personally enjoying films', thereby increasing the fairness and equity of public cultural services provided to the peasants. At the end of the '12th Five-Year Plan' period, the first batch of 185 rural movie indoor fixed screening locations were constructed in the district, which meets the needs of the rural audiences to watch movies during the off-season.

The 'Care Card'

In 2015, the Shenzhen Longgang District Party Committee and District Government put the pilot task of 'Public-Welfare Film Care Cards' into the public-welfare film projection work reform and innovation project. Longgang and Longcheng streets were designated as experimental areas. The pilot audience was designated as 10,000 people who had been residing in Shenzhen for one year, and the pilot cinema was designated as Longgang Film City. 20,000 preferred movie tickets were offered with the choice of two blockbuster films and two new movies in one year for each pilot area, and the 'Care Cards' were sent out twice a month, providing 833 ticket cards each time. Longgang Film City opened a special ticketing channel for the 'Care Card'. Through this special channel, a blockbuster movie can be enjoyed at any time by simply paying ¥5 Yuan along with providing an ID card or factory work card and a verification code for the viewing time.

Distribution Reforms

Preliminary results were achieved in the reforms of the film projection and distribution systems in the rural areas of Zhejiang Province, thus laying out the framework for the integration of urban and rural film public services. Zhejiang Province launched reforms for the distribution mechanism in 2014, and essentially established a competitive and preferential mechanism in the distribution market. In 2015, the reform of the screening mechanism was initiated, and pilot projects for public bidding were implemented in Jinhua, Quzhou and Lishui. In 2016, Zhejiang implemented the sweeping reforms, formulating a plan and quality standards for government purchased screening services, removing all barriers in this sector, encouraging the active participation of social forces and promoting the establishment of market competition mechanism. Zhejiang Province also established a third-party evaluation mechanism to investigate film distribution performance and screening service satisfaction. After three years of practical reforms, it was obvious that the three-in-one public service supply structure of town cinema, rural indoor screening locations and open-air mobile screening locations throughout the whole province had been optimized.

Part 3: Issues

Decreasing Demand for Film and Supply–Demand Imbalances for Rural Audiences

There is weak demand for film most predominantly among the elderly and children. In addition, there is a gap between film supply and peasant demand. The number of alternative products has increased, and strong competition from TV and books is dividing audiences. There are also environmental and climactic factors. It is rainy and hot in the southeast, cold in the northeast and windy and sandy in the west, causing audiences to prefer to stay at home and watch TV and listen to the radio.

Government Officials Do Not Deem the Project Important

Certain local government departments treat the project only as a perfunctory task, and local cadres in charge of the rural film project do not understand the business, while others in charge of its operations are marginalized. These human-related reasons have led to a situation in which some local rural audiences can still only enjoy film as a mere luxury.

Projection Issues

The quality of projection depends first on the quality of the equipment itself. The first batch of state-funded mobile digital projection equipment purchased in 2006 is now nearing the end of its life cycle. Equipment failure rate is high. Equipment wear-and-tear issues affect screen brightness and luminosity, which has declined sharply with age, seriously impacting the quality of projection and the overall viewing experience.

Lack of a Competition Mechanism

Rural cinema operators were initially established in accordance with the municipal and county jurisdictions. In some places, the main body of providers came into being as a result of administrative efforts, combing the project in those regions with strong overtones of economic planning. In most areas, there is only one vendor per city serving the local public with welfare film screenings.

Regulatory System Needs Improvement

Public-welfare screenings in rural areas is a national vanity project, but there is no social evaluation and supervision mechanism for it in most areas. It goes out to the public, yet nobody takes quality issues seriously.

Part 4: Research on the New Era of Rural Film Market Development Strategies

In 2016, screenings in the rural film market were promoted steadily, making the public-welfare film service more effective than in previous years. Local rural cinemas overhauled their film ordering systems, carried out extensive themed screenings, centralized worker training and strengthened oversight. They continued to expand projection pipelines and extended the scope of projection from rural areas to surrounding squares, residential areas, enterprises, military barracks, schools, forests and pastures and welfare homes, and sped up the construction of fixed indoor projection sites.

By the end of 2016, 245 digital cinema operators had been established in rural areas, and 275 exhibition rights had been purchased. Also 3575 films were ordered via the Digital Film Trading Service Platform and a total of 3492 films were ordered by the cinemas. The purchase rate for film exhibition permits reached 9.96 million, of which 5.94 million were commercial films, accounting for 59.62 per cent of the total. Commercial film orders exceeded those for public service cinemas, which ordered more than 1000 films throughout the year, seven fewer than in 2015, showing that the market orientation for rural film is gaining further traction, and the 'enterprise management, market operation' function is gradually taking hold.

Development Opportunities

1. In 2016, the 24th and 25th meetings of the Standing Committee of the National People's Congress passed the *People's Republic of China on the Promotion of Film Industry* law and the *People's Republic of China on the Guarantee of Public Cultural Services* law. The *People's Republic of China on the Promotion of the Film Industry* law clearly incorporates the public-welfare screening in the rural countryside into its plans for a rural public cultural service system. The people's government will invest in perfecting the rural welfare film-screening service network and guarantee the viewer demand in rural areas as a whole. *The Guarantee of Public Cultural Services* law establishes the framework of the basic legal system of public cultural services in China, and provides legal protection for promoting cultural governance, as well as the balanced and coordinated development of public cultural services and the safeguarding of the basic cultural rights and interests of the people.
2. To hasten the comprehensive development of the Pretopia, in October 2016, the Film Bureau of the State Administration of Press, Publication, Radio and Television (SARFT) made a goal of 'comprehensively serving needs of the Pretopia' in the national rural film work conference, grounded in meeting the people's spiritual and cultural needs, as well as launching activities focusing on 2020s 'affluent China's beautiful and rich countryside' National Rural film projection theme.
3. The guarantee of basic service system. Technical support forms a distribution and exhibition network for rural film with regard to supply, subscription, transmission, transaction, exhibition, return and technical services. The policy guarantee system is a top-level design centred around the people at large, founded on meeting their spiritual and cultural needs and aimed at the People's enjoyment of basic cultural rights and interests. Fiscal funds have been legally allocated for the overall protection of the film-viewing rights and demands of rural audiences.

Challenges from Competition

The state has incorporated public-welfare film screenings into the field of public cultural services. Instead of being funded separately with special funds, the government has adopted a bidding system to select providers and encourages social forces to participate in the purchase of public cultural services. Institutional and systemic reform is encouraged for the formation of cross-provincial distribution and projection entities. The introduction of a competition mechanism has put forward a test to the service ability of hundreds of rural film operators.

Development Strategy of the 13th Five-Year Plan

During the 13th Five-Year Plan period, reforms for the system and mechanism of rural film was intensified, transforming and upgrading the system, improving quality and efficiency to bring them in line with the principles of the 'government-led, social participation, co-construction and sharing, reform and innovation' ethic.

1. **To Perfect the Film Service Mechanism and Effectively Mediate Supply and Demand.** Urbanization of rural areas has transformed rural society and demographics. For this reason, optimizing the welfare film service mechanism is a developmental requirement in the new era. Public-welfare film coverage areas should be extended from rural areas to urban districts, schools, factories and mines, migrant worker construction sites, military barracks based on the structural changes in rural society as well as human crowding patterns. Mediating supply and demand for public film services is embodied in the rural film showings and is a core link to the People. To equalize supply and demand, the needs of the people must first be understood and an interactive 'bottom-up, demand-for-supply' menu service model must first be established, so as to effectively link public-welfare film service supply with the people's spiritual and cultural needs.
2. **To Correct the Film Service Supply Structure through a Supply-Side Structural Reform Development Strategy.** The sheer breadth and expanse of China's territory is vast and her various ethnic groups numerous. There are great differences in the human geographical environment in various regions, and film demand is very different across the board. A rational welfare film service supply structure should not only meet the needs of the masses, but also be suited to the level of China's social and economic development. From this point of view, the service supply system should first grasp how to publicize film screenings, integrate school education, health science and technology, poverty alleviation and intellectual support, and traditional Chinese cultural heritage, and construct the framework for public service through market-oriented operations.
3. **To Accelerate the Construction of Township Cinemas and Fixed Projection Sites and Promote the Integration of Urban and Rural Public Services.** Provinces, municipalities and districts can draw on the experience of Zhejiang and other places and formulate plans for the construction of fixed projection venues and township cinemas suitable for local realities. The construction of fixed projection sites should be adapted to local material conditions. The existing facilities such as rural cultural activity centres, ancestral halls, factories, mines and school auditoriums can be adapted and utilized. The construction of township cinemas should proceed from local realities, be guided by the government, operate within the market and attract social forces to participate in the construction of township cinemas.

4. **To Further Standardize Screenings Nationwide and Enhance the Professionalism of Public Film Services.** A system of training projection specialists and improving their skill and integrity to establish a stable team of rural film projection workers with excellent professionalism.
5. **To Adhere to a Dual Public-Welfare and a Market-Oriented Screening System to form a Multi-Tiered and Diversified Rural Film Market to Encourage the Participation of Social Forces and Promote the Socialization of Public Services.** The first reason is to cultivate market players and introduce a competition mechanism with which to break regional monopolies. The second is to accelerate the transformation of rural digital cinema operators, to innovate institutional mechanisms and to form a certain scale of the brand effect through cross-provincial and cross-regional cooperation. Third is to explore the development of secondary market and try to innovate the distribution and screening model by utilizing the construction and operation of township cinemas where conditions permit. Economically developed areas along the eastern seaboard can try to promote the urban film market.
6. **To Establish a Special Fund for the Rural Film Market.** Through a special fund to support the creation of rural film productions, publicity and marketing, equipment refurbishments and upgrades, grass-roots level projection worker training work together to guide the application fund.

Through a summary and analysis of the overall development of the rural film market during the 12th Five-Year Plan period, this author attempted to put forward his research and strategic development models for rural film screenings in different regions during the 13th Five-Year Plan period. However, it should be noted that there are great differences in the level of social and economic development in rural areas of China. All localities must take measures based on their own respective realities and local conditions. The model of rural film development cannot be 'one-size-fits-all'. In addition, for the sustainable development of rural film market, it is necessary to establish an effective supervision mechanism, strengthen the supervision of company operations and market operation and ensure the equitability and efficiency of market operations.

Appendix: The Development Course of the Project of China's Rural Film Projection (1998–2016)

In October 1998, at the National Conference on Rural Film Work held in Zhengzhou, the goal of 'Project #2131' was put forward, that is, basically realizing the goal of 'showing a film in a month at every village' at the beginning of the twenty-first century.

In the year 2000, the state set up a special fund '2131' for the rural film project, which invested ¥23 million RMB annually from 2000 to 2004, focusing on supporting 632 low-income counties in central and western provinces and regions to carry out rural film screenings.

In June 2005, the national pilot project for rural digital film mobile projection technology was launched in the city of Taizhou in Zhejiang Province. The successful experience of the pilot project is popularized nationwide as the 'Taizhou Model'.

In 2006, 'Project #2131' was upgraded to 'The Project of Rural Film Projection', and the National Coordination Group for Pilot Work of Rural Film Reform and Development was established.

In April 2006, 16 cities in Zhejiang, Guangdong, He'nan, Jiangxi, Shaanxi, Hunan, Jilin and Ningxia provinces (and districts within) were selected for pilot projects of rural film reform and development at the National Rural Film Conference.

On June 12, 2006, the China New Rural Digital Film Screening Co., Ltd was established upon approval of the Film Bureau. It was entrusted by the State Administration of Press, Publication Radio, Film and Television to purchase and distribute copyrighted films in rural areas on behalf of the State.

In May 2007, the General Office of the State Council transmitted the notice On Consummating Rural Film Work in the New Period (Document #38 of 2007 issued by the State Office). Document #38 converted rural film from departmental policy to national policy, consolidating policy objectives. Then, specific implementation rules of Rural Digital Film Distribution were promulgated, directly promotes the framework of the rural film market operation.

On 30 May 2007, at the National Rural Film Conference held in Xi'an, an increase in subsidies was decided for each screening in the western provinces from ¥20 Yuan to ¥100 Yuan.

In 2008, Feitian in Gansu explored the path to a win-win way for private enterprises to enter the public service sector and promote the cooperative development of companies and the state in the rural film project; thus, the 'Feitian-Gansu model' was created.

At the end of 2009, the digital translation for minority language of public films was officially launched.

In February 2010, the notice 'On promoting the sustainable and healthy development of rural film projects' stipulated that the funds for sustainable development of rural films should be established by deducting depreciation fees.

From 28 June to 16 July 2010, the first Farmers (Migrant Workers) Film Festival was held in Ningbo, Zhejiang Province.

On 1 January 2011, the State Administration of Press, Publication Radio, Film and Television promulgated the 'Notice on the Adjustment of the Cost of

Public-Welfare Films in Rural Areas', which stipulated that the exhibition fees for public film screenings be adjusted from ¥1 Yuan, ¥2 Yuan, ¥3 Yuan in the east, middle and west of China respectively to ¥10 Yuan per film. Subsidies increased from ¥100 RMB to ¥200 RMB.

On 15 February 2011, the State Administration of Press, Publication Radio, Film and Television released the notice, 'On the readjustment of public service expenses for rural films (#87, 2011)', which stipulated that the royalty fees of a single public film should be ¥7 Yuan.

In 2012, Anji County of Zhejiang Province launched a pilot project for the construction of rural cinemas.

In 2013, Shandong Province launched a pilot project of standardized screening of public-welfare films in Anqiu City.

On 30 August 2015, Shenzhen launched the pilot project 'Public-Welfare Film Care Card'.

From 17 to 22 May 2015, the 2nd National Radio, Film and Television (Rural Film Projector Operator) Skills Competition was held in Beijing. The top three finalists were awarded the title of 'National Technical Expert' by the Ministry of Human Resources Security.

From 14 to 16 June 2016, the Rural Cinema Line Branch of China Film Distribution and Projection Association held a live symposium on the standardization of rural public-welfare films in Anqiu, Shandong Province, marking the 'Shandong Standard' of rural public-welfare films which would then be promoted nationwide.

On 12 October 2016, the Film Bureau of the State Administration of Press, Publication, Radio, Television and Television (SARFT) set a goal of 'comprehensive service for the Pretopia' in the National Symposium on rural film work, aiming to meet the people's spiritual and cultural needs all across the board, and to launch a nationwide focus on the theme of an 'Affluent China's rich and beautiful countryside' in 2020.

On 7 November 2016, 'On the Promotion of the Film Industry Ordinance of The People's Republic of China' was passed and incorporated the public-welfare screening of rural films into the construction plan of the rural public cultural service system on the legal level.

On 26 December 2016, 'Public Cultural Service Guarantee Law of the People's Republic of China' was passed, which established a framework on the basic legal system for public cultural services in China.

In 2016, based on the reform of the film distribution and exhibition mechanism in 2014 and 2015, Zhejiang Province implemented a plan for improving quality standards of government projection service purchasing, which promoted the establishment of the projection market competition mechanism.

NOTE

1. National Press, Publication, Radio, Film and Television Bureau of *The Digital Film Program Management Center* Website: The film with the largest number of feature film purchases is 'What the Family Should Buy', which is a film promoting national policy. The number of purchases has exceeded 600,000.

SECTION II

CULTURE AND AESTHETICS

5. The Internationalization Strategy of Chinese Cinema: Theory and Practice

饶曙光/Rao Shuguang

Part 1: The 'Hot on the Mainland Cold in Other Lands' Dichotomy

China has become the world's second largest film market and the gap with the North American film market is narrowing as we speak. It has changed the pattern of the world film market at a rapid pace of development. In terms of growth, there was a surge of $1.2 billion USD in global box office revenues in 2013, of which the Chinese film market contributed 67%. In 2014, the global movie box office grew by ￥1.6 billion CNY, and the Chinese film market also contributed sizeable gains of 75%; hence, there is no doubt that the Chinese market has become the driving force of growth of global box office (Lei 2015). Chinese film has also established partnerships with ever more countries. By the end of 2014, there were 10 countries that inked co-production film agreements with China, such as China–France, China–South Korea deals. The mainland film market is by all accounts enormous. The sheer growth potential has brought Hollywood film companies and filmmakers out of the woodwork to China seeking to forge partnerships with local production companies.

A retrospective of 2015 reveals that Chinese cinema could be summed up in a single word, perhaps 'high-octane creativity' might be apropos, but the most fitting term has certainly become 'the new norm' of Chinese film development. Chinese cinema was strong and vital in 2015, regardless of whether it is in terms of growth in the number of screens, number of filmgoers or the box office receipts. In the first three quarters of 2015 (January to September), national box office receipts reached ￥33 billion CNY – higher than 2014's total box office take of nearly ￥3.4 billion CNY. Of the ￥33 billion CNY box office take, made-in-China movies accounted for ￥19.7 billion CNY, for a ratio of close to 60% and a year-on-year increase of 75%. It has truly become the driving force for the increases in the Chinese box office (Changxin and Shungshuang 2015). The summer box office favourite *Monster Hunt* surpassed the Hollywood blockbusters like *The Fast and the Furious 7* and *The Avengers 2* with a total box office of ￥2.4 billion CNY. In just seven days of the National Day break, the Chinese box office raked in an estimated ￥1.87 billion CNY with the tandem of *Lost in Hong Kong, Goodbye Mr. Loser*, setting single-day box office, easily besting the previous record set by *Monster Hunt*. Box office receipts for, *Saving Mr. Wu* and *Chronicles of the Ghostly Tower* exceed that of over 90% of the National Day Chinese movies (Xi 2015). High box office films released after the summer season not only had great returns but also won the praise of the media and the audience alike, showing to a certain extent that made-in-China films are commercially and artistically viable, which is a tremendous breakthrough.

All accolades aside, compared with the nearly endless stream of highs and records created in the local market, the progress towards Chinese cinema's internationalization goalmeets with great difficulties . Not only have Chinese films not performed the same abroad, but there have been the occasional downward trends, forming a hot-and-cold disparity that makes the performance in the two marketplaces just like night and day. Data shows that the outlook for international distribution of Chinese films is pretty bleak. In 2012, a total of 75 Chinese-made films by 31 studios (out of a total of 199) were distributed to 80 countries and regions overseas, with total overseas box office revenue of ￥1.06 billion CNY, less than 10% of domestic box office totals, and 48% less than total overseas revenues from the previous year. In 2013, 45 homegrown films (out of 247) found distribution overseas for a total of ￥1.41 billion CNY, an increase of 33.02% over the previous year (2012), but this is still less than total domestic box office receipts. In 2014, the domestic box office take was ￥1.87 billion CNY, compared with 2013. Compared with the year-on-year total of ￥29.6 billion CNY, the overseas revenues account for only 6% of the Mainland box office (Chen 2015). Over the past two years, the box office totals for Chinese films did increase, yet the big is still wide when compared with the increases in film production and film revenues on the Mainland. On the other hand, some of the films that fared well in China are not ideally suited to the North American box office. For example, the North American box office totals for *So Young*, *Lost in Thailand* and *Let the Bullets Fly* were only $9,990, $57,000 and $63,000 respectively (Chen 2015). Of course, there have been many successful examples of recent Chinese films 'crossing borders', but careful analysis shows in no uncertain terms that the overseas box office for these films accounts for a large proportion of overall overseas distribution. For example, in 2010, the overseas box office returns for the Chinese-American co-production of *The Karate Kid* was ￥2.36 billion CNY. The overseas box office for this movie alone accounted for 67% of the total overseas sales of Chinese films (Ying and Jing 2011). Another example is the 2012 Mainland and Hong Kong co-production of

The Grandmaster, which broke the box office record for a Chinese language film set three years prior, with a total North America box office take of $65.9 million USD. The revenue generated from this single film constituted 83% of the total box office revenue in the North American film market at the time (Sijian 2014). Moreover, these commercial Chinese martial arts epics are identical in content, structure and presentation, inevitably causing some viewer fatigue in the European and American markets, thus presenting further difficulties for the Chinese films to get out to the international audience.

Corresponds with the Chinese overseas box office, the embarrassment that is the Chinese 'go global' strategy, which has amounted to a big, fat cold shoulder given to Chinese films internationally. According to the survey data of the *Silver Book: 2013 Annual China Film International Distribution Report* compiled by the China Culture International Communications Research Institute of Beijing Normal University, 'More than half of overseas visitors know little about Chinese movies. Recognition of Chinese directors and actors abroad is low. More than 57% of overseas respondents said they don't know any international film festivals in China' (Xiaoxi 2015). Foreign audience perceptions of China still linger at the age-old Oriental mysticism level; foreign audiences still identify with the legendary Chinese Kung Fu movie. They are still only familiar with Kung Fu stars such as Jackie Chan and Bruce Lee (Huang Huilin, Feng Jiyao, Bai Xuejing, Yang Zhuofan 2013,). In recent years, especially after 2010, Chinese-language films tended to be deaf, dumb and blind on the international art scene, and there is also a lack of award-winning films that represent the current level of Chinese film development. For example, at the 66th Cannes International Film Festival in 2013, Jia Zhang Ke's *A Touch of Sin* failed to take home the big prize; it did however take home the best screenplay award. At the 2014 Venice International Film Festival, Wang XiaoShuai's hotly anticipated, *Red Amnesia* was given the big snub. Although some Chinese films have gained traction internationally, such as the 2014 Berlin International Film Festival where Yan YiNan's *Black Coal, Thin Ice* took home the Golden Bear for best film and the Silver Bear for Best Actor (for actor Liao Fan), the sporadic winnings fall far below the bar set by the grandeur of Chinese cinema in the 1990s, when Chinese films were so often given the red-carpet treatment at international festivals such as Cannes, Venice and Berlin.

All of this reminds us that for now we should face head-on the unchanging 'West strong, China weak' international cultural dynamic, and 'go global' dream for Chinese cinema demands the steely diligence to build an internationalization model that can effectively resolve this dilemma. One that is centred around strategic thinking. The construction of internationalization platform is undoubtedly based on the strategic dynamic of foreign cultural exchange under a comprehensive national strategy that promotes the establishment of a new international cultural order that is mutually respectful, inclusive, fair and logical. Undoubtedly, from a cultural perspective, it is impossible to alter the West-strong-China-weak dynamic in short order. We can only gradually expand and enhance our own voice. We should not go into this focused only on short-term gains, but on the long-term and the future. As an integral part of developing our overall core capacity to internationalize, Chinese cinema's internationalization platform (international communication) must also seek out new thinking, ideas, methods and techniques accordingly.

Part 2: Structural Barriers and the Development of an Internationalization Strategy

Concerted efforts are being made to further the Chinese film 'crossing borders', and those efforts have yielded certain results. Though for now, Chinese film globalization is limited to the business dealings of a number of enterprises. The international investment trends of Chinese film and television companies such as *WanDa*, *HuaYi* and *HuaCe* and the export of commercial films remain largely strategic and have not been upgraded to a more open strategic level or the global level to form a new dynamic of Chinese film's internationalization and create a new dimension for Chinese film's internationalization.

What cannot be ignored are the structural obstacles and issues that have always existed in internationalization. Some experts believe that overseas demand for Chinese film, especially in the West, is nil. If we agree or acknowledge this viewpoint, we must admit that structural obstacles and contradictions do exist, which cannot be effectively overcome and broken through in a short period of time. At the same time, as the Chinese expert, Professor of the University of Southern California's Department of Politics, Luo SiDian pointed out, the desire to enter the United States film market is not uniquely Chinese, but it is a desire that every country with a film industry shares in. Then there is the issue of the structural obstacle stemming from the fact that non-English language movies are just going to be regarded as 'foreign films' no matter what, forming a nearly impenetrable entry barrier to the mainstream theatres in North America (Shuguang 2011). Even Chinese films that do manage to make it into the mainstream cinemas are faced with a group of unsavvy, close-minded viewers in Europe and the United States who just 'stroll in to the theatre one day', and plunk down some cash for a ticket, treating the movie watching experience as a 'mini vacation'. This is exacerbated by the fact that American movies account for 92% of the total of the current North American film market, while European films account for 6% of the market, leaving a miniscule 2% market share leftover for other countries such as India, Japan,

South Korea and China to compete over like dogs fighting over a bone. So, regardless of whether a Chinese film is superior to that of other countries in terms of filmmaking quality, craftsmanship and competitiveness, the fact of the matter is that there is only a 2% share of the North American film market share left over. Even if it were given solely to China, it is still a very limited space for development in the market (Ifeng 2013). In terms of the share of the global film market, in 2014, the global movie box office was $37.5 billion USD, of which the US domestic and overseas film markets totalled $10.3 billion USD and $14.6 billion USD respectively, accounting for 66% of the world market share. China's domestic box office totalled $2.6 billion US dollars (¥16.155 billion CNY), accounting for 7% of the global market share. Of the remaining 27% (less than $5 billion) of the world's film market share, 'internationalized' Chinese cinema occupies $300 million USD (¥1.87 billion Yuan), with the leftover table scraps thrown to other countries like Japan, South Korea, India, Europe, France and Italy (Yang 2015). The film market shows us, in no uncertain terms, the invincibility of Hollywood's dominance. With market, capitalization and technological advantages, films from other countries can be marginalized and excluded from the mainstream theatre chains. The difficulty of 'going international' is not only a problem faced by Chinese films, but also a common conundrum faced by other countries. Just as Zhou TieDong, a film expert and former general manager of China Film Overseas Promotion Company for many years, said that the internationalization of Chinese film is not just about going toe-to-toe with Hollywood, but it is about winning the battle with the filmed entertainment of nearly every country. And only after winning that battle is it possible to secure a small part of the film market. Therefore, perhaps being the lone resistance fighter against the 'Hollywood empire' is just a losing proposition and seeking partnerships and co-productions with Hollywood is 'the force' required to make Chinese cinema's globalization efforts viable (Xiaobo 2015).

At the same time, the fairness and equity of cultural products cannot be fully guaranteed by market behaviour or even by the market itself (Ifeng 2013). In fact, as early as the 1920s, the US government had incorporated Hollywood cinema into its national strategy. In 1927, the powerful Nanking Nationalist regime with countless ties to the United States enabled the United States to put on a display of its strategic design of the Chinese film market. The United States had just launched a market investigation on the makeup of the Chinese film market, especially with respect to the distribution of movie theatres in Shanghai. The report provided a detailed analysis of the viewing habits and aesthetic tastes of Chinese film audiences. In fact, at the US government level, the global promotion of Hollywood movies and the American mainstream values and ideologies contained therein was an important part of American diplomacy. Meaning essentially that the government was and is actively pursuing global cultural hegemony in line with its 'ascension to power'. These government actions are not carried out in an overt way, but rather covertly hidden behind film market behaviour. Therefore, Hollywood has established a global distribution network with which it shapes audience tastes in Hollywood movies. It is not the result of spontaneous market behaviour (Ifeng 2013).

Unprecedented change in the global dynamic is under way. In the competition between Chinese and American cinema, the two are not only economically competitive, but culturally competitive and even confrontational. Therefore, even if Chinese films found a way to 'go global' – by effectively enhancing film's intercultural expressiveness and fully developing a global commercial distribution pipeline, making it impossible for the United States to exclude Chinese films by market mechanisms – the US government also has other means at its disposal, including political measures, with which to prevent the entry of Chinese films. Moreover, the strategic game between the two major powers, China and the United States, has gradually moved from 'guerrilla warfare' to 'all-out war'. This overall strategic game dynamic determines how the American film market will almost never allow Chinese films a smooth path into the film market, especially those that highlight Chinese memes and Chinese values. We must be clear on this, and we must not be blindly optimistic.

From a long-term strategic perspective, this author has repeatedly called for the transformation of the 'Chinese Film Cross-Borders Project' into the 'Chinese Film International Distribution Strategy' and promoted it as a national strategy. In the same vein, a strategic, inclusive and diversified evaluation standard and evaluation system for the internationalization of Chinese films should also be established. We must go beyond simple box office numbers, economic interests and other economic indicators. Meaning that we cannot just look at the total box office and sales revenue figures that Chinese movies have generated in overseas markets. We should also consider the overall cultural significance and evaluate whether Chinese films are impactful. Whether overseas distribution expands the influence of Chinese culture on the international level and whether it enhances China's national image and cultural soft power (Shuguang 2014b). For the internationalization of Chinese films, the soft power in the cultural sense is more important than the box office, and it is more strategic and valuable. Only by thinking about problems from a strategic perspective can we effectively create a new ethic, and a new norm that allows for the internationalization of Chinese films and can cope with the new challenges of globalization.

From the perspective of industrial structure, the book *Competitive Strategy* published by Michael E. Porter in 1980 suggests that companies need to choose one of three strategies – lower cost, differentiated or focus to gain a competitive advantage. These three strategic models provide an excellent reference for the Chinese film industry to utilize in the development its international distribution strategy. Therefore, before determining the global distribution strategy and international exhibition strategy of Chinese cinematic productions, we should also carefully study Hollywood's globalization strategies, learn from the successful experience of the United States, identify our market space and target demographics and use the lower-cost, differentiated and focus strategies to delineate and clarify development ideas in order to better achieve our strategic goals.

Part 3: China's Internationalization Strategy: Multi-Channel, Multi-Level, Collaborative

On the macroscopic level, we must establish strategies for Chinese film's internationalization via strategic thinking; and in the actual practice of promoting Chinese cinema overseas, it is imperative that corresponding strategies be adopted for distribution channels, platforms and content, to aid in distribution paths with the support of multi-channelled exhibition paths with which to delineate the scale of multi-tiered distribution, and to infuse the 'Chinese dream' and the 'Chinese story' into co-productions, thereby minimizing the 'cultural misunderstanding' that happens when Chinese films are distributed abroad, so that the scale of Chinese cinema's cultural influence can be expanded in the international market.

Distribution Paths: Primary and Multiple Channels Side-by-Side

On the path to internationalization, it is necessary to not only stick to the main market and commercial channels, but also focus on tapping into multiple exhibition channels to develop more opportunities and conditions for breakthroughs into commercial channels through multi-channelled partnerships so that we can develop the main channels and the multi-tiered channels side-by-side.

On one hand, it is important to strive to make breakthroughs and do something special in the market and in those commercial channels. Under the premise of being the Jack of our own box office and film market but being the master of none, Chinese cinema should take strive to occupy as much international film market share as possible in order to gain more traction and a stronger voice. The 'traction' here is not only greater traction in the film export game in terms of greater economic strength and scale, but also greater international influence for Chinese cinema (Shuguang 2014b).

On the other hand, while maintaining the primary channels of business, tapping into the wealth of diverse communication channels cannot be ignored. The internationalization of Chinese film is a vast and systematic project. It requires not only the joint efforts of government and NGO channels, but also the effective integration of various resources such as government, market, social, people-to-people and academic exchanges to promote Chinese film culture with the concerted efforts of the whole of society (Shuguang 2014b).

First, at the government level, we must strengthen the efforts to disseminate and promote domestically produced films, such as improving the legal mechanism and trade system for the promotion of Chinese films overseas, increasing policy and financial support, developing overseas distribution and promotional organizations, and priming overseas audiences through joint film festivals, building an overseas marketing platform for Chinese cinema and developing an international business, production, distribution team. However, to some extent the uniformity and homogeneity of communication channels and features has limited the internationalization of Chinese cinema. In this regard, the China Film Association – where this author is stationed – has made a fruitful attempt to open up a private communication channel outside the official platform in the form of partnering with a government enterprise to create a social platform. Its international communication committee has become a comprehensive resource platform for promoting the overseas distribution of Chinese films built upon the strategic foundation of the developmental work for Chinese film's international distribution that is not only limited to financial level of box office returns but is also involved in how to better contribute to the promotion of China's image and Chinese cultural soft power. In terms of talent cultivation, it has attracted a large number of elites in the film industry and academia. Hollywood's top producers, directors, screenwriters have been invited to teach and exchange in China. It also draws on the experience of foreign talent from Korea to strengthen international development of professional and professional film talent and has created a multi-faceted and multi-level communication channel for domestic and foreign filmmakers and cultural communicators (Shuguang 2014b).

Scope of the Message: Drawing a Multi-Tiered Cultural Map

In terms of the scale of distribution, the overseas promotion of Chinese films should adopt a multi-level framework of small and large cultural concentric circles, in accordance with the cultural geography of the 'Chinese community – Chinese cultural circle – Confucian cultural circle – Eastern cultural circle' and expand its sphere of influence layer by layer.

Specifically, the main international market for Chinese cinema's 'global mission' should not be North America, but the importance of the overseas film market should be based on the order of 'the domestic market – Chinese community – Chinese cultural circle – Confucian cultural circle – European and American markets

– African, Latin American market', mainly based on the local market, and from there 'spill over' naturally to Japan, South Korea and the 10 ASEAN countries in the Asian Confucian cultural circle, and from there expand layer by layer to the heterogeneous cultural market in Europe and America. When Chinese films are distributed to the outside world, they must have a clear international regional market position: Chinese-language local business models based on partnerships between the Mainland, Hong Kong and Taiwan, the Confucian cultural film circles with Southeast Asia, Japan and South Korea, all share cultural homogeneity. And in this Chinese cultural circle-produced martial arts films, costume dramas and epic commercial films can be pushed into the North American, Australian, New Zealand and other markets. And for the European film market art films with wax philosophical and humanitarian are more suitable. And as for areas like Africa and Latin America, Chinese films are moving towards these countries more because of the cultural appeal of foreign cultural exchange rather than economic gain, due to the lack of a developed film industry. If we continue to follow such multi-tiered overseas distribution channels, the cultural geography of Chinese films will eventually expand.

Meanwhile, Chinese cinema should be focused on yoking the power of the whole country to conduct an in-detail and in-depth study of overseas markets in different countries and regions, and to diversify audience demographics based on in-depth and all-inclusive visual analysis of the data samples obtained from research. Targeted creative strategies and communication strategies should be adopted, and differentiated marketing strategies should be formulated to provide film products that satisfy different aesthetic conventions and interests and to effectively boost the market competitiveness and market share for made-in-China films in overseas markets.

The Message: Co-productions Tell the 'Chinese Story'

After constructing a multi-channel exhibition path and delineating its scope on multiple tiers, it is desired that the film, as a cultural product, should successfully achieve international distribution and exhibition. At its core, the film's content needs to be suitable for international exhibition.

Current Chinese cinema cannot be accepted overseas, which is related to 'cultural misunderstanding' for factors such as a limited spectrum of content, monotony of genre and a language barrier. Therefore, in order to really internationalize Chinese cinema, the most important thing is to break through the inherent cultural discredit in the process of international distribution. Sino-Xenic co-production is an effective way to mitigate cultural discredits. Co-ventures between China and the United States are primarily to learn storytelling techniques that express shared human values and emotions and tell a 'Chinese story' within the context of a 'world production, global market' operating model. Therefore, co-productions should look to a combination of localization and internationalization. They should seek out common ground while maintaining respect to thematic differences and find elements that can bring about intercultural communication and show commonalities in human nature and use the familiar narrative techniques and expressions of values that are familiar to the world. These films should delve in themes with local characteristics, and in films with a strong Chinese cultural identity and style, to express the depth of Chinese culture and to develop a trademark Chinese film culture that has international competitiveness and influence. At the same time, the Oriental culture and Chinese elements in international co-productions should not only be expressed through amazing visual spectacle but should also be internalized into Chinese cultural connotations and spiritual temperament.

International collaboration, also known as co-production, is the inherent demand for Chinese film to get stronger, especially in promoting the modernization and upgrading of the Chinese film industry. It is also the inherent demand for Chinese film's internationalization and foreign exchange. In the past few years, because of the limited space in the Chinese film market, especially the Chinese film industry's state of being terminally 'cash poor', China has often been painted into a nasty cash crunch corner, needing to participate in the co-venture. Meanwhile the ideas, development and production are controlled by somebody else. Nowadays, the Chinese film market is wide-open, and its golden prospects have created endless reverie, especially that the Chinese film industry is 'not cash poor', and our initiative and its corresponding right of free speech have been greatly enhanced. A few years ago, this author presided over the social science project of the State Administration of Radio, Film and Television, 'The history of development of Chinese and foreign co-productions and its development strategy', and made a detailed analysis, and summary of the occurrence and development of Sino-Xenic co-production, and also tried to predict its future. The various possibilities for development and their space have given people visions of the future. And there has been a general air of optimism expressed in their positions, attitudes and methods. The Art of War advises, 'Know themes thyself, and thou shalt be forever victorious'.

With international co-productions, we have many demands placed on our 'self', such as levelling up in terms of specialization, industrialization and internationalization, as well as promoting Chinese film distribution through international co-productions. In fact, the very development of Sino-Xenic co-ventures signals to us that we have partially achieved our goal. Chinese cinema and the Chinese film industry can develop on par with today's standards, and Sino-Xenic co-ventures have made a tremendous contribution to that end. That said, another dimension to the equation is of knowing 'the other'. In that respect we lack understanding and consideration for the other's needs. Many times, the practice is indeed a bit whimsical. In fact, Hollywood (and of course South Korea) collaborated with Chinese studios because their own film market has limited space for development. They are eager to enter the Chinese market. A careful analysis reveals that many of us have been looking for the quick buck out of these ventures, and excessive pursuit of the advertising effect. We should be soberly aware that compared with many years ago, Americans and Koreans are more demanding and eager for co-productions than we are. We can keep a cool head and a low profile and, take the initiative and strive to lead, and gain more and greater economic and cultural gains for ourselves in the process of collaboration. The key is that we must be a whole entity, and a community of fate.

In the telling of the 'Chinese story', Chinese cinema that is distributed abroad should carry the cultural message of the 'Chinese dream' that pertains directly to the Chinese in terms of their people, history and eras. Infusing the Chinese dream into film will tell the dream of the Chinese people, shape the artistic image of common Chinese folk and express their humanity and ideals in a form adapted and palatable to young audiences. Rooted in the spirit of betterment, cinema will not only be a simple cultural product to be consumed with fast food, but will also enhance China's cultural soft power, display Chinese culture and Chinese characteristics, and realize the modern transformation of traditional Chinese culture and the socialist core values in our cinematic expression (Jingjing 2014). More importantly, it is also necessary to resolve the fundamental issue of value sharing. Why is it that the Chinese dream is connected to the American dream? Why is it that the Chinese Dream is not just a Chinese dream, but a dream that the whole world can share? In fact, it involves the sharing of values, which are the common values and shared by all of humanity as articulated by President Xi JinPing at the UN General Assembly. This proposition contains multiple dimensions: First, it must be based on Chinese cultural traditions and on contemporary Chinese social realities. Second, it must take a Chinese stance and construct a Chinese discourse system to form a Chinese mode of expression called the 'Chinese voice'. Third, it must be international, humanistic and modern and include the intrinsic values that can be accepted with a glad heart by all. If these basic issues are not effectively resolved, it will arguably be difficult for us to create new prospects for the internationalization of Chinese films and form a new dynamic and new order of a new world cinema.

In the act of putting the Chinese story out there for all to hear, we should also consider telling stories in a way that is acceptable to overseas audiences. At present, cinematic partnerships between China and America are still at the stage of learning and experience accumulation. China draws on Hollywood's well-developed team, capital and other industrial experience to foster its own film talents that include an international perspective and expression on a specific operational level. In film production, distribution, screening and other industrial chain links, all the while being in compliance with the international rules of film distribution. At the same time, if China wants more voice and control in its international co-productions, the first order of business is to expand the scale of investment and increase its ability to take the lead in the projects it undertakes. Second is to partner with the powerful film companies from abroad. To reach an equal and collaborative relationship with the big international studios means that Chinese films need to come up a great deal in terms of financial and technical standards, talent level and even boost the entire film industry as a whole (Shuguang 2014b). Ultimately, to enter the global market with 'co-captaining' to expand the international market scale and international cultural influence of Chinese films.

Conclusion

Richard Gelfond, CEO of IMAX Corporation predicted that China's box office will surpass the United States in 2018, and by 2025 it may become twice as large as the United States (Shuguang 2014a). Although this rosy vision for Chinese cinema may become a cosy reality in the foreseeable future, we must not be blindly optimistic when we are cheering for positive developmental momentum, but we should take the rose-coloured glasses off and judge the naked realities as they are. In fact, in today's globalized context, huge cultural barriers and 'cultural deficits' still exist in cross-cultural film exchange. China needs to formulate a globalization strategy for Chinese cinema based on the realities of a changing cinematic era and maximize the cultural value and capital value of Chinese cinema to further consolidate the local film market, effectively promote the internationalization of Chinese cinema, and explore and adopt Hollywood's long-term cultural game as the way to win. We should establish a more equitable and rational new cultural order and new film order and work systematically to expand its voice and influence (Shuguang 2014). As Chinese filmmakers continue to improve their core capabilities, the bar will be set ever higher for Chinese film technology and modernization standards, which will happen right in tandem with the continued development of China's film distribution channels. With the diversification and variegation of this process, Chinese cinema is likely to become the leader in the spread of Chinese culture. This is how the internationalization of Chinese cinema will become like 'water flow cutting a channel' and 'the channel leading the flow of water', and Chinese movies will go from, 'others telling us stories' phase to the 'others listening to us telling Chinese stories' phase. Only through the establishment of side-by-side national-international, multi-level, multi-channel overseas film distribution systems that integrate the creative powers of the Mainland, Hong Kong and Taiwan can we make our way up to the spotlight on the international film stage to be the powerful face of culture and the industrial community.

REFERENCES

Changxin, Liu and Shungshuang, Liu (2015), 'Box Office of the first three quarters exceeded the total amount of last year: The Chinese film has become the driving force', *Nanfang Daily*, 22 October.

Chen, Qiu (2015), 'Overseas movies box office only accounts for 6% of the Mainland box office: Chinese film earns "extra money" still needs "shot in the arm"', *Wuhan Morning Post*, 24 May.

Ifeng (2013), 'Experts talk about Hollywood: Chinese movies have "crossing borders" phobia', ifeng entertainment, http://ent.ifeng.com/movie/special/dayingxianghlh/detail_2013_03/25/23497346_2.shtml. Accessed 1 January 2018.

Huang Huilin, Feng Jiyao, Bai Xuejing and Yang Zhuofan (2014), 'The International Communication Research of Chinese Film Culture in 2013', *Modern Communication, Journal of Communication University of China*, 2.

Jingjing, Ren (2014), 'The Chinese dream and the internationalization of Chinese film', *Wenhui Daily*, 26 February.

Lei, Li (2015), '2014 China Film Market Impact Research Report release: Chinese film contributes 75% of the global box office increases', *Guangming Daily*, 7 January.

Shuguang, Rao (2011), 'Globalization and China's film globalization strategy', *Journal of PLA Academy of Art*, 2.

—— (2014a), 'Improving film quality and optimizing the film ecology: A retrospective of 2013 Chinese film and speculation on its future', *China Film New*, 9 April.

—— (2014b), 'Secretary-General of the China Film Association: Unable to see the success or failure of Chinese film's internationalization from the box office', http://www.chinawriter.com.cn/ news/2014/2014-08-06/213791.html. Accessed 1 January 2018.

Sijian, Liu (2014), '"The Grandmaster" hits the North America box office', *The Mirror*, 9 January.

Xi, Zhang (2015), 'In the first three quarters, the domestic Chinese box office broke 3.3 billion: What is the measure of a blockbuster on the Mainland?', *China Culture Daily*, 26 October.

Xiaobo, Wu (2015), 'Why aren't Chinese movies popular overseas?', *China Youth Daily*, 26 October.

Xiaoxi, Liu (2015), 'Belt and road: New opportunities and new missions in the development of Chinese films', *Modern Literary Magazine*, 1.

Yang, Liu (2015), 'China becomes the global box office growth engine', *People's Daily*, 7 January.

Ying, Bai and Jing, Gao (2011), 'Chinese film bogged down overseas: Experts say, learning from world film', 3 May.

6. Seven Visions: Rooted in the Traditional, Steeped in the Nouvelle — A Study of Zheng DaSheng and his Films

万传法/Wan ChuanFa

Part 1: A Singular Realization

A simple peek at the Zheng DaSheng's creativity reveals the multifacetedness of his vision, which this author believes can be summed up as: movement, stillness, change, conception, struggle, harmony and transformation – oft referred to in ancient times as, 'the wisdom of the seven sages' – whose earthly incarnations were frequently depicted as figures partially obscured within scenes of 'thick misty mountain swirls and branching plum blossom curls', whilst the seven great sages, 'emanated light bright as the sun's glow, as radiant as the heavenly dipper and bull's halo'. Not just bright enough to reflect one's own image, but bright enough to reflect all in creation. The seven phases referred to in this text are used to interpret the Tao of the great sages. Yet what is specially referred to in this text is a framing with two reference points in order to make us know what is established by these seven facets. One is spontaneity, the other liberation, both of which are related to his upbringing. Zheng DaSheng, who was born into a prestigious and learned family – focused on education, bright and studious, and wise and distinguished throughout its ranks. This is the environment that nourished his 'mercurially philosophical' side, which is something that should not be taken lightly. It is the very thing that determines a person's breadth of mind and depth on character. It was his rich scholarly homelife that immersed him in the arts from a young age. Being steeped in the likes of traditional Chinese theatre, visual arts and film awakened the Zen of his 'art consciousness', which determined not only his own achievements, but his future as well.

Part 2: A Pair of Factors

There are two elements that still affect him today, namely 'the avant-garde and the worldly', along with 'tradition and egoism', which stand in opposition to one another – conflicting yet complementary, separate yet overlapping, independent yet interdependent, isolated yet interconnected.

The 'avant-garde' element finds its roots in his time at the Chicago Institute of Film Art. It was the year 1990, and Zheng DaSheng had just graduated from the film department at the Shanghai Theater Academy and thereafter made a bold move – to bravely venture out of his homeland to master the craft of film. One factor in his decision was that he felt there to be a void in the 'avant-garde spirit' in China, the other was the powerful new zeitgeist that broke out in 1980s China that ignited a powerful curiosity for Western style art (Bin and DaSheng 2003: 91). An inquisitiveness and a dream that he carried with him all the way to the School of the Art Institute of Chicago (SAIC). He once commented,

> I chose to study commercial and industrial film at a school whose entire mission seemed to be centered around the avant-garde, standing in stark contrast to the monolith of capitalism. Every department was exploring new possibilities, toppling long-held notions and reforming hypotheses. People there held doggedly the out-with-the-old-in-with-the-new ethic. They were always like, 'I can do it this way', or 'Why can't I do it that way?' It was totally extreme.
> (Bin and DaSheng 2003: 92)

The cultural differences he faced and the culture shock he endured are detailed in an article entitled, 'Confessions of an Indie filmmaker'(Zheng Dasheng,2000), which painstakingly chronicles his 'avant-garde experience'. A single frame dissolves into a grid, cutting a piece of celluloid into eight equal parts, a shot moved at a leisurely pace, slowly becoming compacted into a six-part grid, still moving lethargically, then becoming four parts, then three and two (such is the limitation of 16mm film editing), and finally moving into a hysterical flickering like an insane blitzkrieg dive-bombing the retina. Opening to a languidly panoramic pan taken from a crude workprint to the middle taken from the original negative, and on to the end taken from a restored composite positive. The shots continue in a rapid succession, forming a scene that is made alive with an unending interplay of elements. This was a black-and-white film, in which, after two or three viewings, a transposition of black and white, positive and negative, deficiency and excess, truth and fiction, reality and imagination began to take place, leading to a state of confusion, which characterized Zheng DaSheng's academic avant-garde assimilation. Actually, it was the film *Pedestrians 1, 2, 3* that earned him praise from teachers and students alike, as well as a scholarship.

Zheng DaSheng's 'tradition vs. egoism' factor likewise finds its roots in his time in Chicago, but its inspiration was the result of a direct comparison. When referencing his and his fellow students' creative works, he described them in the following manner:

> There are sure be certain commonalities, but the overtones in every individual's work are uniquely their own. There was this girl I once knew from Argentina and Canada who wrote poetry in French that she would then transcribe to the human body and put it in her films. She produced shots of the warmth of nature through the lens that brought out an almost orgasmic joy of the lushness of the forest, and the still beauty of its tranquillity – literally vacillating between two extremes. My films also feature their own moments of natural beauty, but when played side-by-side, the difference was plainly evident. But I found that the reason why I shoot landscapes featuring lofty mountains and still waters is because I am steeped in the ink wash painting tradition, but the lakes, mountains and groves featured in my films are decidedly different from hers. Though we shot it in the same season and in nearly the same location, yet the overall effect achieved in my films is the polar opposite of hers.
>
> Personality and gender differences aside, there are most certainly other factors hidden deep beneath the surface, which have given me a new awareness. Unconsciously becoming a consciousness. One that is increasingly detailed and powerful – an egotistical need to come to terms with my own cultural background – and from that standpoint to say where I've come from. It was this burning need that became of prime importance.
>
> (Bin and DaSheng 2003: 94)

It was this very thing that caused Zheng DaSheng to wax introspective, prompting him to read the *I-Ching*. He began listening to Tang Dynasty music at every given opportunity and delving into his cultural heritage. He was bound and determined to return to his homeland after graduation. In his own words, the next goal was exceedingly clear – to 'discover China' (Bin and DaSheng 2003: 92).

A search that began from exploration of the 'avant-garde and worldly' to 'tradition and egoism'. It is most likely what Zheng DaSheng did not initially expect, but it is this path that gives his work a greater clarity of vision and lends a fuller panoptic scope to his work than that of other Mainland directors. Through the focal point of the ego, the contrast between the two elements, 'the orthodox and the avant-garde' gradually transformed after returning to his homeland. Through a myriad of changes, the soul remains the same. From the very outset, these two constituents were like a seed buried deep in the mind, one in the left brain and the other in the right, forming the duality of his nature, with each side working together in perfect harmony. His entire catalogue of films to date that can be categorized under the 'traditionalist and avant-garde' dichotomy are: *Ah-Tao, The Death of Wangbo, The Curio, DV China, Fleeting Time, The Inspector and the Prince, Falling City, Useless Man, Corrosion* and *Bangzi Melody*. Of course, this list should not be taken as gospel truth, but as a general rule of thumb.

Part 3: Three Phases

Zheng DaSheng's edge over the competition became increasingly pronounced in the application of the two elements, 'traditionalism and avant-gardism' within his work. His work may be more diverse than the other directors, for example film-TV crossovers, documentaries, films, TV series, opera, plays, promotional films and the like. Yet, no matter the project, only the cream whose artistry reaches the highest level can truly make, 'countless directors vie for credit'. To give the reader a better sense of his work, this essay will categorize his films into three phases.

The first is from *Ah-Tao* to *Fleeting Time*, which includes *The Death of Wangbo, The Curio* and *DV China*. This is his 'China discovery' phase – a period of artistic exploration and life experience. It is apparent from interviews with Zheng DaSheng that the production of *Ah-Tao* mirrors his own experiences in the May Seventh Cadre School. The simple pleasures, true comradery and bitter sorrows that Ah-Tao, Yi Lan and other girls go through are a reflection upon the director's own experiences from that time. *The Death of Wangbo* is a ponderance on history through a self-interrogation process. His search for Chinese literary spirit and his depictions of Chinese scholars comprise an extended 'self-portrait' of sorts. And, *The Curio* is his musings on the relationship between 'history, relics and mankind'. The film poses the thought-provoking question: is it 'man acting upon objects' or 'objects acting upon man?' The film can be seen as Zheng DaSheng's contemplations on the 'cultural roots' of a nation. Meanwhile, *Fleeting Time* was made as a commemoration of his dearly departed father. In the film, the role of his father – played by Yao AnLian – is actually an intense psychological projection of DaSheng's own ego. This film was a trip across time from his father's 'absenteeism' (portrayed in *Ah-Tao*) to his father's 'absent presence' (as portrayed in *Fleeting Time*). Zheng DaSheng completed a diachronistic journey that began from 'the passage of history' to the 'passage of the present'. Stylistically, his films traverse the gamut from 'essay film' (*Ah-Tao*) to 'lyrical film' (*The Death of Wangbo*) to 'drama' (*The Curio*), to 'documentary' (*DV China*), to 'neorealismo Italiano'

(*Fleeting Time*). Most importantly, it was at this stage that he completed a spiritual and life journey of 'China discovery'.

The second phase includes only one film, the opera film entitled *The Inspector and the Prince*, which draws upon influences ranging from the stage play, *The Crucible*, to the propaganda film, *Harmonious China*, to the traditional Cantonese opera *Tong Yun*. Despite the lack of a vast body of work to characterize it, this phase undoubtedly represents a major breakthrough for the director and is unanimously proclaimed as a 'quantum leap' or 'turning point' in his development. The film, which took home the eighteenth annual Golden Rooster and Chinese Movie Awards for best Chinese Opera film, was a major breakthrough in terms of the experimentation, exploration and reflection embodied within its carefully crafted frames. It also marks the beginning of a concept that formed his own aesthetic ideology that had a profound and far-reaching effect on his subsequent productions. Director ZhuFeng had high praise for this film, believing that the directorial concepts in *The Inspector and the Prince* were not merely there to put a traditional Chinese opera to the screen via filmmaking techniques, but rather an attempt to expand upon the limitless possibilities of the film genre itself through a cinematic interpretation of traditional Chinese opera. It is an interplay and fusion between these two genres, which simultaneously pushed the boundaries of both Chinese opera and cinema itself by borrowing a convention from a Chinese film industry still in its embryonic stage – cinematic opera. The film *The Inspector and the Prince* is an 'avant-garde cinematic opera' with its own powerfully self-aware aesthetic consciousness (Feng 2016: 4).

The third phase, which is often referred to as his 'great developmental phase' or his 'aesthetic consciousness phase', begins with *Useless Man* and includes *Falling City* and the five-part series *Corrosion*. In these films he essentially took the aesthetic concepts begun in *The Inspector and the Prince* and began consciously employing them in a series of other productions. And it was at this point in his career that his passion and eagerness to get on to the next discovery became particularly palpable in this body of work. Though each piece had its own look, and some were even two sides of the same coin, for example, *Useless Man* and *Falling City*, each was nevertheless a piece in a greater puzzle. This process was finally taken to new heights in *Bangzi Melody*. If *Useless Man* is Peking Opera, then *Falling City* is Kun Opera, and *Corrosion* is a five-part series of operas, and *Bangzi Melody* is made in the epic historical Bangzi opera tradition. At this point, we, the viewers, have glimpsed total perfection. Regardless of the theme, the era or the story, as long as it is entrusted to Zheng DaSheng's masterful hands, the final product is sure to be a great 'film', and in incomparable presentation of 'theatre'.

Part 4: Four Cases

Four of Zheng DaSheng's films have been selected for analysis here to better acquaint ourselves with his creative nuances. The films from the first stage will not be discussed in much depth from this point on, as they have largely stolen the limelight thus far. For related materials, please refer to Zhen (2007) and Zheng and Yan (2003). The cream of the crop from the second and third stages has been handpicked, specifically, *The Inspector and the Prince*, *Useless Man*, *Falling City* and *Bangzi Melody*, with the latter being given centre stage.

The Inspector and the Prince is a co-production between the Shanghai Peking Opera Troupe and the Shanghai Film Group and was met with overwhelming acclaim. Mister Shang ChangRong – Shanghai Peking Opera Theater's own distinguished performing artist who played the part of Yu ChengLong – had high praise for the film, summing it up in a succinctly verbose manner, 'It was an exquisite juxtaposition of fantasy and reality, weaving in and out of modernity and antiquity'. While mister Guan DongTian – Shanghai Peking Opera Troupe's own distinguished performing artist who played the role of Kang WangYe – expressed,

> The piece is a valuable creative experiment in contemporary opera film. The director was literally speaking to the audience through the film medium, trying every novel filmmaking trick in the book in an effort to break through the peculiar limitations of the four-act play format of the stage. It transitioned smoothly and masterfully through the introduction, elucidation, transformation and on to the conclusion with an exquisitely crafted interplay between fantasy and reality. The piece was full of elements that sought to upend the formulaic conventions of the traditional opera film.
>
> (Wei and Lili 2009: 5)

Personally, this author feels that the film broke through the longstanding 'to adapt stage to film or film to stage' conundrum, not only imbuing film and stage alike with 'life', but also with a contrasting complementarity, causing a qualitative leap in the world's first 'film-stage' montage technique experiment, and all of the rich innovations that come with it. The innovations that are considered to be the most impressive are:

> A 'latent' traditionalism was exposed under the 'rawness' that was so ahead of its time. The main thing that resonates in the film is the brassy boldness of its stripped-down quality: Essentially, everything in the film is stripped down. The locations, staging, lighting, sets, music and even on down to the musicians. Zheng DaSheng's explanation for this was, after filming *The Inspector and the Prince*, theatre's five and six at The Shanghai Film Museum – his dream premiere spot

since he was all but knee high – had been torn down, 'terminated with extreme prejudice' if you will, which provided him with the powerful motivating force to preserve it on celluloid (DaSheng 2013:165). He has always held the musicians' performance to be an externalization and manifestation of the hero's moral makeup (Haiyan and Xue, 2016(5): 8), making these two points the reason for the 'rawness' that Zheng DaSheng employs in his work. But in a statement made before rehearsals for a stage performance of *The Crucible* began, Zheng DaSheng mentioned about the 'raw textural and raw structural' treatment he was employing, which drew its inspiration from Deconstructionist theory and methodology (DaSheng 2010). Taking these two statements together, this author feels that the 'raw' used by Zheng DaSheng is most certainly the dictates of his ego-complex; on the other hand, long before *The Inspector and the Prince*, he had witnessed his desired effects in certain things he attempted in *The Crucible*, which was the manifestation of the energy brought on by his edginess. It is for this very reason that this author believes it was the addition of the cutting-edge 'rawness' that allowed the 'hidden' traditionalism at the centre of the piece to emerge in such an unexpected manner, a prime example of which is the Prince getting drunk at a wine ceremony, as it brought out an inherent traditionality.

The 'transformations' in the film obliterated the stodgy 'constancy' of traditionalism. In days of old, making opera films either took place on location or completely on a stage, but primarily the latter. These films, though artistic in nature, are mostly just there as records and archives, what with their strict adherence to conventions and formula. But a forward-thinking pioneer, Zheng DaSheng, a man who has put his mind to the task of innovation, threw a monkey wrench into this well-oiled works of 'constancy'. Zheng DaSheng later mused,

> 'So how does one go about properly negotiating the middle ground between film and stage, truth and fantasy?' After ruminating on the question, I decided to 'disregard' the intrinsic aesthetic dilemma present in this kind of film. I just let it go. I disregarded the presupposed duality of the premise. And when that doesn't stand in your way, then you can overturn and re-make the premise from scratch, and from there you can go on to discover new breakthroughs, and consciously 'crossover' into new realms.
>
> (DaSheng 2010)

Thus,

> Dissolving the bounds between the historical, and the modern, real locations and studio backdrops, the definite and the indefinite, plot and performance,

and characters and performers. Traversing, interweaving and mobilizing every possible cinematic audio-visual element, to freely interpret operatic performance. And, the freedom this affords you is what you get from putting the avant-gardism you learned into actual practice; to always push to reformulate the premise and to initiate change.

The pioneering 'breakthroughs' in the film broke out of the 'orderliness' of tradition. A symbol of the avant-garde is 'fragmentation', whose completeness lies in reorganization, and reassembly. In *The Inspector and the Prince*, the overall sense of 'segmentation' was rendered cinematically through 'splices' and 'reassembly'. Case in point, the climactic drinking contest scene that made use of overhead shots, undercranking, zoom-ins, intercutting and jump cuts throughout a full aria performed on a stage. A montage of quick cuts and splices later, a lucid and memorable spectacle is created that vastly surpasses what could ever be possible solely through the theatrical medium.

This is not to say that this stage play's grand entrance into the world of the avant-garde was meant to replace its theatrical counterpart, it was only meant to break the bonds between 'the cinema and stage, the real and virtual, the isolated and concentrated', to achieve the liberal aims of the transcendental ego. For example, the prison search scene or the conjugal reunion scene, juxtaposing back and forth between the real world and the fantasy world, as if entering a no-man's land where desolated turns to be populated, and film follows stage and stage follows film. Director Zhu Feng believes that *The Inspector and the Prince* is where 'Chinese expressionist theatre' becomes 'Chinese expressionist cinema' (Feng 2016: 4). However, and this point the author must stress that, the true success of *The Inspector and the Prince* lies in his discovery of a way to seamlessly blend 'traditionalism and avant-gardism', where the traditional 'activated' the avant-garde. It was the pioneering elements that helped carve out a niche for the traditional, and the traditional elements just shone all the brighter for the avant-garde ones.

Useless Man and *Falling City* should be analysed together, not simply because the two were filmed contiguously, but because the two were conceptualized together. 'These two novels both occur during Tianjin's period of decline in 1937', Zheng DaSheng expressed,

> but one is a series about a character in a small town, and the other is the story of a big family. The original idea behind the story was to explore what happens when a city has gone into decline but causes a different kind of decline for many people living within its borders. For the same city at the same time, it is seemingly different faces and existences for people in different classes and different

walks of life. And so, I wanted to use a loose contrast between *Useless Man* and *Falling City* and not draw such tight, point-by-point parallels.

(DaSheng 2013: 51)

It is for this reason that this author has grouped the two together and analysed them as a single unit. Although the two films are completely independent and can be studied separately, the author believes that putting the two together like this seems to play closer to director Zheng's original concept. By comparison and contrast, it was discovered that the two films have the following characteristics:

A. *Useless Man* represents the 'avant-garde', while *Falling City* represents the 'traditional'. As previously outlined, Zheng DaSheng's early aesthetic sensibilities began to deepen with *The Inspector and the Prince*. The 'dualist' concept was most likely a one-time trial. And, the viewer of *Useless Man* becomes a first-hand witness to a sort of avant-gardist experiment, 'through means such as, narration, split-screens, encircled and obscured subjects, titles flying across the screen, juxtaposed vintage photographic and phonographic elements, dynamic shifts between saturated and desaturated imagery, slow and fast motion shots, first-person perspective, moments of exaggeration and even anachronic music' (DaSheng 2013: 52), all of which work to make the vivid and affected style of *Useless Man* look remarkably true-to-life and true-to-spirit. The story begins with a narrator telling the story of what happened in real life, at which time the story becomes 'fictional', but after the protagonist bursts into the narrator's niche, the story becomes 'true'. Meaning, the hero steps out of the confines of the narrator's story. However, when he asks the on-site audience, 'I'm telling the truth, how come you don't believe me?' the 'truth' reverts back to 'fiction'. This 'truth, fiction' narrative pattern is open-ended, modernist and labyrinthine. *Falling City*, on the other hand, breaks from the capriciousness of *Useless Man*, putting the characters into a traditional pavilion setting and revived the 'court lady' acme of beauty, which he had been fixating on. The sister-in-law character in the film is representative of the beauty, purity and strength of tradition, the fullness of which can be drunk in by the eye of the beholder.

B. *Useless Man* represents 'Peking Opera', while *Falling City* represents 'Kun Opera.' It is not known whether it was set up to be this way during Zheng DaSheng's initial conceptualization stage, but judging from his modern films, such as those outlined above, he made the rollicking *Useless Man* into Peking Opera and the serene *Falling City* into Kun Opera. One work is masculine, the other feminine. One reaches outward, the other looks inward. One is exciting, the other placid. One is direct, the other reserved. One is overt, the other covert.

One drifts around, the other stays put. One is hotly emotional, the other coolly stoic. One emphasizes action, the other dialogue. One is like the opera, *Where the Roads Meet*, the other *The Peony Pavilion*. The two offset each other brilliantly.

As previously stated, *Useless Man* can be categorized as 'allegro', while *Falling City* can be categorized as 'largo'. After making a sort of, 'two-for-one' production, Zheng DaSheng was clear on the fact that he wanted the audience to see differing life reactions simultaneously, and to see similar stories interpreted differently. To better understand *Useless Man*, it is best to see *Falling City*; and to better understand *Falling City* it is necessary to see *Useless Man*, which is the dynamic duo's very reason for being made.

2017's *Bangzi Melody* is Zheng DaSheng's latest masterpiece. During a premiere in the 'Theater Five' in the Shanghai Film Museum at the Shanghai International Film Festival, the place was packed with wall-to-wall people and the energy in the room was palpable. The year of its release, *The Inspector and the Prince* came charging out of 'Theater's Five and Six' with a bang, and now *Bangzi Melody* has made a triumphant return to 'Theater Five' (of course not the original Theater Five), which is not just simple turn-taking, but a representation of how his films have scaled to new aesthetic heights.

Bangzi Melody has accrued a great deal of positive word-of-mouth and spontaneous praise. Noted film director Peng XiaoLian expressed,

> The film is very well-made, and the acting is great, as the cast is made up of actual locals. It really draws you in to the authenticity of its rustic environment. The cinematography is great, so much so that it immerses the viewer in the story. The production design is excellent, as you get a real sense of the environment of the time and the real stuff they used in their daily lives during that era. The music is great too. The director really packed the film full of the local opera culture, which constituted the language the film. The direction is just excellent, exhibiting total mastery over the craft!
>
> (XiaoLian 2017: n.pag.)

'It is a spectacular example of mature filmmaking at the highest level. The camera movement, performances and dialogue were just first-rate' (Ling 2017: n.pag.). '*Bangzi Melody* is truly excellent! The absurdist and unforgiving tone, the realistic yet exaggerated performances, the highly stylized visuals and the various links between characters, space, sets, staging, action and music have created a multifaceted and thought-provoking country fable' (ChuanFa 2017: n.pag.). Though comments like these literally litter the map, the film's own internal mechanisms will be analysed for the purposes of this essay and not external comments like the ones stated above.

Parallel Operas

My Wife Is Princess and *My Husband Is Kuei-zi* are featured within the movie. Zheng DaSheng set up an ingenious 'mirror image plays' format; thus, the opera *My Wife Is Princess* and *My Husband is Kuei-zi* are one and the same story. *My Wife Is Princess* is a famous Shanxi opera that tells the story of Tang DaiZong offering his daughter, princess Sheng Ping's hand in marriage to Guo YiZi, the King of Fengyang's seventh son Guo Ai. During the king's sixtieth birthday, his son and son-in-law bowed to him in reverence of the auspiciousness of the occasion, with only Princess Sheng Ping abstaining from showing her respects. This controversial act drew the ire of Guo Ai, who took her back to the palace and beat her soundly. In the film, Kuei-zi is undoubtedly the 'golden child' in the town mayor's eyes, as he was the one who had 'fought for righteousness against corruption and nepotism', which led to the town procuring life-saving rations and making him the town hero in the process. But now, in order to redistribute the nine hectares of land that Kuei-zi is 'squatting' on, the villagers launch an all-out 'attack' on him, in which they surround him with spears, capture him and haul him off to the local insane asylum. The rehearsals for *My Wife Is Princess* are presumably reality, while the attack on Kuei-zi is fantasy, but a simple peak beyond surface reveals the rehearsals to be totally devoid of substance, meaning that *My Wife Is Princess* is merely a hollow shell – a void. The attack on Kuei-zi is clearly what is real. Thus, in the limbo state between reality and fantasy, the attack on Kuei-zi becomes the true substance of *My Wife Is Princess*. The film contains several layers of meaning, and deepening its message when the two plays, which had no clear relation up until that point, begin to assume a montage-esque interplay: Kuei-zi had been holding nine-and-a-half hectares of land, making him a landlord of sorts, and it was then that the film's hidden theme, 'attack the landlords and redistribute the land', came up for air. A theme that is deeply rooted in the Communist Party's long-standing land policy. It is truly a case of art imitating life ... and history. Beyond that, the 'Guo Ai' contingent who attacked the 'golden child' Kuei-zi included the mayor, a Lu LaoHe-type cadre, as well as the ordinary villagers (other than Xiao Fen) and beyond that, even his own flesh-and-blood took part in the attack. In a furious call to arms, Kuei FengZi, the 'fair-haired boy' of the day, found himself deserted and isolated by the very people who had professed to admire him. He was subsequently exiled and incarcerated in a chaotic spectacle bearing quite a striking resemblance to another period in history. It not only foreshadowed later historical events, but also allegorized a people's national portent.

'Exposed' and 'Hidden' Parallel Structure

If we look holistically at the aforementioned 'parallel operas' as a whole, the 'exposed' elements are those that reference politics, history and ethnicity, and are apparent on the surface. Then there are the 'hidden' elements, like Zhang KueiSheng beating his 'golden child' – his daughter Cai Yun – as a measuring stick of reason and morality. It is at this moment that Zhang KueiSheng actually becomes Guo Ai, which replicates what happens in *My Wife Is Princess,* in the sense that Zhang KueiSheng receives a prize that allows him to ascend to the 'top' for beating the 'golden child' – namely, among other things, the nine-and-a-half hectares of land and free workpoints that allow him to get ahead by receiving a disproportionate pro-rata.

However, what it does not share in common with *My Wife Is Princess* is, in the opera, Guo Ai had a happy life following the beating incident, whereas the Guo Ai of the film subsequently descends into madness, becoming a 'maniac', which is a major trauma that is both a penance to be paid, and a reward/punishment, collectivist/individualist, personal/family interests' dichotomy or binary opposite relationship. However, Zheng DaSheng's critiques and ideas do not stop there. Just as every character in the film can possibly become like Guo Ai, which is an 'overt/covert' complementary structure, one that takes the prevailing human and ethnic nature – for example everyone is a bully or madman – and puts them on the judgement seat to be handled as 'God' sees fit.

Folk Opera and Official Opera Parallels

There are also parallels between folk opera and official opera running concurrently through the film. Folk productions of *My Wife Is Princess* had previously fallen out of favour with the powers that be, and the props, sets and costumes were falling apart with age. However, times were changing, and at that point in the film the opera had been 'officially ordered' to be performed, showing that a paradigm shift in the dominant ideology on the part of the leadership had taken place, and the entire rehearsal for the opera was an ideological indoctrination process. Slowly the opera became an officially sanctioned production, with the 'officialization' of the piece actually being the gradual stripping away of reality itself, which caused indifference, clandestine dealings and self-interest to become the status-quo. Arguably, it was through this parallel structural relationship that Zheng DaSheng revealed certain historical and factual implications.

In addition, we can find others such as parallels between 'realism and expressionism', 'rationalism and irrationalism'. And it is in the construction of these parallel relationships that allow us to see 'dual-essence' aesthetic system that Zheng DaSheng set up for the film. These 'dual-essences' can be referred to as 'twin-turbines'. The 'essences' here refer to the 'traditional' and 'avant-garde' present within the film. The traditional elements are concentrated on discovery, guardianship and bridging, while the avant-garde elements are concentrated on reconceptualization of the premise, analysis and recombination. They are tangible – e.g. Xiao Fen representing conservatism and Lu LaoHe representing politics, but also intangible. Though it is a deep structure they are always in motion and at work.

Part 5 – The Five Characteristics

To sum up, it is apparent that the following five main characteristics were gradually formed in the creative mind of Zheng DaSheng:

1. A 'Theatrical Spirit' that Centres on 'Traditional Opera'

A 'theatrical sprit' centring on the sense of identity felt in his own 'traditional style operatic productions', which he found so long ago when he went looking for China. One fact must be clarified at this point, Zheng DaSheng being 'tradition-oriented' does not mean that he is obsessed with tradition or that he blindly clings to tradition. It is through this tradition-centricity that he has developed his 'expert-craftsman' approach. His 'traditional opera spirit' is embodied in the following ways: (a) Operatic elements appear in nearly all of his films besides the opera-film *The Inspector and the Prince*. *Bangzi Melody* goes without saying, as well as *Useless Man*, *Fleeting Time* and *Ah-Tao*, in which operatic touches are skilfully interwoven throughout. (b) Many of his films are edited to the drum or gong beats of traditional Chinese opera. 'In editing, I should have both a feature-film mentality and a strict adherence to the signature rhythms of Peking opera percussion' ('Theatrical film' 2016: 8). (3) In his usage of Chinese opera, there is sometimes a figurative cinematic structure, for example, the use of the opera, *Where the Roads Meet* in *Useless Man*, which is an 'opera within an opera', where the film takes place in its entirety. (4) The externalization of Chinese operatic structure as a narrative structure, for example *Corrosion* is nearly an opera serial. (5) The 'essence' that is communicated through Chinese opera has become Zheng DaSheng's conscious creative principle. Especially, the all-important 'creative breath' of Chinese opera that is used extensively in works such as *Falling City*.

> I talked to my art director and cinematographer about the fact that we wanted to compose shots with the doors, windows and hallways of the Chinese style courtyard as much as possible. And to create the most neutral and ambiguous

foreground space. The Chinese courtyard serves to create space, but at the same time it's permeable. I told my D.P. that it was the same as the relationship between the leading man and leading lady.

(DaSheng 2013: 54)

Through the 'space/permeability' interpretation, Zheng DaSheng found a suitable flavour for the characters, structure and rhythm of the film. Moreover, it is essentially a traditional Chinese opera practice. (6) The aesthetics of Chinese opera, especially in terms of 'freeform aesthetics' have become something of a conscious pursuit for Zheng DaSheng, which is represented in the likes of *The Inspector and the Prince* and *Falling City*.

2. A 'Theatrical Energy' Created by Avant-Gardism

For Zheng DaSheng, who went abroad to study the avant-garde and at the same time went through arduous training to apprehend it, the craft has become an inextricable part of his knowledge and aesthetic systems. It is not unlike what is ingrained naturally by traditional family education in a family of scholars. It will be with him forever. Therefore, one aspect of the avant-garde is seen throughout Zheng DaSheng's work; moreover, it is the 'inspiration' for the 'theatrical energy' in his work. This 'avant-garde as means to an end' ethic is spelled out in detail as follows: (1) Avant-gardism is a technique whose imagery, timing and rhythm create a sense of novelty in his films. (2) Avant-gardism is a skill that was employed in an experimental montage technique in the film *Fleeting Time*, where he employed silhouettes and audio-visual montages to bring to life the dream of a policeman, portrayed by actor Yao AnLian, who fantasized about becoming an army general. The resulting imagery was not just vividly expressive, but downright jaw-dropping. (3) Avant-gardism is a structural approach that gives films an extremely original narrative structure, of which the aforementioned film *Useless Man* is a perfect example. Employing it gave the ending of the film an open-ended feel and created an ambiguous middle-ground between truth and falsehood, expanding its narrative artistry. (4) Avant-gardism is meaningful and conceptual, and its application has made Zheng DaSheng's films stand out. *The Inspector and the Prince* and *Bangzi Melody* are classic examples.

3. A Focus on Complex Texts and Serial Opera's Multifaceted and Multilinear Structure

Zheng DaSheng's later work trended increasingly away from a single narrative tendency and application and began to become increasingly focused on complex text and serial opera's multifaceted and multilinear narrative structure. The above-mentioned *Useless Man* and *Falling City* are examples of his attempts at complex text and multifaceted structures. With *Corrosion*, Zheng DaSheng adapted Mao Dun's eponymous trilogy into a serial of five independent but closely related instalments, closely mirroring 'serial opera' in structure. The five parts were separated into main plotlines about individuals like Lu MeiLi, Hu BaoSu and Zhang QiuLiu. These stories were told individually but combined into a multiple narrative structure. The protagonist of the first part becomes a supporting character in the second part. The stories then intersect and combine to form a story with a clear thread but a multiple narrative pattern. Peng XiaoLian realized this when he commented,

> DaSheng has gone from simply telling stories to embracing the multiple narratives. *Bangzi Melody* starts out exploring each individual and character's life circumstances and begins to show their fate through the economic conditions of the village. Over a large expanse of time it throws the characters' needs right at the audience. It is expressed in the actors' dialogue, through lighting and through the language of the director's lens. It is multi-linear and shows us all the warts and quirks of real life. This is film!
>
> (XiaoLian 2017: n.pag.)

4. The Impulse to Push the Envelope Beneficial for Expanding His Repertoire

Armed with his avant-garde sensibilities and an inspiration rooted in traditionalism, Zheng DaSheng has been fighting to break down stereotypes and taboos. Something inside compels him to use every means at his disposal to add new dimensions to his work, in terms of characters, story and ideas. One may wonder, and yet be won over and awe-struck by how he has the sheer audacity to use certain tricks and techniques that may have previously been considered impossible. *The Inspector and the Prince*, *Useless Man* and *Bangzi Melody* are just such masterworks. For example, in *Bangzi Melody* when Kuei-zi entered the millhouse with two women, Zheng DaSheng employed techniques such as quick cuts, handheld shots, wide angles, the subjective camera, montage and counterpoint to express with amazing accuracy, beguiling uniqueness and staggering impressiveness, the contrast between Kuei-zi's perceived psychological time and actual clock time. This is an experiment in the avant-garde, and to an even greater degree, the pursuit of the penultimate – a pursuit involving an understanding from multiple artistic angles, and the wisdom to know how to bring every element into play.

5. An Aesthetic System Built on a Fusion of Traditionalism and Avant-gardism

Starting from a search for a personal visual style for *Ah-Tao*, to successfully borrowing from avant-gardism to offset traditionalism in *The Inspector and the Prince*, and then on to the creation of 'dual-essences' for Bangzi Melody, this is the aesthetic concept of 'a traditional and avant-gardist fusion'. It is not the simple 'you-and-me-together' fusion that we might expect, but it involves a progressive relationship. (a) The façade of traditionalism is cut away with the 'cutting-edge' of the avant-garde and the unwanted is then discarded. (b) The traditional form is refined with the 'fire' of the avant-garde. (c) Tradition is alchemized with the 'elixir' of the avant-garde. (d) The traditional is remoulded and repolished with the 'hand' of the avant-garde. (5) Harmonic resonance is created and power is reciprocated with the 'dual powertrain' of the avant-garde and the traditional working together.

There have been virtually no one who has progressed to study or practice 'avant-garde' cinema in Chinese history; therefore, most of them 'turned inward' in their aesthetical pursuits, but Zheng DaSheng's practical avant-garde experience put him in the driver's seat of 'twin-powertrain' or 'twin-turbocharged' aesthetic that became a reality. From *The Inspector and the Prince* and *Bangzi Melody*, we the viewers have been able to appreciate the treat that is the allure of Da-Shengian aesthetics.

Part 6 – Six Sides and Seven Visions

Besides the five aforementioned characteristics, Zheng DaSheng explored a great many additional aspects. Due to special limitations we will concentrate the discussion on only six. (1) **Bridging gaps, crossovers and fusion**: Zheng DaSheng's method of crossover and fusion was unlocked long ago. His technical demands listed in his professional summary were to aggressively push the envelope and challenge himself to fuse new elements with his work. For example, he incorporated deconstructionist concepts and filmmaking techniques into his direction of stage play *The Crucible*. He borrowed from the flashback concept so often seen in movies, in that he handily cut in silhouetted projections and key moments in the story, taking the narrator and the scene of the action and staging them on dual planes, one placed behind the other, where the action happens simultaneously. The theatricality of it was obvious, but it played out like a cinematic live-action spectacular, with montage-like segments that easily and effectively beefed up the traditional theatrical look, feel and pacing to the production. (2) **The broken narrative**: Similar to the real asymptotic line, there is also an asymptotic line in Zheng DaSheng's films, but it is not the real asymptote, but a freeform line that makes up the broken narrative of Zheng DaSheng's work. For example, in *Bangzi Melody* five elders sit under the images of Karl Marks and Joseph Engels. It goes without saying that the moment was born spontaneously. (3) **Extensive use of non-professional actors:** For example, the individual playing the role of Su HongDa in *Useless Man* is a crosstalk comedian. The performer playing the role of *Er Sao* in *Fallen City* had no previous film acting experience. And in *Bangzi Melody*, there was a host of localities in the background and local opera performers in the cast, yet under the godlike direction of Zheng DaSheng, their performances reached almost supernatural perfection. (4) **Use of locations:** The sumptuous western Hunan locations in *Ah-Tao*, the beauty of the ancient Beijing settings in *The Curio* cannot be overstated. In *The Inspector and the Prince*, the entire space seems to be virtually 'alive'. And in *Useless Man* and *Falling City*, Shanghai piers stood in for old Tianjin, and the audience could not tell the difference. And even more amazing is, in *Bangzi Melody* an entire town became one giant set that both served to tell the story and enhance the film's expressiveness under Zheng DaSheng's masterful direction. (5) **History and time:** Thus far, *Fleeting Time* is Zheng DaSheng's only modern drama, almost all the others are period pieces. He has stated that people and situations from history are nearer and dearer to his heart. He strongly values the old and weakly values the present. But in watching his films, there is a strong sense that the people and events he references are real, and there are many reasons for this. But the main one is that he is fond of imagining himself on a certain street at a certain time to meet with real historical figures – a kind of thought experiment. (6) **Mainstream commercial viability:** Beginning from his humble roots as an 'indie filmmaker' and on to *Bangzi Melody*, Zheng DaSheng has made remarkable artistic achievements, but the curious thing is that he has yet to enter the mainstream a commercially viable helmsman. Some critics believe that in contemporary Chinese film, he is the alternative to the business of showbusiness, and that he shies away from controversy and gossip, and focuses solely on film itself, and has a fairly broad body of work, which is probably because of the magic of 'home video' and the fact that he has invested his own money into his projects. But it is precisely because of the nature of his work that he has made a name for himself (Qiqi 2017: n.pag.). These kinds of reviews have pegged his work under the 'art film' label. But, in the views of this author, this label is both wrong and right. The correct is that Zheng DaSheng is very much committed to the artistic development of the craft of film. The incorrect is that nearly every one of Zheng DaSheng's films, although made on a shoestring, is basically a state capital. Therefore, this author holds that Zheng DaSheng is on the cusp of entering the mainstream. So, let us return to the seven visions of DaSheng. From *The Pedestrian* on, we have seen the tireless champion of film art. His search for 'tradition and self' has allowed him to see tradition in its truest form, and to begin to consciously receive tradition into his heart and soul and become its fiercest guardian. His pursuit of avant-garde and his experience out there on the cutting edge have allowed his time on the path to bravely forge ahead for 'change and innovation' to change him completely. It is highly commendable that he has been doing his art within the context of 're-envisioning', and learning from the shortcomings of his last film. He is a born thinker. And the man is no Salieri – he has the talent to back up the hype. At the same time, he is no Mozart, in the sense that he has remained grounded and has not gotten caught up in his own hype. He was born curious. The fact that he is so keenly able to perceive and appreciate diversity has strengthened his resolve to be well-rounded. The fact that he is a prodigy and a master has qualified him to be a true reformer. At this point, the 'seven faces of DaSheng' shaped by his seven visions have given us a clearer understanding of him as a director. It is arguably due to the very fact that he received avant-gardist training and a traditionalist education that he is today's true representative of the Shanghai school of filmmakers, who are open, diverse, progressive and neocentric. He also represents the future of Chinese filmmakers, who are, free-spirited, conscientious, magnanimous and tenacious.

REFERENCES

Bin, Li and DaSheng, Zheng (2003), 'On the road of the movie: Interview with young director Zheng DaSheng', *Journal of Beijing Film Academy*, 4, p. 91.

ChuanFa, Wan (2017), WeChat, 8 June.

DaSheng, Zheng (2000), *The Self-Supply of the Single Film: Avant-Grade Today*, 9th, Tianjin: Tianjin Academy of Social Sciences Press.

—— (2010), 'A summary of his professional films', 9 September, unpublished.

—— (2013), 'Tianjin's past, images in memory: *Useless Man* and *Falling City*', in Zhen, Ni and Yuan, Xu (eds), *Chinese New Director Micro Interview*, Beijing: China Film Press.

DaSheng, Zheng, Jian, Pu, Lisheng and Lin, Zhen, Li (2013), *Falling City*, four dialogues, *Contemporary Films*, 1.

Feng, Zhu (2016), 'Avant-garde and redemption', in Li Yizhong and Li Zhenlin (eds), *Hai Shang Ying Tan (The First Series)*, Shanghai: Shanghai People's Publishing House.

Haiyan and Xue (2016), 'The Dialect about Opera Film between Zheng Dasheng and Shang Changrong', *Shanghai Theater*, 5.

Ling, Zhang (2017), tweets, 19 June.

Qiqi, Su (2016), 'Theatrical film: Prospects for the future are still wide-open – Zheng DaSheng and Shang Changrong's dramas', *Shanghai Theatre*, 5.

—— (2017), 'Facing history: In the reflection of realism and expressionism – Talking about Zheng DaSheng *Bangzi Melody*', DeepFocus Wechat Public Account, 16 July.

Wei, Nie and Lili, Guo (2009), '"Movie" and "Drama" intertextuality and narrative modern innovation: Peking Opera film', The Inspector and the Prince Seminar, *New Films*, 3.

XiaoLian, Peng (2017), 'Why *Bangzi Melody* is so good', 5 July, http://www.pmovie.com.

Zhen, Li (2007), 'The traveling monk in the mirror – Zheng DaSheng and his films', *Contemporary Film*, 9.

Zheng, Tan and Yan, Zhang (2003), 'The traveling monk's films – The analysis of young director Zheng DaSheng's work', *Journal of Beijing Film Academy*, 4.

Zheng DaSheng's Filmography

1990: Graduated from the Shanghai Theatre Academy Directing Department
1994: Graduated from the Chicago, Art Academy, Film Department
1996: Directed the multimedia CD-ROM 'Ancient Chinese Art'
1997: Directed 20 episodes of the TV series 'All Girls Condo'
1998: Directed CD-ROM multimedia CD, 'Drama Master Huang Zuolin'
2000: Directed the TV movie 'Death of Wang Bozhi' (CCTV Movie Channel)
2000: Won the Best TV Film Award at the 20th Golden Rooster and Hundred Flowers Film Festival; won Best Film or TV Program Baihe Award
2000: Directed the TV movie 'Ah-Tao' (CCTV Movie Channel)
Received the Special Award of the 8th Annual Shanghai International Film Festival Jury; Best TV movie Baihe Award
2001: Directed the TV movie *The Curio* (CCTV Movie channel)
2001: Won, Best Director of Film or TV Series Award at the 9th Beijing University Student Film Festival
2001: Nominated for Best Film or TV Series nomination at 21st Annual Golden Rooster and Hundred Flowers Film Festival
Directed four episodes of the TV Series, *Liao-Fan's Four Lessons*, 'Traditional Chinese Moral Code'
2002: Second Annual Chinese TV Art 'Double Ten' Top Ten Director
2002: Directed the documentary *DV CHINA*
2002: Silver Award at the Austrian International Film Festival
2002: SWISS FILMS International Documentary Film Festival Beyond the Truth
2004: Directed the regional theatre Kun Opera production of, *The Palace of Eternal Youth* (Shanghai Kun Opera Troupe)
2005: Directed the digital film *Fleeting Time* (CCTV Film Channel); shortlisted for the French 2005: Hans International Film Festival; directed 20 episodes of the TV series, *Lang Tao Sha*

2006: Directed the drama, *The Witch of Salem* (Shanghai Drama Center); directed the Yue opera 'Tang Yu' (Fanghua Yue Opera Troupe); won the 'Hundred Years of Yue Opera' drama Gold medallion

2008: Directed the Beijing Opera film, *The Inspector and the Prince* (Shanghai Troupe)

2008: Received the 13th China Film China Watch Award for Outstanding Drama Film Award

2008: 18th China Film Golden Rooster Award for Best Drama Film; featured filmmaker at the 5th 'Vanguard of Glory' Film Festival

2009–2010: Shanghai World Expo China Pavilion theme film 'Harmonious China' (Expo Bureau, Shanghai Film Group Corporation)

2009–2010: Showing at the World Expo, Hundred Years of Classic Drama production of Kun Opera 'Peony Pavilion' (Shanghai Theatre Academy Opera Institute)

2009–2010: Winner of the 4th Shanghai Federation of Literary and Art Circles 'Twin Merits' Artist Shanghai 'May 1st' Labor Medal Award

2011–2012: Directed film *Useless Man* (Chinese Writers Publishing Group, CCTV Movie Channel)

2011–2012: 20th Beijing University Student Film Festival Best Low-Budget Film Award and Director Award

2011–2012: Received the first prize of the 13th Movie Channel Baihe First Prize Award for Best Film

2011–2012: directed the film, *Falling City* (Chinese Writers Publishing Group, CCTV Movie Channel)

2011–2012: Selected as the 'World Focus' unit of the 36th Montreal International Film Festival

2011–2012: Won the 7th Chinese Youth Image Forum Annual New Cinematographer Award

2013: Director's Criterion Series, 4K film 'Corrosion' (adapted from Mao Dun's eponymous novel; CCTV movie channel, China Writers Publishing House)

2013: Won first prize of the 15th Movie Channel Baihe Award for Best Feature Film

2014: Selected for the Shanghai Film Critics Society '2015 Top Ten Chinese Movies'

2014: Director/Producer 37 episodes of TV Serial, *Code*

2015–2016: Directed the film *Bangzi Melody* (Shanghai Film Group)

Creator, Director of Kun Opera, 'The Songs of the Songs' (Memorial of Tang Xianzu, the 400th Anniversary of Shakespeare's Death)

Creative, director 'Non-heritage' Ethnic Theater 'The Buyi Octave'

(Compiled by: Wan ChuanFa)

Acknowledgement

This chapter is the result of the 'Cultural and Art Science Research' project of the Ministry of Culture (project number: 14DC17).

7. A Kaleidoscopic View of Wang Han-lun's Celebrity Image

岳莹/Yue Ying

What is celebrity? Toby Miller believes that the formation of stardom began when the film industry generated attention towards the wonders of cinematic technology then to the characters in film (actors), and towards the links to the three developmental stages the star's career/life paradigm (Miller 2012: 21). Richard Dale pointed out that the image of a star is sweeping, multimedia and intertextual. Even if the star's screen image has the advantage of being firmly entrenched, it is also influenced by other 'private individual in the public eye' factors, which have different ascendancies in the different stages of the star's image (Dale 2012: 29). Therefore, to analyse a star's image, it is necessary not only to observe how it was 'created' on the screen, but also to examine its connotations at the private and public levels. Wang Han-lun, who is credited as 'The first movie star of the Republic of China' in history, as the public's muse in the field of modern cultural production in Shanghai, has been given complex and multiple meanings under the joint construction of many ideological discourses.

Part 1: 'The May Fourth Movement' Women's Liberation Zeitgeist and the Origin of 1920s Urban Culture in Shanghai

Originally known as P'eng Chien-ch'ing, Wang Han-lun was born in Suzhou in 1903 in a prominent feudal clan. At that time, Western culture had begun to take hold in the East, and soon after China transitioned from the late Qing Dynasty into the Republic of China. It was because of this changing of the guard that she had the opportunity to be sent to the St. Mary College of the Shanghai Church Girls School when she was a teenager. It was there that she received an East-West mixed education with an emphasis on Enlightenment Age values, which cultivated P'eng Chien-ch'ing's temperament. The influence of modern Western education instilled in her the self-awareness that traditional women lacked. The turbulent times in which she lived, as well as her arranged betrothal by her elder brother and his wife to a Manchurian bureaucrat named Zhang after her father's early death, caused her to begin to ponder the irrationality of gender inequality in society and subsequently fuelled her hatred and contempt for institutionalized male chauvinism. These complicated life experiences laid the basic foundation for her future contact with and acceptance of women's liberation.

During her youth, there were three separate women's liberation movements launched in China, and the advocates of the New Culture Movement pushed for women's issues to be completely rethought from the ground floor up. People began to realize that women's liberation held the same importance as human rights. And as a filmed product, this time brought the use of film, an emerging media, into full play.

In 1913, in the tenth year after the birth of P'eng Chien-ch'ing, directed by the film pioneers of the Republic of China, Chang Shih-ch'uan and Cheng Cheng-ch'iu, Hsin-min Film Company and the Asiatic Film Company produced a short story entitled *Die For Marriage*. The film is written around the custom of buying and selling marriages in Cheng-chou's hometown of Chaozhou. The film shows the cumbersome process of a couple who had never met before being brought together by matchmakers into the wedding chamber. It is the first feature film recorded in the history of China.[1]

The film looks raw and amateurish, and actually more like a home video of 'regional theatre'. Both the male and female parts were played by male actors of the 'regional theatre' at that time. Rather what this means is, life in the middle class was quite different from how Western films liked to portray it during the fledgling period of cinema history. For the first time there was a Chinese film about marriage and women. Since then, issues such as women's liberation, economic independence and autonomy have become the focus of longstanding focus of Chinese cinema, which is closely linked with women's liberation and anti-feudalism. If the 1905 film *Dingjun Mountain* provided Chinese cinema its genesis based in quintessential Han theatre, then *Die For Marriage* created a separate feminist, realist, family-oriented, socially conscious tradition for Chinese stories, which provided a reasonable opportunity, unprecedented at that point in history, for the aspiring starlets in 1920s China to get seen onstage in emerging performing arts theatre groups.

Shanghai in the 1920s was experiencing the freest and most open era since the Xinhai Revolution of 1911. Far removed from the influence of political elements, against the backdrop of the battle between consumerism and the old and new ethos, modern urban pop culture quietly began its development unnoticed and unabated, while entertainment and capital markets opened up new urban spaces. Lu Xun once said that the culture of Shanghai at that time was a 'business' culture. The urban spaces closely matched the daily life of the citizens: department stores, mandarin-duck-and-butterfly romances, alleyway taverns, electric trolleys, Paramount clubs, playhouses, cinemas and casinos, all of which crossed the old with new in a bizarre motley crew of stylistic hallmarks all jumbled up in the cinema of the time.

The urban landscape of this period is inseparable from the establishment of modern feminist imagery. With the popularity of Hollywood stars, foreign women's fashion stores came into vogue bringing with them imported stockings, high heels and cheongsams, which became the symbols of modernity for the Chinese women's groups that advocated wearing modern clothing. Those who had sampled the taste of modernity could no longer stomach the sight of the masculine characteristics that the new theatre actors dressed in drag splashed up in extreme close-up across the silver screen (Cheng-Ch'iu 1925). Cheng Cheng-ch'iu once recalled the difficulty of finding an actress when he first made a movie. Even the director himself felt that acting was disgraceful.[2] Ten years went by, and radical changes in social aesthetics led to changes in the structure of performing arts. Compared with the conservative atmosphere in the filming of *Die For Marriage*, female actors' appearance on screen was no longer taboo. This was the social backdrop for the first generation of female stars who led the way, such as Wang Han-lun.

Part 2: 'The Silver Screen's First Tragedienne': The Symbol of Traditional Oriental Woman Aesthetic in Cinema

The 1923 film *An Orphan Rescues His Grandpa* by The Star Motion Picture Company really changed P'eng Chien-ch'ing's fate. At the time she had recently divorced her unfaithful husband for consorting with Japanese sex workers and was working as an English typist in Shanghai's Hongkou. She got her big break when she met Jen I-p'ing, one of the founders of The Star Motion Picture Company, at a friend's house. The Star Motion Picture Company had just shot four films back-to-back that mimicked the style of Western cinema, all of which were box office bombs. Chang Shih-ch'uan and Cheng Cheng-ch'iu revamped their business strategy and film themes and produced the film *An Orphan Rescues His Grandp*a in a last-ditch effort to save the company from total meltdown. The film turned out to be an unabashed blockbuster. It tells the story of a family's disputes over inheritance.

Rich old tycoon Yang Shou-ch'ang (played by Cheng Che-ku) lost his son in his later years. To seize the family fortune, nephew Tao P'ei (played by Wang Hsien-chai) and Lu Shou-ching hatch out a plan to accuse Yu Wei-ru (played by Wang Han-lun) of infidelity, successfully driving Wei-ru out of the house. A few months later, Wei Ru gives birth to a son and names him Yu Pu (Cheng Hsiao-ch'iu). At ten years old, Yu Pu attends a school built by Shou-ch'ang, who also has a residence there. The grandparents and grandchildren have never met, though Yu Pu, who is polite and well-mannered, is favoured by Shou-ch'ang. Yu Pu often goes to his place to play. One day, Tao P'ei and Shou-ch'ing go to Shou-ch'ang to solicit money. After being reprimanded, their desires turn insidious, but just then Yu Pu shows up. Shou-ch'ing is arrested, Tao P'ei is seriously injured and Yu Pu is hurt as well. Tao P'ei comes clean and the family is finally reunited (Jihua 2005: 60).

Both Chang and Cheng felt that P'eng Chien-ch'ing's presence was very consistent with that of a young mistress from a large feudal family, which prompted them to cast her in the film as the widow Yu Wei-ru. The film was a huge smash after it was released and caused a sensation throughout the country and even Southeast Asia. The picture saved The Star Motion Picture Company and a Chinese film industry struggling to lift itself out of the doldrums at the time. The film resonated with every segment of society and people of all walks of life. Women and children, young and old were moved to tears. Newshawks reported the buzz surrounding the film at the time, 'Business is hitting on all eight, ticket sales are just ducky; dolls at the petting pantry say it could be a pip, the picture is the bees knees!' P'eng Chien-ch'ing threw the doors to the market wide open with her outstanding performance in the film, which became the focus of after-dinner conversation in Shanghai. Seeing her great market appeal, The Star Motion Picture Company signed P'eng Chien-ch'ing to a long-term contract, promising to pay ¥ 20 Yuan per month for transportation fees, and another ¥ 500 Yuan per film (Xiaonan 2008). Shortly thereafter, P'eng Chien-ch'ing broke from her feudal clan and changed her name to Wang Han-lun, thus establishing her as the first bona-fide starlet of the Chinese cinema.

The success of *An Orphan Rescues His Grandpa* was mainly due to its moralistic and didactic theme of poetic justice that was consistent with Ch'eng Chen-ch'iu's personal ideology. Cheng Cheng-ch'iu was deeply in tune with the sympathies and psychology of the Chinese audience, which he brought into play in the creation of a family morality play, consistent with the traditional Chinese cultural sentiments. Its influence on subsequent Chinese films was far-reaching, especially for the storytelling techniques it utilized, such as the closed dramatic structure and dramatic conflict, which are used even now. These storylines stress mythological qualities and coincidental happenstance. Looking back, the series of slightly exaggerated misunderstandings and coincidences in *An Orphan Rescues His Grandpa* seem a bit unrealistic, but the audience was not the least bit concerned about a flaw here or a wart there, as they were emotionally invested in the story. They laughed and cried. And once the happy ending with the family united in blissful love, they left the theatre grinning from ear to ear in satisfaction.

Images of family togetherness as an aesthetic trend for the Chinese audience was described in detail in the section of the official trade report of Hollywood, 'Chinese film and TV taste':

> The social issue known as 'the eternal triangle' in modern movies is powerless to effectively impress the Chinese audience. A central ethic for the Chinese is their deep filial respect for the elderly and they cannot understand things from any other perspective. Moreover, historical films have always been able to attract a large audience, and love stories, especially one that plays out like an amorous rustic elegy, will always have the power to impress the audience […].
> (*The China Film Market*, pp. 3–4, quoted from Oufan 2008: 58)

This is a testament to the emphasis on tradition present in the Chinese film audience's viewing tastes. From this perspective, examining Wang Han-lun's rapidly rising popularity due to her performance in *An Orphan Rescues His Grandpa*, it is hard to ignore the psychological connotations within the affinity the audience had for the character of Yu Wei-ru, whose image represented the female ideal on screen and gained sweeping emotional recognition from the audience. She combined into a single persona, the traditional Chinese ethics of the 'three virtues and three obediences', namely ,the guiding virtues of, 'The subject bows to the ruler, the child obeys the father and the wife belongs to the husband', as well as the three obediences, necessitating a woman to, 'Obey her father at home, her husband when she marries and her son if her husband should pass away'. The female character groomed under this Oriental ethos should be gentle and wise, but at the same time be humble and long-suffering. It is an ethic essentially requiring the woman to be subservient and meek in character, to be stoic and elegant, and calm and reserved. In other words, she is duty bound to bear her own tragic fate along with convoluted emotional underpinnings of an entire ethnic group just to satisfy Man's glib musings on the role of motherhood and women.

Wang Han-lun's star rose at various points in her life. The audience's perceptions and image of her were more derived from the symbols created by her onscreen persona, and their images that were underscored by these ideal female characters she created, such as Yu Wei-ru. 'We never knew who she was as a real individual, we only knew the images that appeared in media texts' ('Contemporary Western film theory selection' compiled by C. Xihe and X. Hong, in Dyer 1979: 6). On a textual level, the only basis for a star's very existence is the symbolic images seen on film, and its comprehensibility as the meaning of the character can only exist within the domain of this intertextuality ('Contemporary Western film theory selection' compiled by C. Xihe and X. Hong, in Dyer 1979: 6). Even if it appears in a non-screen form, the audience will continue to understand the textual symbols beyond the onscreen form, so the image of the star will often become fossilized and extremely difficult to alter.

Following *An Orphan Rescues His Grandpa*, Wang Han-lun went on to star in *The Death of Yuli, A Child Worker, The Poor Children* and other tearjerkers for

The Star Motion Picture Company. *The Death of Yuli* was the first script written by Cheng Cheng-ch'iu on women's issues. It depicts a young widow who sacrifices love and obedience for her morals, eventually dying a tragic death (Jihua 2005: 64).

After that, Wang Han-lun left The Star Motion Picture Company and made three films, *The Discarded Wife*, *Between Love and Filial Duty* and *The Love's Dream* for the Great Wall Film Company. Being similar to her own personal experiences, *The Discarded Wife* was Wang Han-lun's favourite. In the film, Wang Han-lun plays a woman who is abandoned by her husband. In order to survive, she performs menial chores in a bookstore and is continually humiliated by her boss. In grief and anger, she joins a social feminist movement and refuses her husband's request for reconciliation, causing him to retaliate by taking away her social standing. In bitter desperation, she steals away into the wild. In the mountains she encounters a robbery. Sick and destitute, she ultimately dies in the nunnery. *The Discarded Wife* refers to the women's occupational issues that were rarely shown in Chinese films in the 1920s. Although the plot never breaks from the narrative thread of the tragedy of a woman ultimately abandoned by society, its awareness of female voice was unique for that time. A poet wrote a lyric about Wang Han-lun's performance in the film, 'Wang Han-lun as Wu Chi-fang …'

> Anguish stains a brow swashed, with colors splashed an air a woman quashed, the details of a life limned and lined; with the pain of neglect anguish sublime; the shame of abuse, the terror of plunder, the cruelty of death; tracing the temper of a woman in limine, framing the demeanor of a woman in decline, casting an expression of delicate poise, facing what remains a life without choice.
> (Mo 2000: 33)

Wang Han-lun was later typecast into the tragic widow roles for her role in *The Discarded Wife*, earning her the title of, 'The Silver Screen's First Tragedienne', which later became the symbol of her professional image.

Part 3: Shanghai Chic – The Creation of an Offscreen 'New Woman' Identity

In recent years, celebrity research has entered a 'star-power' phase.

> The traditional film-power research model recognizes the identity of the star within the context of the film, while the star-power model is free from the shackles of this context. The celebrity image is separate from the film context whose existence is dispersed by a series of factors from outside of this context.
> (Watson 2012: 10–12)

For example, eminent scholar John Ellis said, 'Maybe a Nicole Kidman fan just admires her as a person, but not her because of her films'.

From this perspective, Wang Han-lun's celebrity image clearly reveals a dichotomy between her screen performance and her offscreen existence, the relationship between the individual and the character, and the public and private space.

A 1925 issue of *Cinema Journal* published a personal account by Wang Han-lun:

> I was fond of the spirit of our women's self-reliance. The 'self' in self-reliance means to support one's own self … I wanted to find another path, to blaze a new trail, to do something great for the glory of our women's honor … Later I threw myself headlong into the film business … I made up my mind to sacrifice myself, to fight the good fight for womanhood.
>
> (Han-lun 1925)

P'eng Chien-ch'ing had become a legitimate celebrity after the release of *An Orphan Rescues His Grandpa*, her eldest brother and sister-in-law however – the leaders of her feudal clan – thought that she had besmirched their family name by becoming an actress and wanted to banish her to the family's ancestral home in Suzhou. P'eng Chien-ch'ing saw through the heartless hypocrisy behind their façade, and with that broke from the family and changed her surname to Wang. Her name Han-lun was transliterated from the English name HELEN, and from there she embarked down the path of 'new woman' self-reliance. The words she had written in her personal statement ring true with strength and power, thus reflecting the strong personality of Helen Wang's 'new women' and her determination to break the feudal bondage that shackled her.

In her personal statement, she mentioned that the spirit of women's self-reliance was to support oneself, a sentiment that was right on par with the 'new women' concept of the May Fourth Movement. Visionaries of the day who advocated women's liberation generally held the belief that '[t]he biggest reason why Chinese women are bound by society is because the economy is not independent'. The prerequisite for women to truly be liberated was for them to win economic independence. Only at such time when they could fully support themselves would they ensure selfhood and completely attain 'personhood'. Under such a zeitgeist, 'economic independence' became a symbol of women's 'modernity', and the celebrity effect of silver screen starlets who represented the career girl was undoubtedly role models outside of affecting the audience from on screen. For example, after garnering fame, stories of how she broke the chains of the feudal family and ventured to Shanghai to earn her own bread spread like wildfire in the media, inspiring more and more young cosmopolitan women follow in her footsteps and fight against the patriarchal system, to also become a 'rebel girl'.

Moviegoers in the 1920s began to concern themselves with the offscreen private lives of movie stars. By then, the movie star had been completely removed from the context of the movie and began gaining attention as a celebrity. From 14 August to 14 September 1926 The Shanghai New World Entertainment Center held a film festival, during which there was a vote for the 'Queen of Cinema'. The nominees were Wang Han-lun, Chang Chi-yun, Yang Nai-mei, Hsüan Ching-lin and Li-ming Hui. The competition was intense. Ultimately, Chang Chi-yun won the 12 candidates with 2,146 votes, becoming the first 'Queen of the Cinema' in the history of Chinese showbusiness.

The first generation of Chinese female movie stars represented by Helen Wang was the poster child for Shanghai urban culture. They were the highest profile thought leaders in the city. Their personas, attire and everything they stood for became the object consumption for Shanghai citizens, thus concentrating attention on the star's look in the public realm, as well as the comments and criticisms made by people in all walks of life. They were the very first true 'modern girls' in any Chinese metropolis. The meaning of 'modern' here has nothing to do with the onscreen image of these female stars, but rather represents a trend in social aesthetic tastes and values.

Hsü Ch'ih-hen wrote a bio about Helen Wang in a 1927 issue of Chinese Film Spectrum,

> Ms. Helen Wang ... is a woman of wit, she is fond of English, and is in fact enthralled with the subject, which has thus afforded her a great many female friends from Western countries, with whom she has had a great many dialogues on a great many subjects. This has caused a monumental shift in her thinking. As purported, their careers afford European and American women the chance at self-reliance. How can the Chinese dame be so unconventional? She must test of herself and make a new start down a new path for the womenfolk of China.

Chang Shih-ch'uan recalled his impressions from the first time he met Helen Wang. Everyone said of the 'modern' woman, 'She was that rare no phonus balonus modern Shanghai sheba, sporting those keen glad rags of hers, we just knew she was hip to the jive. We took one look at her and went cross-eyed, we were positively goofy'.

(Shih-ch'uan 1935)

The film industry in the 1920s had become the epicentre for commercialization of the modern Chinese women. The female image was mass-produced and commercialized as a consumer object, which was an inevitable result of the commercialization of the urban economy and the increasing prevalence of mass consumption since the opening of Shanghai to the West. The starlet's physical proportions, gossip, and various aspects of their private life had become the main fashion news sought out by newshawks and pushed out to the masses through urban tabloids.

A column that ran in the magazine *Film Life* in 1920s evaluated each of the body parts of female stars, summing up the most prominent physical characteristics of starlets, under the title, 'the trademarks of a Starlet' (Wei 2012: 78).

Helen Wang was the only starlet with small feet. 'Three-inch Golden Lotus' became a prominent symbol of her personal image that was repeatedly bandied about in media discourse. Even though she had announced her retirement from acting in the 1930s and no longer appeared on the screen, her offscreen lifestyle was still fodder for the tabloids.

Part 4: Social Myth – The 'Jilted Runaway Lola' and 'Covetous Lola'

Roland Barthes believes,

> Myths are a product of the naturalization of a certain class's ideology, presenting the emergent ideologies as natural and timeless history of relations that will help uphold their position of dominance in society, denying its special dominance and positing its meaning as timeless, thereby mystifying or obscuring their true origins and concealing the discourse patterns of social ideology.
>
> (Fiske 1999: 115–30)

For example, society's demand for women is that they should devote all themselves to the family and take on the duties of housework and mothering children. Regardless of whether they like it or are good at it, once they enter the family discourse, they should feel good about their role of assistant to the husband and teacher for the children – the 'good wife', complementing her husband's role of the indefatigable breadwinner and provider. This is the basis for the formation of basic family unit in society. We are born into this division of roles between men and women, but social myths conceal its ideological origins, positing that these distributions are natural. Ostensibly, it would seem that distribution is fair to both men and women, but in essence it hides the political operation of capitalism and consolidates the rights of men (Fiske 1999: 115–30).

Although Helen Wang was a celebrity in the social hierarchy, with far more rights and freedoms than that of ordinary women in society, she couldn't shake off the social myth that stacks the deck in favour of men's rights. The following is an excerpt from a contemporary newspaper article about her:

> Helen Wang's image in film is mostly that of a widow and a discarded wife, and her own marriage was terribly unfortunate. At the age of 16, Helen Wang lost her father and was married off to Mister Chang of Manchuria. Her husband's continued abuse was nearly unbearable. Helen Wang filed for divorce and her husband gave her 300 Yuan to expedite the divorce proceedings. In 1933, Helen closed her beauty parlour and went to Hangzhou to attend a wedding with a young gent named Wang Chi-huan and invited the famous scribe Chang Shih-chen as a witness, but this marriage did not last long.
>
> (Taiyao)

Here the media's positioning of Helen Wang as 'a woman who is unlucky in love' is obvious, which is essentially the same as her tragic onscreen roles played. Ostensibly, the narrative structure refers to the example of 'new women' in the era; Helen Wang rebelled against the patriarchal system and left her family, becoming the first economically independent professional woman, but though she obtained a measure of Social standing, social myths surrounded her as 'The Discarded Wife' and 'the jilted woman'. She could not climb the social ladder on account of her brave departure. The media portrayed the tragedies of her life as having their roots in her family life, which actually counteracted the portrayal of her getting out from under her husband's thumb as a courageous act and her social role was once again sent back one of subordination to the male.

Following Is a Depiction

The first paragraph describes how Helen Wang's star rose after the release of *An Orphan Rescues His Grandpa*, but Helen Wang felt that her share of the proceeds was unreasonable. She was unlucky in marriage being betrothed to a husband with a violent streak ... her first marriage ended. In the second marriage, she was greedy for security and stability, demanding that all her partner's money be given to her, consequently losing both love and money, and the marriage ended after only a year (Yibei 2013: 60).

The description of Helen in this article reads, 'But Helen Wang maintained that the distribution of proceeds was unreasonable', and here the author either consciously or unconsciously insinuates that she was a money grubber. The article plays down the possibility of the film company putting the squeeze on her, and then went on to shape her image as greedy and insecure, demanding that the other party's money be given to her, and ultimately losing both. And on her marriage, it insinuates that her marital misfortunes came down to being too greedy for her beau's money. Perpetuating the myth that women should be forced into humiliating circumstances, thereby whitewashing the inherent unfairness of *manus* marriage.

Helen Wang described her departure from the Star Motion Picture Company thus:

> The continuous night shoots made my eyes so dry that I couldn't tear up. Then the director thought of using carbon lamps to illuminate the eyes in an effort to stimulate tears. Afterwards, my eyes wouldn't stop watering. I asked the company to help me with medical treatment, but I was flatly denied. 'There is no such clause in the contract' they told me. Now I'm behind the eight ball. My eyes keep watering and can't be cured. There's nothing anyone can do about it.
>
> (Wang 1956: 62)

Obviously, these hidden facts, in addition to Helen Wang's own description were selectively ignored by the newspapers and magazines. Behind the collective aphasia in the media is the myth that the sacrifice of a famous woman is not worth mentioning. It actually reflects the ideological values that maintain the absolute patriarchal authority. Starlets are nothing but dolls and decorations to be in front of the camera and manipulated by the director at will.

Regarding the beginning and end of the second marriage, Helen Wang's personal statement appeared in an issue of Cinema Weekly in 1934:

> Mrs. Hsu's said how well-heeled Chi-huan's family was, he prepared case dough with a thousand-yuan worth of silver coins as well a set of gold adornments to secure the marriage. I felt that marrying him would put me on easy street… then upon entering the Wang family, I came to know that Chi-huan suffered from alcohol insanity, he was given to violent mood swings, unpredictable behavior, and he would even force me to eat the smegma between his toes and the mucus from his nose. Whenever I went out, there would be someone on a bicycle tailing me. A life such as this was like Hell on earth.
>
> (Taiyao)

Helen Wang's second husband's horrendous behaviour is obvious from this description. She was a successful woman with a successful career when she retired from showbusiness and opened a beauty salon. She was rich and famous and had received a fine education. However, she still believed that she needs to rely on a man with a good family to guarantee security the rest of her life. It was because of Mrs Hsu's stories of the lavish wealth of Chi-huan's family and that she would be given a thousand pieces of silver and an allotment of gold and gold adornment that she rushed into marriage. Yet the myth that 'finding a rich man is a woman's guarantee of happiness' was inescapable. From this perspective, it is not only the society's requirement for women to bow to the power of the patriarch, but even women themselves regard themselves as dependent on a man, showing silver screen starlets and women of notoriety also exist in the patriarchal system. And the nature of the affiliation is no different from that of the average woman.

Part 5: The Fight Against 'Prying Eyes' –Multiple Identities Buried in History

Helen Wang's notoriety as 'The Silver Screen's First Tragedienne' and her two failed marriages are well-documented in history, but her identity is much more than that. She was the first Chinese actress to leave her clan and become a runaway. She worked with three different film production companies. She went on a long journey to southeast Asia to make a propaganda film in the area and took a film company to court. She started her own production company and was actually the first female filmmaker in Chinese history. She opened a beauty salon in Shanghai and became her own boss. She was proficient in English, amazing at acting, quiet in temperament and dressed in modern style of the day that was representative of the 'new women' in China after the May Fourth Movement. She was a trendsetter of her era, the victim of patriarchal society. She lived through a whole host of political changes, and lived a life of great glory and bitter torment.

These brilliant facets to her identity – all undisputable facts – were long ago silenced with all but a rare few having fully explored them. Due to the fuzzy divisions between historical stages and the lack of case studies, people who have tried to do research on Helen Wang, have lumped her in with a group of other actresses from the same period. Thus, some of the qualitative conclusions often come from a few specific films and her unsatisfactory marriage, which have worked tone gate the richness of her individual screen image.

Helen Wang' experienced all manner of social changes and political movements. Her personal efforts were more often than not, to adapt to the tides of the times, to carve out a niche for herself to survive in the torrential storms of the ever-changing times. The influence of the women's liberation trend in the wake of the May Fourth Movement determined the trajectory of Helen Wang's life and every important choice she made, reflecting the moxie of a woman who faced head-on everything the historical period in which she lived dished her way. And in the face of a new social zeitgeist, this starlet made her choices, learned her lessons and absorbed it all with the character and temperament of a 'new woman'. One of the main lines running through Helen Wang's complex multifaceted profile was her eternal fight to be free of the omnipresent authority of the patriarchal society, and to fight tooth-and-nail to find a way out.

Her first struggle was against the clan. She changed her name and broke from the feudal clan. In the social context of the time, being the first to do anything was not considered an act of courage. Then there was the struggle against the production company. Helen Wang was very forthcoming about her disputes with Great Wall.

> The compensation promised by The Great Wall Film Company promised never materialized. I finished work on *The Discarded Wife* and immediately sent me to act in another film. Never in my wildest imaginings could I have thought a film company would deprive me of my rightful earnings, so I went off to work on *Between Love and Filial Duty* and *The Person in the Boudoir Dream* back-to-back. This time the company simply said that there was no dough to pay me. I had no recourse but to sue Great Wall. Although I won lawsuit, I got nothing but a blank check and a kiss off in return. Great Wall was on thin ice, and I was chiseled again.
>
> (Wang et al. 1962: 57)

On the run-in with Sir Run Run Shaw's Unique Film Productions, a.k.a., The Tianyi Film Company:

> When I was filming in Singapore, the newspaper ran a feature saying an audience with me was for sale for a ¥ 50 yuan fee. I didn't know it at the time, but someone had set up a Helen Wang office and then some glib lollygagger tried to sell me off to a big shot with 13 wives. While I was there I had no privacy, they even snooped through my personal letters ... every day of those months I spent in Southeast Asia was like a nightmare.
>
> (Wang et al. 1962: 57)

After these experiences, Helen Wang realized that even the glamorous screen starlets could not escape the exploitation and insult visited upon them at the hands of the corrupt film company. To fight against the patriarchal system, she started the Han-lun Film Company in 1928, in an attempt to gain independence from the control of any company – though things did not go well. The film *An Actresses Revenge* a.k.a., *Blind Love*, was written by Bao Tien-hsiao and directed by Bu Wan-tsang. Helen later recalled how Bu Wan-tsang often went off to the race track and missed shooting days. In order to prevent delays, Helen Wang had to purchase a Moviola and slowly edit the film at home, forcing her to wear simultaneous producer and director hats. At the beginning of the next year, she distributed the film domestically, from the northeast to the south of the Yangtze River, getting up-close and personal with the audience. The film was a bit hit, and the response was so enthusiastic that even orders came from abroad. However, Helen Wang had no gas left in the tank. She became disillusioned and felt that the life of a woman in showbusiness was just too arduous and taxing. She retired from the film industry with the money earned by *An Actresses Revenge* and opened the Han-lun Beauty Salon at Hsia-fei Road. During Shanghai's 'isolated island' period, the Japanese government urged her to do propaganda for them, but she pled illness and closed down the beauty salon.

As an enlightened 'new woman' with superior education and a star with a clear sense of independence and self-reliance, Helen Wang rebelled against her own destiny as a star in the 'public eye'. Her personal struggles and personal self-expressiveness represented the efforts of China's first generation of female stars to ascend to the position of independent 'new women'. She repeatedly emphasized that the purpose of her 'sacrifice of individuality' by getting into showbusiness was so that, 'The Chinese women could breathe a collective sigh of relief'.this self-aware woman made an indelible contribution to the historical development of Chinese cinema and modernizing Chinese women's thinking. The only question remaining is, how to prevent an oversimplified approach to evaluating the image and legacy of the early movie stars represented by Helen Wang from getting in the way of their multi-angled evaluation, and how to make a more logical explanation for many historical phenomena of that time.

REFERENCES

Caihong, Zhang (2008), 'The early Chinese movie stars and the imagination of Shanghai urban culture', *Journal of Zhejiang College of Communication and Media*, 5, p. 5.

Cheng-Ch'iu, Cheng (1925), 'Can new actors not star in pictures?', movie star special issue, *Young Master Feng*, 4, March, p. 3.

Dale, Richard (2012), 'The body in heaven: Movie stars and society (Abstract)', in *Selection of Contemporary Western Film Theories* (compiled by C. Xihe and X. Hong), Beijing: China Film Press, p. 29.

Dyer, Richard (1979), *Celebrity*, London: British Film Institute.

Fiske, John (1999), *Introduction to Communication Studies* (trans. Z. Jinhua), Taipei: Yuanliu Publishing Co., Ltd.

Han-lun, Wang (1925), 'The true story about me and the film industry', *Motion Picture Magazine*, 1.

Jihua, Cheng (ed.) (2005), *The History of Chinese Film Development*, Vol. I, Beijing: China Film Press.

Miller, Toby (2012), 'Introduction to stars and performances', in *Selection of Contemporary Western Film Theories*, 2nd ed. (compiled by C. Xihe and X. Hong), Beijing: China Film Press, p. 21.

Mo, Chen (2000), *The Old Track of the Film*, Nanchang: Jiangxi Education Press.

Oufan, Li (2008), *Shanghai Modern: A New Urban Culture in China (1930–1945)*, Shanghai: SDX Joint Publishing Company.

Shih-ch'uan, Chang (1935), 'After I became a director', *Celebrity Biweekly*, 1:3, May.

Taiyao, En (n.d.), 'The first Tragedienne of the screen: The story of Shanghai women's movie star Helen Wang in the Republican era', http://blog.sina.com.cn/s/blog_62b67b4301011jgk.html. Accessed 1 January 2018.

Wang, Helen (1956), 'My acting career', *Chinese Cinema*, 2, p. 62.

Wang, Helen et al. (1962), *Regrets about Yesteryear*, Beijing: China Film Press.

Watson, Paul (2012), 'Overview of celebrity studies', in *Selection of Contemporary Western Film Theories* (compiled by C. Xihe and X. Hong), Beijing: China Film Press, pp. 10–12.

Wei, Zhang (2012), 'Anxiety of image – "Modern Man" and "Modernity" in early Chinese films (1921–1937)', Ph.D. dissertation, Capital Normal University.

Xiaonan, Wan (2008), '"Rising star?" Fallen women? – The movie stars of Shanghai in the 1920s', *Journal of East China Normal University (Philosophy and Social Sciences)*, 2, p. 74.

Yibei (2013), *Fringe and Nora*, Changsha: China South Publishing & Media Group.

NOTES

1. On Qian Huafo's oral narration of 'The beginning and end of the establishment of Asian Film and Television Company', was reprinted in the inaugural issue of 'China Film', and quotation was taken from Jihua (2005: 18).
2. Cheng Cheng-ch'iu 'Speaking of Chinese cinema', originally published in Shanghai *Big Newspaper* on 3, 6, 15 and 24 December, quoted from Caihong (2008: 5).

8. The Impact of Hong Kong Cinema on Mainland Cinema after the Return of Hong Kong

赵卫防/Zhao Weifang

Weaknesses in the Mainland Chinese film industry post–Hong Kong return notwithstanding, the industrial experience and aesthetic advantages of Hong Kong cinema have been a guiding light for Mainland cinema. That was just experiencing growing pains from reforms before Hong Kong returned to China. In this context, the developed visual style and systemized industrial model of Hong Kong, such as the aesthetics, creative characteristics, capital operations, release scheduling, and promotion and distribution, have provided important insights into the development of the Mainland Film industry. At the turn of the twenty-first century, especially around the time of the signing of the Closer Economic Partnership Arrangement (CEPA), the Mainland film industry opened up the industrialization process and improved by leaps and bounds. Its soaring wings bear the strong imprint of Hong Kong in terms of systemization, cinema franchising, aesthetics and genrefication. Even to this day, the creative sensibilities and narrative conceptualization, cinematic expressiveness, the wealth of talented people and management experience in Hong Kong cinema are still a strong driving force for the development of Mainland cinema.

Part 1: The Impact of Hong Kong's Genre Experience and Creativity

Genre aesthetics is a basic element of 'Hong Kong-style'. Hong Kong cinema has been accumulating quite a number of genres in a century of development. There is action, comedy, crime, superhero, erotica, drama, philosophical, musical, opera and the list goes on and on. Genre composition in Hong Kong cinema has shaped certain aesthetic experiences, such as the genre adherence principle and restraint principle. Genre composition in Hong Kong cinema is dynamic, and creative practices are moving in step with the times.

With the integration of the cinemas of the two places since Hong Kong's return, genre experience and creative ideas of Hong Kong cinema have become the main driving force for the development of cinematic aesthetics on the Mainland. Many Hong Kong–Mainland co-productions existed before Hong Kong returned to China. This exposure to Hong Kong cinema has given rise to an age of genre enlightenment in Mainland Chinese cinema. After the return, especially after the signing of the CEPA, Mainland cinema embarked on an aesthetic path whose main drag is genre creativity. The wealth of genre aesthetics of Hong Kong cinema functions as also part of greater Chinese cinema and has been very influential since entering the Mainland. Subsequent Mainland films have broadened in scope, aspect and perspective, effectively extending and expanding by classic Hong Kong classic genre film exponentially. Besides action, comedy and their respective sub-genres and cross-genre, there have been Mainland entries into a whole host of genres, including chick-flicks, costume films, monster movies, sci-fi, suspense, disaster, war, fairy tales, teen movies, courtroom dramas, superhero films, sports movies and many others. At the same time, there are hybrid genre films that combine two or more genres.

Based on the genre film, domestic Chinese cinema began draw lessons from a composite of the superior resources and experience of *Crouching Tiger, Hidden Dragon* (2000) and some-odd Mainland, Hong Kong and Taiwan productions, along with Hollywood experience, which led to the adoption of the commercial mode of production. This mode finds its roots in the 2002 film *Hero*, a film whose creative and marketing teams are obviously steeped in the stylings of the Hong Kong contingent. The film martial arts choreography was handled by Hong Kong's renowned, Tony 'Siu-Tung' Ching. The entire action choreography and stunt team was from Hong Kong. It was surmised that Hong Kong action filmmakers could provide a guarantee of a successful action movie. In addition, cinematographer Christopher Doyle and leading cast members, such as Jet Li, Tony Leung and Maggie Cheung all found their international stardom in Hong Kong. And so, the Hong Kong contingent has trumpeted the bluster of the 'blockbuster' in the Mainland film industry, leading the boost of Mainland films from aesthetics and systemization standpoints. Subsequently, production teams made up of Hong Kongese, Taiwanese and other Chinese-speaking production teams have hit Mainland China's shore and begun producing large-scale Chinese-style films. These blockbusters are consistent in terms of financing channels, production methods and genre aesthetics. Most of them tend to be of the costumed action variety and are completely consistent with cinema of the Chinese nation and the modernity of global cinema. Aside from capturing the imagination of the local Chinese audience, they are fighting to find a footing in the global mainstream commercial market.

The route of Hong Kong film genrefication has also lauded certain principles, namely the adherence principle and the restraint principle. The former means that there should be only one principle genre in a film, with other genres playing only a supporting role. Genres like action, comedy, suspense and drama are primary, and most of these genres should be given main-genre status in the making of a film. The restraint principle means that the use of genre elements in the making of a genre film must exercise a certain degree of restraint and must not be abused due to the fact that said elements have a commercial value. A large number of artistic practices in Hong Kong genre films have proved that the use of genre elements in a film should generally be limited to no more than three, so that aesthetic and commercial functions of the genre can work. Otherwise, the main genre cannot be separated, and multiple elements collide with each other and the effect is offset, eventually degrading into a chaotic farce. In Hong Kong genre films, all successful films follow the restraint principle.

The genre films in Mainland China after Hong Kong's return follow closely the artistic practices of Hong Kong genre films, and also aforementioned principles. The main genre is only based on the classic genres of Hong Kong films, such as action, comedy and suspense, and do include all genres. For example, in the first decade of the new century, the blockbusters with high levels of aesthetics and systemization in Mainland cinema are based on action and comedy. Then, action, comedy, suspense and drama are still the main subjects in the story of genre diversification. The action and suspense genres, which have always dominated the market, are represented by *Detective D* (2010). The action and suspense elements are still the main trend. Feng XiaoGang's comedy stylings, female-centric chick comedy and the new style of farce comedy represented by *Lost in Thailand* (2012) and *Jianbing Man* (2013) have been the main staples of the comedy genre in the Mainland film market. The teen movies based on the drama genre have also become a staple of the said market. Adhering to genre parameters has also become the Ace in the hole for Mainland cinema.

With the profound interactions between Mainland China and Hong Kong, the Mainland genre film creations mostly are strictly followed by the genre parameter principle. Especially considering some single genre of films such as 'Xiaogangist comedy'-stylings, martial arts films and teen movies have produced strong value with respect to aesthetics and systemization in the light of the strong move towards systemization of the Mainland film industry. But films are going the cross-genre route in increasing numbers; combine three or less genre-specific elements to create film with more word-of-mouth and market power and become the driving force for Chinese film to down barriers and cross chasms. But there are also some Mainland genre films that do not follow the genre parameter principle. The issues came to a head in genre film production in China in 2010, where a score of films showing absolutely no restraint came to the market; among them were *A Chinese Odyssey Part One: Pandoras Box*, *Flirting Scholar 2*, *The Fantastic Water Babes*, *Virtual Recall* (2016). And the proof is in the pudding, with most of these films failing to achieve anywhere near their expected performance. Even though some films did achieve a degree of commercial success – the catch is, if the film itself is below par, there is no value to add, and no developmental prospects. This also contradicts the very nature of the restraint principle in film production as it is practised in Hong Kong and on the Mainland.

However, the genre composition in Mainland films is not simply a description of the genre of Hong Kong but used Hong Kong's creative conceptualization ability to innovate and invent new genres. The innovative concept of Hong Kong genre films has played a key role, particularly in the historical mode of the development of Mainland China film.

Since the beginning of systemization, a notable mode in the development of film aesthetics in Mainland China genre film is the homogeneity that sprang up starting in the late 2010s. A serious trend towards homogeneity in big-budget Mainland productions of the 2010s began when the focus was transferred solely onto the epic costumed martial arts films with stunning visuals and sound. These formulaic productions have a similar level, and they are widely criticized for their weak narratives, lack of meaning and low value orientation, which has led to a slowing in ticket sales for these high-concept Chinese cinematic offerings and has consequently led to imported films having a higher market share in 2012 than their Chinese counterparts. At this point, the high levels of creativity of diversity of genre have become the game changer for Mainland cinema. The same holds true for Hong Kong where genre experience and creativity have played a major role.

First of all, after 2010, the classic suspense factor borrowed from Hong Kong films has increased narrative intelligence in these big-budget productions in action genre. In the Hong Kong cinema, the new martial arts films such as *One-Armed Swordsman* (1967) and *The Hitman Chronicles* (1967), released by the 'Shaw Brothers' in the late 1960s, began to form a suspense narrative tradition. At that point, the martial arts film, the whodunit, the superhero film, the thriller, the zombie film, the gambling film, the gangster film, all carried the suspense narrative forward. This narrative tradition generally uses suspense to create a tension or create a feeling of suspense, which can more capably highlight the narrative intelligence, creating a strong narrative tension to attract audience's eyeball and better realize its own distribution demandability.

At a time when Mainland movies are mired down in the muck of meek narratives and formulaic aesthetics, the suspense narrative traditions and action genre in Hong Kong films are fused together to form a new breed of hero – suspense action films with Chinese characteristics. This kind of film is no longer boxed in by a tired, old linear narrative with fighting and killing, but now has an added suspense factor with a more sophisticated narrative, having subsequently become the primary factor attracting audiences. The martial arts action then becomes just an icing on the cake. The first directors to put this into artistic practice in the Mainland after the 'move North' were Hong Kong directors, Tsui Hark in the film *Detective D* (2010), and Su Chao-pin and John Woo in the film *Reign of Assassins* (2010), and Peter Chan in *Swordsmen* (2011). Case in point, *Detective D* raised the suspense stakes with a burning question from the very beginning…how is it that several characters could spontaneously combust? Was it really murder? Who is behind it all? From there, the story is all about finding the murderer. This is a typical suspense film, and in the Hitchcockian suspense tradition, there is a bit of horror and tension to it. The success of these films has led rapidly to follow-ups with other entries into the action genre. The action–suspense film has once again become a mainstay of the HK–Mainland co-productions and Hong Kong films in 2012, such as *The Silent War* and *The Bullet Vanishes*. After 2013, the suspense film still proved to be a co-venturing champ, and includes films like, *Painted Skin 2* (2013), *Young Detective Dee: Rise of the Sea Dragon* (2013), *The White Storm* (2013), *Control* (2013), *Overheard* (2014), *Last of The Best* (2014), *Cold War 2* (2016) and other such genre films have dominated the market. Under the influence of the Hong Kong factor, Mainland films have been introduced to a brand-new 'defamiliarization' path, which it has been traversing extensively to resolve homogeneity issue.

Second, once Mainland filmmakers were done innovating on Hong Kong's classic comedy genre, the palpable artistic moxie at play helped refine the comedy genre on the Mainland, leading to a comedy revolution, which manifests itself in three forms: the first is, after the 'move Beijing-ward', HK-style farcical elements have been successfully transplanted and revolutionized. At the outset of CEPA, Hong Kong director Jeffrey Lau worked to incorporate these elements into the films, *A Chinese Tall Story* (2005) and *Metallic Attraction Kungfu Cyborg* (2009), but it soon degraded into outrageous parody and absurdity. The effect was not 100 per cent successful. After 2010, the Mainland environment became opposed to homogeneous aesthetics, and the incorporation of Hong Kong comedy stylings in Mainland comedy films was extremely successful. The comedies of this period combined the traditional 'Hong Kongese' farce comedy with characteristic Mainland comedic elements, thus forming a wholly new comedy genre. Prime examples are *My Own Swordsman* (2012), *Just Call Me Nobody* (2012), *Lost in Thailand* (2014), *A Hero or Not* (2015), *Goodbye Mr. Loser* (2015), *Lost in Hong Kong* (2015) and *Mr. Donkey* (2016), among others. These films have both Chow-esque 'absurdity' and exaggerated farcical elements, as well as many innovative comedic elements used in Mainland China. Second, the revolution of the comedy genre in Mainland China under the influence of the Hong Kong contingent in this period is reflected in the New Year's film. Spring Festival films from Hong Kong are a major brand. The Hong Kong filmmakers who have 'gone north' have replicated their Spring Festival offerings, mainly based on remakes and sequels. Highlights of these offerings include, *All's Well End's Well* (2009) and *All's Well Ends Well Too* (2010), produced and directed by Bak-Ming Wong, whose 'doubly-happy event' series continued the 'doubly-happy event' of late 1990s Hong Kong. This film series emphasizes the importance of the family to the individual and emphasizes that the family is formally the harbour of the mind, and it does this by way of constant parody and pastiche. For example, in *All's Well End's Well Too* 2010, Sandra Ng had a time travel to the role of He LiYu who was played by Maggie Cheung in the 1992 version. Peppered with scenes depicting elements of hot topics on the Mainland, such as 'cat-cat catch games', 'social angst' and 'wealth-flaunting', which have created a new comedy genre. The third new form is the 'chick flick'. This genre innovation dominated by the Hong Kong contingent during this period is reflected in the emergence of the chick flick with Asian characteristics, which was born out of the Hollywood chick flick genre. It made its debut in Hong Kong in the early 1990s and subsequently became a feminist drama genre film with strong 'Hong Kong flair'. The theme of this genre as it plays out in the Hong Kong variety features a very obvious inspirational theme. The heroine who has lost her greatest love realizes she has not lost everything. She has to continue her life strong and confident; the seemingly lost love will wait for her at the turn after she succeeds. Hong Kong actresses Sammi Cheng and Miriam Yeung have won over female audiences with their image of hip, businesslike and slightly neurotic cosmopolitan women. With the integration of the Hong Kong and Mainland film, Hong Kong and Taiwan chick flicks have skipped the border and crossed the strait, as it were. *Perfect Dating* (2009), *Go LA LA Go!* (2010), *Love is Not Blind* (2011) and other films are the acme of this genre. In 2012, a number of co-produced chick flicks hit the theatres, such as *I Do, Color me Love, Wo De Lei Ren Nan You, Marry a Perfect Man, Lacuna, My Sassy Hubby* and many other films, which have become important co-production genre film in the past years. These Mainland 'chick flicks' have inherited the same elements of their Hong Kong predecessors – the feminist viewpoint, the inspirational romance, the urban fashion and the sly wit, but at the same time certain internal transformations took place that gave them stronger Mainland Chinese characteristics. Comedy is more suitable for Mainland audiences. One of the most important factors is that this type of 'chick flick adds the uniqueness of the old-maid', or, 'leftover woman', as she is known in China, which is more likely to capture the attention and imagination of Chinese women. Post 2013, this genre has continued to be an important part of the HK–Mainland co-venture line-up. The cream of the crop includes the *Tiny Times 1.0 series* (2013–14), *Seeking Mr. Right* (2013), *Soulmate* (2016), *Love You* (2017) and others. Films of this genre have become an important brand to Mainland viewers.

Third, the Hong Kong filmmakers have been integral in the broadening of fantasy genre in the Mainland film industry, in films such as *Journey to the West: Conquering the Demons* (2013), *Monster Hunter* (2015), *Chronicles of the Ghostly Tribe* (2015), *Looking for Dragons* (2015), *The Ghouls* (2016), *The Monkey King 2* (2016) and *Journey to the West: The Demons Strike Back* (2017), among others. Hong Kong's substantial genre experience was a key influence on genre innovations in Mainland China during this period. Most of these fantasy films were produced by Hong Kong filmmakers. New genre creation manifests itself mainly in the creation of new worlds and new images. Such films generally create a conventional world with opposing forces that is different from the ones in traditional film. In addition to humanist values, this kind of world also contains the ideas and values of all kinds of extra-terrestrial creatures such as humanoids, demon, ghosts and aliens. It is a sprawling world in which humans and heterogeneous creatures coexist, and the types of ghosts, spirits and demons seen in Hong Kong cinema have provided an excellent reference in the creation of these new worlds. The creation of its new image elements includes both the shaping of new graphical and pictorial elements of the genre, such as the images of a new race of demons represented by the Huba in *Monster Hunter*. The new image also includes the synthesis of images of real people and alien creatures often seen in anime imagery. For example, in *Journey to the West: The Demons Strike Back*, a real man provided the physical performance for the battle between Sun Wukong – the Monkey King, and the Red Child, who was rendered in CGI animation. This reflects the genre awareness and creative power present in the 'Hong Kong aesthetic'.

The genre experience and creative concepts from Hong Kong cinema have been guiding creative practices of Mainland filmmakers since the turn of the century. On to the second decade of the new century, 'Internet thinking' has also begun to strongly influence these creative practices. Netizen movies have once become the strongest embodiment of the power of the Internet's influence on Mainland films. However, after all the hoopla died down, Hong Kong genre experience began to keep pace with Internet thinking and once again has gotten back in the driving seat and has again begun leading Mainland filmmakers. Neo-classic examples of filmed excellence in the genre are *Mermaid, Operation Mekong* (2016), *Kung Fu Yoga* (2017), *Journey to the West: The Demons Strike Back* (2017), *Shock Wave* (2017) and many others. Under the sure and steady hand of the Hong Kong filmmaking contingent armed with the Excalibur of genre experience brought a swift and decisive defeat to online films, both in terms of box office and word of mouth, showing that Hong Kong cinematic experience and vital creativity possess artistic supremacy.

Part 2: Hong Kong Style Humanism Boosts the Speculative Value of Mainland Motion Pictures

Hong Kong-esque genre experience and creative concepts are guiding Mainland's genre compositions, and in the link-up of HK humanism and Mainland values, the speculative value of Mainland film has shot up considerably. This improvement is no more clearly embodied than in Mainland commercial cinema and main-line films.

Even though Hong Kong cinema has always been known for its commercial aesthetics and entertaining qualities, a Hong Kong-style humanistic concept has been created that demonstrates Hong Kong's unique values. This Hong Kong-style cinematic humanism refers to the fact that its thematic form has gradually evolved from focus on nationalist sentiment to focus on individual survival and emotion. It generally refers to the pure care for humanity, and basically does not take traditional morality and values into practical consideration in its value expression. For example, the 'mafia' characters in Hong Kong cinema. If judged in accordance with traditional values, they would undoubtedly be written as negative characters. But, most Hong Kong films do not portray them according to such standards. Instead, they represent them as individuals in society and often portray them as heroes – a prime example of the Hong Kong humanistic concept adhered to in Hong Kong cinema. And one that avoids conceptualizing binary opposition into stories, not only reflecting individuality and novelty, but to a greater extent highlighting the complexity of human nature.

After the return, Hong Kong-style humanism has also influenced the creation of Mainland films with the integration of the cinematic practices from the two areas. At the beginning of CEPA, this concept was directly taken to the Mainland by Hong Kong filmmakers. Due to the disparity in mainstream values between the two regions, co-ventures were not successful at that time, as they had not yet become 'acclimatized'. Gratefully after 2005, due to the joint efforts of the filmmakers of both Hong Kong and Mainland China, this situation has changed. The Hong Kong-style humanistic concept was successfully paired with the mainstream values of Mainland China beginning at the dawn of the 2010s. Hong Kong-style humanism was localized on the Mainland, making its way most prominently into co-produced films. The elements of the Hong Kong-style humanistic concept and the mainstream values of the Mainland may stand in direct opposition, but the essence of humanist artistic expressions are now preserved on celluloid, thus enhancing its speculative value.

First of all, the introduction of the Hong Kong-style humanist concept into mainstream commercial cinema has made it more reflective. The most important embodiment of the migration from South to North is the effective intermingling of the core values of the two places: particularly the introduction of humanism. In recent years, some successful Hong Kong filmmakers have initiated co-productions with Mainland producers, such as *The Stand-In* (2010), *Little Big Soldier* (2010), *Ip Man* series (2009–16), the *Overheard* series (2010–14), *Kung Fu Jungle* (2014), *Dearest* (2014) and others that reflect the migration. The film that best embodies the intermingling is *The Stand-in*, directed by Teddy Chan. The film tells of Sun Yat-sen, a revolutionary thinker planning on going to Hong Kong to organize an uprising. The Qing government sends a hit-man to assassinate him. Several members of Hong Kong grassroots organizations die rescuing him. The country's ideals in film and the theme of patriotism are undoubtedly right in line with the Mainland mainstream values. However, the revolution and its leader Sun Yat-sen are protected by a group of ordinary individuals who do not understand the real meaning of revolution. Their motivations are not based on the belief in the revolution, nor do they have the evolved concept of 'saving the nation and the people', living up to the Mainland's expected revolutionary significance while satisfying the needs of the HK humanist narrative. What makes these people rescue Sun Yat-sen is love, familial love or even human nature at its most basic level. The humanism glorified in the film effectively closes the gap between the Mainland values and Hong Kong humanist values, not simply reflecting the Mainland values, but also replacing the conceptual narrative with the humanist narrative, whilst displaying the essence of the Hong Kong humanistic concept, reflecting the depth of human nature, thereby gaining speculative value. Another example is *Dearest*, directed by Peter Chan, the theme of which is ostensibly about 'anti-trafficking', which is consistent with the mainstream values of the Mainland, but on a deeper level it reveals and expresses beautifully the complexities of human nature, in the anguish of a family of the lost child as well as the family who fraudulently adopts the child. In its attention to individual survival and emotional state, the film corresponds perfectly to the Hong Kong-style humanist concept and reaches into the very depths of human nature, not only preserving the essence of humanity in Hong Kong-style humanistic concept, but also enabling Mainland motion pictures to gain a sense of human empathy and artistic novelty without losing their mainstream value, thereby strengthening their artistry.

Mainstream films with Mainland characteristics made by Hong Kongese filmmakers, but produced entirely on the Mainland, represent a major breakthrough. Mainland China's mainstream cinema is one of the primary media used for conveying Mainland ideology and promoting the mainstream values of the Mainland, though the oft-criticized issues plaguing Mainland ideological dissemination, i.e. formalism, conceptualism and superficiality have seriously affected its promotability. The main-line films made by Hong Kong filmmakers take Hong-Kong style humanist concepts and fuse them with Mainland popular values, promoting these core values and simultaneously exhibiting the multidimensionality of the human condition. The end result was a big increase in the speculative value of these films, while simultaneously avoiding the previous superficiality and formalism issues, thus strengthening the films' visual value and comprehensively increasing the artistic values of Mainland China's main-line films.

There are four main-line films from this period whose artistic quality and speculative value were empowered by the influence of Hong Kong contingent. They directly represent national revolution or major historical events in the history of the Chinese Communist Party. Such as, *The Founding of a Republic* (2009), *Beginning of the Great Revival* (2011), *The Xinhai Revolution* (2011), *The Founding of an Army* (2017). Besides being conceptualized and produced according to a genre model, in these genre films, the leaders were brought down from their high horse, being portrayed as populist leaders with multi-dimensional fallibility and a nature identical to the common man, in accordance with the grammar of the Hong Kong-humanist concept. This allowed for the films to obtain profound speculative value and strong visual value.

The second type of modern film that portrays the current Chinese spirit is, *American Dreams in China* (2013). For example, the film combines the 30-year reform in Mainland China with the entrepreneurial history of the young people of the generation, depicting the changing times on the Mainland with exquisite visuals and attentive detail; the mainstreamness of the film goes without saying. The way it is presented in the film is a profound reflection on human nature. Three college students with different personalities befriend each other at school. Later, they join forces and start a business partnership. But their widely divergent personalities, lifepaths, lifestyles and even emotional experiences elicit a number of conflicts in their business pursuits. Ultimately they do realize their dreams. The screenwriter did not overplay the main-line angle, but instead tried to find a way to integrate Mainland culture with the essence of Hong Kong film.

The third type is a film that incorporates action, war and suspense with a philosophical nationalist sentiment. Such as, *The Light Goes Out* (2014), *Wolf Warriors* (2015), *My War* (2016), *Operation Mekong* (2016), *Extraordinary Mission* (2017) and *Operation Red Sea Action* (2017). These films have undoubtedly gone mainstream owing to their nationalist narrative. The appealing genre and impressive display of humanism in the films is the main way to obtain visual value and speculative value. Of these films, *Operation Mekong*, directed by Lin ChaoXian is a model for effectively linking Hong Kong-style humanism with the nationalist consciousness in mainstream Mainland values. The film as a whole tells a story about saving the Chinese people through a show of national strength and willpower and requires every living individual to complete this grand narrative. For example, the role of Fang Xinwu, who struggles to live up to humanist standards and is torn to the end, directly violates his discipline and murders the drug dealer who killed his girlfriend. It is a selfish act that does not live up to the ideals of the 'selflessness, honesty and justice', which come up consistently in the Chinese film from the Mainland. Worse yet, it even seriously deviates from this quality. However, it is through these acts that are the antithesis of, 'selfless, honest and righteous' that bring the film closer to reality and highlight the human compassion, thus giving the film profound artistic value and non-conceptualist narrative impact.

The fourth type of film is the remake of revolutionary films, such as *The Taking of Tiger Mountain 3D* (2015) directed by Tsui Hark, *Railroad Tigers* (2016) directed by Ding Sheng and Jack Chan appeared. These films directly pair the personal heroes and human complexity of Hong Kong-style humanist concepts with the classic revolutionary stories from Mainland China and compose revolutionary tales of humanity from a humanist perspective. For example, in *The Taking of Tiger Mountain*, Yang Zirong, who is steeped in full-on blood brother loyalty, has a decidedly different image and personality from the classic red-star-over-China socialist figures in the classical revolutionary stories, which is the expression of the Director's attention to the characters in the story as individuals. In, *Railroad Tigers*, the 'Great, Daring, Quixotic' image of the, 'railway guerrillas' in classic red films has disappeared without a trace, and in its place are characters written with very humanist sentiments. For example, the captain of the railway guerrillas in the film was humbly and submissively going between with the Japanese and the Flying Tigers. Fan Chuan, an anti-heroic former warlord who looks like he has lost hope in the War of Resistance, chooses to protect himself. Yet, patriotism nevertheless lays dormant under that rough and tumble exterior. These characters all have their own strengths and weaknesses stemming from their nature, giving full embodiment to the human complexities in times of war.

In these main-line films, multi-dimensional human characteristics are combined with classic red cinema, deepening the humanities elements and speculative value of the film. In addition, under the influence of the Hong Kong contingent, the mainline films have tended to converge with commercial films. These films are sustained by commercial genre elements. They fully displays the artistry of Mainland values and strengthens the entertainment and visual value by Hong Kong-style. They also retains the essence of the humanism of the Hong Kong-style and has acquired profound aesthetic value. In this context, Mainland film, including the co-produced variety, has gradually been set upon a path to win-win that is genre innovation and speculative value. New mainstream blockbusters based on the 'Hong Kong-style' aesthetic have been widely and enthusiastically received by the Mainland audience and is moving in a very positive direction.

Part 3: A Nudge from Hong Kong Cinematic Products and Experience Puts the Mainland over the Top

At the beginning of the new century, the Mainland film production system began to take its industrial development, and lack of experience. The developed film system experience of Hong Kong cinema has given tremendous boost to the development of the Mainland film industry with respect to the systemization and diversified seasonal marketing models, as well as a large number of 'Hualiwood' productions backed by value brought from marketing, promotion and quality acting.

The film system appeared in Hong Kong in the late 1930s and provided a foundation for its industrial development. Before the 1950s, the traditional model of the Hong Kong film industry was based on the production model. After the 1950s, large-scale film companies such as the 'Shaw Brothers' were the first film production companies to put the 'vertical integration' model into practice, which vastly improved the industry chain and the overall health of the industry. By the early 1970s, Golden Harvest Entertainment Ltd (known colloquially as Golden Harvest) launched the satellite system, consisting of a parent cinema operator and a film production subsidiary. In the early 1980s, the satellite system developed into a cinema operator model, led by cinema chains. With the transformation of the Hong Kong film industry model, the distribution chain in the industrial chain has been promoted to the highest end beyond the production process, which has greatly improved the industrial development of Hong Kong film.

Due to the long term planned economic system in place on the Mainland, production and distribution were out of touch; there was no concept of joint interests, and the distribution industry were depressed and lacked initiative. The whole industry was fragmented and unresponsive. In 1993, the Mainland film system and cinema-franchising system underwent major reforms, and the centralized purchasing and marketing model of the China Film Corporation was cancelled, which put film production directly into the hands of provincial distribution companies. This resolved the aforementioned issues to a certain extent, but did not completely solve the most critical problems, namely fragmentation and the lack of joint interest in production and distribution, which exacerbated production and distribution issues. In June 2002, the State Administration of Radio, Film and Television again reformed the film distribution and franchising mechanism and began to implement a film system similar to the Hong Kong film industry model. This mechanism was introduced into the film system of film production, distribution and cinema franchising, that is the distribution company is responsible for the promotion and distribution of the film production taking place over a large territory, and even nationwide. Many of the original provincial companies have become producers that are not limited to the province but are capable of film development nationwide. In just a few short years, more than thirty of this new type of production companies with joint-assets and cinema chains doing business under a market structure and system replaced the planned economic system that came before, enabling the production company to cross the previous provincial, municipal, county and other multi-level distribution companies, directly connected with cinema operators in large areas and even across the country, unifying filming and screening, which has greatly enhanced the film production on the Mainland and has become the most important part of the Mainland film systemization strategy. After the reform of the cinema-franchising system, the Chinese film industry quickly embarked on the rapid development model.

Although the cinema-operator system has changed Mainland China's film system, in the process of reform and implementation, the 'vertical integration' of the integrated production and distribution model in the Hong Kong cinema system marketing model was not integrated completely, and this was done purposely to avoid a resurgence of monopolies, and more so to unify the framework for film production and exhibition. Therefore, the cinema-operator system in the Mainland hasn't undergone the same operator segmentation as Hong Kong, and there is no specific audience or market segmentation. This will inevitably lead to uniformity of exhibitors, in which, the Hongkongian practice of segmenting cinema chains has brought about certain changes to the massive unified cinema-operator model on the Mainland, leading to Hong Kong EDKO Film Ltd making such strong headway with its subsidiary Broadway Cinemas in the Mainland. Broadway Cinemas brought audience segmentation in its operations into play and maintained certain differences in the films that were released. For example, different cinemas were set up differently for various audiences. One theatre would play popular blockbusters, while the smaller theatres would show dramas. There was also a special art theatre division, where artistic films only favoured by smaller demographics would play. This kind of market-oriented cinema-franchising strategic practice of segmenting set consumer groups has increasingly obvious implications for unfurling the development of cinema franchises in the Mainland operator logjam. The emergence of art film exhibitor alliances is the most practical manifestation of this influence.

With the sweeping reform of the film system on the Mainland, Hong Kong entertainers have also begun investing in the construction of cinemas in the area during this period, further refining the development of the film industry on the

Mainland. After CEPA went into effect, Shaw Brothers Ltd, Golden Harvest, Ultimate Movie Experience and other companies have also established joint ventures or wholly owned cinemas in China. By the end of 2013, Hong Kong had invested in the construction and renovation of more than 232 cinemas in 27 provinces and municipalities in the Mainland, with a total of 1,116 screens. (People's Network Financial Channel (2014), 23 January, http:// finance.people.com.cn/n/2014/0123/c1004-24207821.html.) Since then, a number of Hong Kong cinema-operators have 'gone north'. Among them, Orange Sky Golden Harvest has more than 50 cinemas in Beijing, Chengdu, Changzhou, Dongguan and Chongqing on the Mainland, making it the largest Hong Kong company in the cinema industry in the Mainland. The Broadway Cinematheque and UA of Hong Kong, EDKO Film Ltd have also begun constructing cinema chains on the Mainland. The UA Cinema launched in cities with development potential such as Dongguan, Shanghai, Wuhan and Chongqing. The goal is to make high-quality boutique cinemas. To differentiate itself from others, IMAX Hall is one of the trump cards for the development of the Mainland market of the UA Cinema brand. See-Yuen Ng invested in the UME cinema chain.Jackie Chan invested the Jackie Chan Cinema with the Sparkle Roll International Cultural Industry Investment Co., Ltd. in the Mainland. Both of them have also become an important base for Mainland sales. The establishment of these theatres has led to the construction of high-end cinemas in Mainland China, which has enhanced the quality of cinemas chains in the industry in terms of cinematic culture, construction technology, operational systems, film output and hardware and software facilities.

The multi-marketing models' focus on seasonal marketing is another manifestation of the influence of Hong Kong cinema on the Mainland after Hong Kong's return, primarily in terms of its influence during the Chinese New Year. Timing releases is an important point in Hong Kong's film production and systemized operations. One of the most important exhibition times for Hong Kong film is the Chinese New Year. In the mid-1990s, the concept of the Lunar New Year film season in Hong Kong was introduced to the Mainland during this time. The Jackie Chan film, *Rumble in the Bronx* was the first film to be introduced the Mainland carrying the New Year's Film tagline, thereafter gradually becoming the golden harvest season in Mainland China. A few years later, the enlightened aesthetic practices of Hong Kong New Year's films began appearing on the Mainland. In 1997, the Beijing Forbidden City Film Company started using Feng XiaoGang to launch the first genuine New Year's film, *The Dream Factory*, on the Mainland. The film was conceived and promoted as the first Chinese New Year film even from the pre-production stage and triggered the Mainland comedy phenomenon. After 2002, the Chinese film industry began following the Hong Kong New Year's film concept and began to make the transition to the New Year's film with a Spring

Festival timed release date. In addition to comedy films, there were other genres of films that began to be released as Chinese New Year movies in the Spring Festival. At the same time, the Lunar New Year film season is no longer limited to the New Year's Day or the Spring Festival period, but from the end of the last month of the year, and running through a long period between Christmas, New Year's Eve, the Spring Festival, the Lantern Festival and Valentine's Day. The concept of the schedule has also become an important means of film publicity and distribution on the Mainland. In every stage, Mainland films will be created and marketed according to the commercial operating model and commercial film standards, forming a local marketing method with local features, thus improving systemization.

In addition to the seasonal marketing, the corporate culture strategy based on the star system of the Hong Kong film industry also had a major impact on the Mainland film industry during this period. Mainland Chinese film companies, be they private or state-owned, must focus on yoking corporate culture and creating stars, as this is an important means of enhancing their competitiveness. Each large-scale production company owns a talent agency or a workshop where stars' unique, individual persona is crafted. Quite a number of stars' images have been carefully crafted and packaged in this manner. Establishing a corporate culture with stars' personality characteristics and making that the most important competitive resource for the company is the order of the day. Private companies such as *Huayi Brothers Media Group, Bona Film Group* and *Chengtian Entertainment* are in possession of the most star resources, and for the star brokering and packaging methods each have their own characteristics. Star resources have become an indispensable part of core competitiveness.

Hong Kong's modern diversified marketing model continued during the period of the Mainland's film promotion, and new developments sprang from it. In particular, more ideas for promotion in the Internet era are constantly being developed and utilized, such as e-commerce pre-sales, fan marketing and microblog marketing. Regardless of how diverse and innovative the marketing methods of the current Mainland films are, the experience, such as bringing distribution to a leading position, the entire industry taking actions according to the market-based, has come largely from Hong Kong.

The injection of talent is another important aspect of the Hong Kong film industry which can provide a boost to the development of the Mainland film industry. Of the wealth of talent Hong Kong has contributed to the Mainland, producers are the most important and greatest in number. Among them, Bak-Ming Wong, Albert Yeung, Bill Kong, Peter LAM Kin-ngok, John Chong, Charles Heung, Nansun Shi, See-Yuen Ng are the best and brightest. The production companies they control are some of the most powerful film companies in Hong Kong, and they all have very strong film distribution networks. Since the 1990s, they have planned to develop business through partnerships with the Mainland. After CEPA, they have put their focus on investing more production resources into the Mainland. Their 'Northbound' paths are not the same, and their influence and contribution to Mainland cinema are different, but each and every one of them has been an inspiration and an influence on Mainland motion pictures, in terms of systemized development paths, and production and marketing concepts.

Of all these esteemed producers, Bak-Ming Wong has been the one most interested in working with the Mainland. Under his direction, Oriental Entertainment Holdings Co., Ltd, which he was the head of until January 2017, put all their funds into the Mainland. Both the studios and the post-production facilities he built on the Mainland were set up with common development in mind. Bak-Ming Wong emphasized that all would develop according to the rules of the Mainland, and advocated the concept of 'big productions', suitable for the vast Mainland market. His co-ventures include *The Seven Swords* (2005), *Dragon Tiger Gate* (2006) and *Flash Point* (2007), *IP Man* (2009), *All's Well End's Well* (2009), *Ip Man 2* (2010) and many more. These films focus on the market concept of 'big China', matching the 'big production' to the Mainland market. Simultaneously, Oriental Entertainment insisted that the primary creative team must be Hong Kong filmmakers. The co-ventures were produced strictly up to Hong Kong standards by HK filmmakers, editors, directors, actors, cinematographers and sound engineers to ensure aesthetic and artistic quality.

Emperor Entertainment Group Co., Ltd, headed by Albert Yeung, divided funds and allocated a portion to develop the Mainland and overseas productions. Before CEPA, Albert Yeung was already working with some state-owned production houses and private film companies on the Mainland and created relatively developed production models and distribution channels. So, after CEPA, the company made full use of these resources and contacts to collaborate more closely with the Mainland. In choosing leading creators, Emperor Entertainment who chooses more filmmakers from Mainland China is different from Oriental Entertainment who only uses Hong Kong filmmakers. Following with this concept, Emperor Entertainment has co-produced nearly 50 films after CEPA, and works with state-owned enterprises such as China Film Group Corporation and Shanghai Film Group Corporation, as well as private enterprises like Huayi Brothers and Poly Bona Film Distribution Co., Ltd. There have been some co-ventures that have had good box office returns and hold significant influence on the Mainland in recent years, such as *The Knot*, *The Myth* (2005), *The Sun Also Rises* (2007), *Forever Enthralled* (2008), *The Message* (2009), *The Founding of the People's Republic of China* (2009), *Detective D, If You Are the One 2* (2010), *Aftershock* (2010), *Let the Bullets Fly* (2010), *Beginning of the Great Revival* (2011), *To the Fore* (2015) and many more. Albert Yeung has become the Hong Kong producer with the largest number of co-productions with the Mainland and holds more influence on the Mainland.

The route of Bill Kong's collaboration with the Mainland has not been the same as that of Bak-Ming Wong and Albert Yeung. First of all, EDKO Film Limited, which he heads, works on both production and distribution and has established a number of cinema chains on the Mainland. Second, the co-productions Bill Kong has undertaken with the Mainland have primarily been large-scale productions and have accrued huge box office returns in the Mainland market and have had a significant influence on the Mainland. For example, at the beginning, it mainly cooperated with the New Screen Picture Film Company in the Mainland. He has mainly invested in the films directed by Zhang Yimou, such as *Hero, House of Flying Daggers, Curse of the Golden Flower, A Simple Noodle Story* and *The Flowers of War*. He has also been responsible for the overseas distribution. After 2011, Mr Kong continued to expand the Mainland's international blockbuster road, and invested in *Journey to the West: Conquering the Demons, American Dreams in China, The Golden Era* (2014), *Monster Hunt* and many other major films. Therefore, Mr Kong is the most important individual to help the Mainland film industry improve. He has become the producer with the greatest influence on the Mainland film industry.

Unlike the above-mentioned producers, Peter Lam is taking a path that crosses Hong Kong and the Mainland and seeks development in both areas. His Hong Kong Media Asia Company has ramped up the scale and space of co-productions and has opened up the film market in the Mainland and even Asia proper through the integration with film companies in Mainland China. Peter also believes that Hong Kong's own films make their way out of Hong Kong. He has stuck to his goal of making movies for the local Hong Kong market and becoming the producer there. In terms of collaborations with the Mainland, Peter Lam, Charles Heung and other main leaders of 'Media Asia' have adopted a more multi-dimensional approach, by first expanding their distribution channels, working with the CCTV film channel, expanding their distribution channels outside of the cinema and jointly distributing films with the China Film Group Corporation. Second, he has established cooperative ties with Shanghai Media Asia Co., Ltd, focusing on the collaborations with the domestic heavyweight film giants, Huayi Brothers and Poly Bona Film Distribution Co., Ltd.(Jiaming, Chen 2013) In the time since CEPA was signed, 'Asian Media' and the Mainland have co-produced some influenced films, such as, *A World Without Thieves, Confessions of Pain* (2006), *The Banquet* (2006), *The Warlords, Triangle* (2007), *If You Are the One* (2008), *Look for a Star* (2008) and *The Founding of a Republic*. Peter Lam has also become an important figure in the acceleration of the development of the Mainland film industry.

Producers are the backbone of Hong Kong cinema, and affect Mainland cinema at the talent level. In addition, a large group of acting talent has become key to the development of film on the Mainland. Large numbers of Hong Kong editors, directors, performers and their aesthetic contributions have been discussed above. Others have made important contributions to the development of Mainland cinema, for example, action choreographers such as Woo Ping Yuen and Siu-Tung Ching; cinematographers such as Christopher Doyle, Arthur Wong and Peter Pau; art directors such as William Chang and Chung-Man Hai; editors such as Chi-Leung Kwong, Marco Mak and Angie Lam.

Under the influence of Hong Kong filmmakers, scores of Mainland filmmakers have completely rethought their aesthetic concepts and changed their industry perceptions. Most of the Mainland filmmakers are trained by Mainland institutions, and they are also deeply influenced by the traditional consciousness of the Mainland, in terms of their educational background and expressive conceptions. Even though they have experienced many stages of commercial changes, their understanding of the market is still not as profound as Hong Kong filmmakers. After the HK co-venture experience, these and many other Mainland filmmakers have not only gained epiphany-like inspiration but have also learned from the wealth of film ideas and flexible expressiveness of Hong Kong cinema, thus enabling them to experience major breakthroughs, and cut through the shackles that were holding them back in terms of narrow expressive concepts, clichéd narratives and creative shortcomings. The imprint of the Hong Kong contingent in Mainland films has become increasingly pronounced with time, and throughout the process, the Mainland contingent also benefited at the systemic level. From talent training to the specific film techniques to marketing and promotion. They are all up to par with advanced film industry concepts. Mainland filmmakers and Hong Kong filmmakers have together created a new corpus of Chinese-language films that will emblazon the name of China onto the hearts and minds of the world.

REFERENCES

Jiaming, Chen (2013), 'Hong Kong Discussion Media', *Openness and Limitation: The Past and Present of China and Hong Kong Co-productions, Zhang Shaoqiang, Liang Qizhi, Chen Jiaming,* Oxford University [China] Press, pp. 104–105.

People's Network Financial Channel (2014), 23 January, http:// finance.people.com.cn/n/2014/0123/c1004-24207821.html. Accessed 1 January 2018.

9. The Celebrity Face: Contemporary Celebrity Culture – Body Obsession and Physical Fetishism

陈晓云/Chen Xiaoyun

There is a spectre haunting the film and entertainment industries. The celebrity question is like a two-headed monster rearing its quarrelling heads behind our backs. On one hand, the celebrity's paycheck, income and everything related to their daily life are receiving unprecedented attention. Their private lives are frequently turned into a reality show or TV series broadcast on various media platforms. The drama in their lives is even more dramatic than their movies and TV series. On the other hand, showbusiness is built on the celebrity and the films they star in, but it often appears 'empty'. This seemingly contradictory phenomenon is the manifestation of the convoluted and contradictory nature of a Chinese film industry under construction. It is part of what the audience can perceive sensorially and apprehend experientially, though they may not be entirely clear on the internal workings of the film industry. Being that the stars are present in all links in the film production chain, from filming to distribution to screening, and industry and social influence, the star system is an integral part of the film industry and is also the foundation of a well-established film industry system. This has given rise to the celebrity influence felt throughout society and the public sphere – from the groupies to the fans, it has become a significant social and cultural phenomenon in our modern world. This is the context of discussion of contemporary celebrity culture throughout the remainder of this chapter.

The Celebrity Face: Body Fascination and Material Worship

No matter how we appraise the value of a film, we cannot steer clear of Chinese-produced 'event movies', like Zhang Yimou's, *Hero* and *The Great Wall*, regardless of whether they are in 'textual' or 'system' forms. Significantly enough, *Red Sorghum, Ju Dou, Raise the Red Lantern, The Story of Qiu Ju, Shanghai Triad, To Live* and other films successfully yoked local power to 'manufacture' internationally influential movie star Gong Li. Starting with, *The Road Home*, Zhang Yimou 'manufactured' another movie star, Zhang Ziyi of 'transnational' significance. Beginning with *Hero*, the very first Chinese blockbuster film was born. It presented a completely different portrait from his previous film on choosing actors and celebrities and was different from the early works of the *fifth generation* of Chinese directors that value the director's expressiveness over the actors' performances. The celebrities in *Hero* include both Jet Li who is the most influential Kung Fu star in Chinese-cinema world after Jackie Chan and Bruce Lee, and Tony Leung, Maggie Cheung, Chen DaoMing and Zhang Ziyi, who can be called 'prestige stars' (McDonald 2015: 31). Donnie Yen joined their ranks after the success of the *Ip Man* series years later. Being that it had an all-star cast, the film follows the basic formula for a commercial blockbuster. Next, *House of Flying Daggers* and *Curse of the Golden Flower* have roughly similar traits. *The Great Wall* was a more transnational co-venture, which incited heated debate and criticism because of the all-star cast of Hollywood superstars Matt Damon, Pedro Pascal, William Dafoe and Mainland stars Jing Tian, Andy Lau and Zhang HanYu. All-star casting in 'Sino-blockbusters' such as *The Promise, A Simple Noodle Story, The Warring State*, etc., had already been denounced by detractors, but this time it became the focus of debate due to the glaring discrepancy between actress Jing Tian's privileged position and her actual acting chops. After the release of *The Great Wall*, comments surfaced on the Internet stating that Jing Tian's image is closer to one of the heroes in a revolutionary film than a contemporary Chinese superstar, being aesthetically speaking such a far cry from Director Zhang Yimou previous 'Mou Girls' like, Gong Li, Zhang Ziyi, Dong Jie, Li Man, Ni Ni and Zhou DongYu. In response, Jing Tian made a set of self-deprecating pictorials with an 'art group aesthetic' in a nostalgic style on the Chinese microblog, Weibo.

Coincidentally, another topic related to the celebrities has also started from the 'face', which is the so-called 'Little Pretty Boy' – known in China by the Internet meme 'xiao xian rou', literally, 'little fresh meat'. Currently Chinese film is chock-full of too many out-there meme-like 'concepts', such as 'earthy air' and 'explosive fund', among others. The loose 'definition' for 'Little Pretty Boy' from various texts refers to the body or face. However, it is essentially not limited to this. The debate on culture behind 'the face of a celebrity' is being followed even more closely. In fact, celebrity recognition begins with the celebrity's physique, rather than getting into the cultural connotations behind their physical façade. This probably explains in part at least, why people either instinctually like or dislike a certain celebrity. In celebrity body image, the face may be the first part to draw interest, as well as other parts of the body, voice, movements and 'embellishments' such as clothing and accessories. Preferences for certain faces and body types are not something belonging to this era alone. One could even say that, 'judging by appearance' is just the way things have always gone down. Although it was replaced by 'lust at first sight' in a television dating program, *If You Are the One*. Ultimately, lust at first sight more emphasizes the visual stimuli aspect. Moreover, it could be argued that there is nothing inherently wrong with having a preference for certain types of faces, considering the celebrity and the fan's individuality. However, if one or a kind of 'face' becomes a prevalent aesthetical trend in a particular era, the implicit ideology behind the phenomenon is definitely worthy of further research.

In discussing the term 'Little Pretty Boy', one cannot help but think of two other words related to male celebrity. First is 'creamy boy' from the late 1970s and early 1980s, the other is 'young beaux', both of which certainly sound much neutral to the ears than the term, 'Little Pretty Boy'. The emergence of stars in that era stood in great opposition to the earlier 'hero' image of the silver screen, a sort of rightsizing of the '**Glitzy, Dapper, Superior**' ethic, and is also based on the demands for scholarly, culturally enlightened, humanist expressions of the era. The screen introductions of Ken Takakura and Alain Delon quickly established a new understanding of 'the man' or 'the true man', in a way that is different from customary aesthetic expressions, but this is only the superficial, extrinsic motivations of that era. The reason why audiences flatly rejected the 'creamy boy' is the demands of the times at the beginning of the Open-Door Policy, and the call for collective 'power' in that era. What can be gathered from study of film texts is that Tang GuoQiang's, *Wreaths at the Foot of the Mountain* and other films were made in the name of subverting the 'creamy boy', and the 'the pursuit of the real man' value orientation. Although Chinese cinema seeks a real man like Takakura or Delon, it has yet to find him. In the late 1980s, actor Ge You led and deconstructed the spirit of this unfinished ethic, but the rejection of that of the 'creamy' reflected a positive trend. Later, the male aesthetic trend of the 'metro-male' triggered by the TV series *Meteor Garden* seems to have received more positive evaluations and even became the icon of masculinity for a generation of women. So, 'the pursuit of the real man' on the screen in the 1980s, as presented in the narrative of the film of the same name, so often turned out to be nothing but an exercise in futility.

In a genderist sense, the current popularity of the 'Little Pretty Boy' is often interpreted as a certain preference for male after a feminist awakening and is related to the spread of concepts of the 'mama's boy' and 'tough chick' at the sociocultural level. Naturally, this interpretation has its own logical merits, but convincing information and discussion on the subject of what kind of girls would favour and love such a man, and whether their emotions stem from a sense of 'screenism' or from 'reality' has yet to present itself. On the other hand, celebrity culture reflects the cultural traits of youth, immaturity and androgyny, and the resulting lack of values and subsequent value vacuum that is prevalent in the current film culture is worthy of further exploration.

Another question is, what is the real definition of 'Little Pretty Boy' as star? The celebrity from post-1949 films and on, not the Hollywood variety mind you, is unique animal. So, the word 'celebrity' in China has always had its own peculiar connotations that are far removed from those of the Hollywood icon. '22 great stars' as one of the 1960s moral compass variety, were not in the commercial or star system sense, but much closer to the popular 'exemplary war hero' or 'model worker'.[2.] As the stars in the sense of the 'review' or 'recommendation', most of them made them famous to the Chinese audience for their image as workers and peasant soldiers. Chen Qiang, who is famous for playing a villain, seems to be an exception. Due to the special system of Chinese filmmaking in that era, such a 'selection' is more honourable and removed from economic interests. Even the celebrities who emerged at the beginning of the reform and opening-up era, such as Chen Chong, Liu Xiaoqing, Zhang Yu, Siqin Gaowa, Pan Hong, Tang GuoQiang and Guo KaiMin, and other celebrities who appeared afterwards, such as Jiang Wen and Gong Li, were not fully imbued with the meaning of a star system, again, due to the film system. Perhaps in this sense, discussing the local position and method of Chinese filmmaking, there is a possibility of a tentative exploration in the celebrity industry, which can largely relieve the 'tension' between Western theory and Chinese texts.

'Fan BingBing on the Red Carpet', and 'Yang Mi at the Airport', these silly Internet memes splash the lives of the today's popular celebrities across the mediasphere. Naturally, getting people discussing celebrities' acting skills across the blogosphere may be like trying to squeeze water from a rock, case in point, this is what they had to say online about the acting skill of a popular female actress, 'We can't talk about what she doesn't have.' But this does not mean that when discussing a celebrity, the 'acting' side of things gets left out. Celebrity performances can usually be divided into two different levels: film performance and cultural performance. The former refers to the part of the star playing a role in the film context, which naturally involves an appraisal of their presence and acting skills; the latter mainly refers to side performances including red-carpet show, product endorsements and glimpses into their private life. Celebrities are often a collection of these two performances. To put it another way, it is the product of the combined effects of different contexts, such as the film and media context. The celebrities discussed above are actually framed more in the latter sense. Not only because some stars' films are lacking in the sense of artistic or cultural quality, but even if many so-called 'A-List stars' are often difficult to find their representative works, in which, their images, the quality of the movies can be balanced and correspond to their personal income and public influence. That's exactly why public and critical outcry on the issue of stars astronomical salaries originates from. In this sense, the absolute number of payouts, or the precise ratio of their gains as compared with other segments of society (such as scientists) is not up for debate. The crux of the problem is that if you discuss the commercial value of the star, the core is the ratio of input to output, 'is both a valuable asset and an expensive burden' (McDonald 2015: 11). Film Box office numbers can be looked at in the same manner.

Celebrity Value: The Unity and Paradox of Culturism and Commerciality

As some scholars have pointed out,

> The Hollywood star system is a cultural and commercial phenomenon. As part of the symbolic content of the film, celebrities are suffused with significance in culture, because they reproduce the meaning of human identity through performances on the screen. At the same time, the celebrity is also a symbol of economic value and an asset used by the film market. Its goal is to increase production financing, obtain income and secure profits. Thus, symbolism and economics are closely interlinked with the Hollywood star system.
> (McDonald 2015: 4)

In other words, 'In film culture, the star becomes the crossover point of meaning and money' (McDonald 2015: 6). The combination of culture and commercialism is almost an intrinsic quality of the film. Naturally, it has become the basic characteristic of the movie star. The combination of 'myth and capital' of idol and commodity is staggering; it is neither a coincidence nor a contradiction. The star and the idol, and the star and the commodity are two aspects of the same reality. This reality is the demand of people in the twentieth-century capitalist society (Moran 2014: 80).

In the cultural sense, if the celebrity's face, body, voice, movements and clothing are embellishments for the body which form a signification, and if it is a 'signifier', then the connotations behind the body image are implied allusions to the star's body, as a 'referent'. Béla Balázs believes, 'Visual culture that has been revived with the birth of film and has made the beauty of the body an important experience for the masses' (Balázs 2003: 301). The main carrier of this visual and cultural experience is the movie star. Edgar Morin called the movie star a 'demigod' in the preface of the third edition of *Movie Stars: The Myth of Star Worship*. 'These demigods, these creatures originating from the dreams of film performances, are studied here as a modern myth' (Moran 2014: 1). He holds, 'Stars are creatures that are both human and divine. In some ways, they resemble heroes from mythology or gods on Mount

Olympus. They trigger certain beliefs or religions' (Moran 2014: 1). Regarding the mythical expression of stars, the book, *Understanding Movies* also states,

> Stars directly or indirectly reflect the needs, desires and anxieties of the audience. They are the fodder of dreams, so that we can have the deepest fantasy and obsession. They are like gods, being worshipped, admired, extoled, as a deified image. Just like in ancient times.
>
> (Giannetti 2016: 255)

There is no doubt that the celebrity is the most influential 'visual myth' of this era.

The face and body constitute the most basic and primeval visual representation with which the movie star uses to stir the audience and is also the basis by which the star is recognized. When discussing Greta Garbo, the greatest actress in the silent film era, Béla Balázs admitted that her prestige was 'fame by virtue of beauty'. Of course, Garbo as a movie star is not so simple, as of course, Garbo's stardom cannot be explained away so cavalierly, because, 'Beauty is something that acts on the senses, it possesses a certain sexual charm, but beauty can't make such a tremendous impact on tens of millions of people in the world'. There are many beautiful women in the world. Garbo's superb symmetry in and of itself does not give her such an exalted position. According to Béla Balázs, 'Garbo's beauty is not just a symmetry of lines, not just a decorative beauty. Her beauty also encompasses an attractive appearance that expresses her inner state of being very clearly'. In his view, the beauty of Garbo is a sad, suffering beauty, a more elegant and noble beauty (Balázs 2003: 303–05). Garbo's understated performance in *Queen Christina* is a subtle performance for film rather than a melodramatic performance for the stage, and is endowed with a deep understanding.

The star system fits in snuggly with archetyping and the studio system; thus, productions within the system are made largely based on commercial demand, and actors are usually 'typecast' into their roles.

> Mary Pickford charmed audiences by playing the ingénue. That deep and mysterious air surrounding Greta Garbo made her an important topic of conversation. John Wayne was famous for playing the sharpshooting cowboy who killed bad guys than you can count. Humphrey Bogart was always the frustrated hero and stubborn private detective. Errol Flynn was the quintessential male archetype and James Cagney was that perfect tough-guy. Then you had the forever femme fatale in Rita Hayworth or the wise and stoic type in Katharine Hepburn. Their image never changed throughout their lifetime.
>
> (Mujun 1982: 28)

The stars' archetypical presence stems from the stars themselves and the screen image they portray, and objectively contributes to the stereotyping and replication of that presence, which can partially explain why the look, hairstyle and movements of stars like Audrey Hepburn, Ingrid Bergman and Marilyn Monroe have always been widely imitated.

Richard Dell believes that capital, investment, spending and the market are the basic elements of a star as the most dynamic factor in the Hollywood economy. The star represents the form of capital mastered by the studio and is the guarantee and commitment of investment. The star accounts for a large part of the investment budget and is used to promote the film and plan the market (Dyer 2010: 15). In another way, Dyer affirmed the commercial value of Greta Garbo as a star. 'The famous tragedienne Greta Garbo was most certainly a gold mine for Hollywood, but she also brought with her art to the studios' (Sadoul 1995: 257–58). And Béla Balázs believed, 'Greta Garbo was the most famous star in the world, not based on aesthetic standards, but on a better, more appropriate, and absolutely perfect standard – the number of dollars her reputation made her' (Balázs 2003: 30).

The commodity value attributes of a movie with a major star attached not only determines the extent to which the media characteristics of the film are magnified into the personal image of the star – face, body, clothing, accessories, etc., as body embellishment – but also determines a film's production and run at the box office, extending the performance and impact of its development, distribution and screening. However, stardom is actually a double-edged sword.

> Even in the most prosperous periods of Hollywood's illustrious history, the star could never guarantee the success of a film. Oftentimes stars come in and out of the public's good graces. Even when their fame is at its zenith, they may make some films that not many people want to watch.
> (Dyer 2010: 16–17)

This contradiction is almost ubiquitous.

> There is an economic paradox in the center of the Hollywood star system. On one hand, because the stars have box office value, the film industry fawns on them; on the other hand, the astronomical level of compensation paid to the stars raises the cost of production, thus limiting the potential for film profitability, and the film industry complains about it incessantly.
> (McDonald 2015: 138)

This paradox is even more apparent in contemporary Chinese cinema. On one hand, in the context of the raucous *carnevale* that is popular culture, the daily pleasures of kaleidoscopic multi-sensory experiences that are used to dispel the hardships and drudgery of daily existence with a carnivalesque *joie de vivre* have become an almost universal pursuit. The superficial obsession with the famous faces often obscures thought and conversation about the cultural values implied thereafter. The resulting 'fans', as groups that form celebrity clubs and have united common love for 'following their favourite star', can almost be regarded as an upgraded version of the latter, while there are some consistent correlations within them, such as fanaticism and irrationality. In the different dimensions of the network structure, this massive and anonymous group ubiquitously maintains the object of their affections in their own way, even if their love is not necessarily recognized by its idol. Furthermore, the verbal expression of said love is almost without exception, sensitive, direct and pervasive. The 'Do you how diligent he is to have gotten to where he is' verbal logic and the fanatical rituals for the stars they love all refer to this group and are even cultural symbols of the present era.

If the film context constitutes the field of the stars 'film performance', then the film festival is one of the main and iconic areas of its 'cultural performance'. 'The film festival is like a big religious ritual. The stars go down the altar and bear witness to their own glory. And at any moment, the fanaticism may give way to madness, and admiration may develop into hysteria' (Moran 2014: 49). Also in this sense, the star's red carpet performance is even more interesting than the performance in the movie itself. This is the reason why certain phenomena worth discussion have arisen. In one respect, the 'Red-carpet Star' frequently enters the red carpet show at famous international film festivals including Cannes, yet said star has no films entered at the film festival either for competition and exhibition. In another respect, some film awards, especially film awards in China, are an affirmation of the absurdity of acting as 'cultural capital'.

It could be argued that 'culture' is compensation for what is lost in 'commercialism', though such compensation does not necessarily hurt 'culture' or even 'business' itself; but then, when 'commercialism' becomes a deficiency, it suddenly falls into a 'null' dilemma.

Star Evaluation: The Possibility of Constructing an Evaluation System

The star's colossal compensation and flippant phoned-in performances are film industry-wide issues resonating throughout the entirety of the industrial chain. However, the stars are the most visible part of the industry, therefore making them the centre of focus.

The reality in China is that there is widespread selective attention in their preference of celebrity image. Most of them choose stars with simple star rankings and personal tastes, thus lacking an effective objective evaluation mechanism.

This is related to the fact that the film industry is underdeveloped. The value of the stars and the public image of the star's personal influence the development of film.

Cases of thoughtless investing in the film industry are many and multitudinous. When *capital* becomes the core of a *cultural* industry, the 'creative' part simply gets left in the dust. From superstitions about 'big data' to fetishism of 'franchise flicks', rampant industry-wide investors are pretty much just out there firing blind. In light of this feckless shotgun approach to investing, box office and word-of-mouth win-wins become like an occasional winning lottery ticket that comes floating out of the sky onto your head as if by an act of sorcery. It theoretically could happen, but it would be a 'once-in-a-lifetime' freak occurrence – a 'dark horse' as is often termed in the movie business. The overexposure of celebrities, and most especially the proliferation of 'little pretty boys' is the most oft mentalated manifestation of this phenomenon.

And in that vein, there is the drama/narrative issue that has come to an impasse. Chinese cinema is deadlocked, and it is hard pressed to free itself anytime soon. And a return to 'common sense' is too much to hope for. Common sense at the screenwriting/narrative level would only require that the story conforms to basic logic. When the narrative tends towards hollowness, the handsome but empty face of the 'little pretty boys' then becomes the most visual form, and the interplay between emptiness and eye-candy will all the more cruelly point and mock the inferior quality of the film. The pale and empty 'famous faces' in the film *Tiny Times* is exactly the same as the empty context of the film itself. The 'acting' does not make a bit of difference, though one would be hard-pressed to find any 'acting' in the film, but moreover the issue is with the script itself, along with the roles, which have 'empty' written all over them.

Therefore, it is a pressing issue to provide instructive, theoretical, forward-looking and operational academic support and information consultancy evaluation system to government departments, film and television institutions, and colleagues and universities, regardless of whether it is for production, use and consumption in the celebrity or for the sound development of the film industry. This system should base researches on celebrity science , related theories, and big data.

One of the evaluation systems already in place is a fairly quantifiable, relatively invariable and frequently stable part, which can include star salaries, celebrity box office, advertising endorsements, online news search volume, blog/microblog fandom and more. In the era of big data, they can theoretically acquire a relatively reliable and cache of credible material. The reason why 'in theory' is emphasized is that in the current film industry, box office numbers are highly suspect in many cases; there are also uncontrollable or unmeasurable variables in the sense of a star's salary and other personal income. This phenomenon needs to be further improved by relevant mechanisms.

A noteworthy and fascinating phenomenon is this, what is being sold in the international film market is a movie, not a movie star; so, it is very different from the electronics or automotive industry. For the film that is introduced to the market, the movie star is more like an intermediary or a bridge, but the star will actually influence and even pre-decide the box office of a film. For a large number of fans, their dominant motivation to enter the theatre may not be the quality of the film, but actually because their favourite star is in it. In this sense, the value of the 'XX million box-office celebs' is only in their publicity, because the factors for a film to get box office returns in the first place are rather complicated. How to evaluate the star's contribution to the box office is quite a complex issue.

And different stars themselves often have obvious differences. 'The status of A-List stars depends on their ability to accumulate economic capital through box office and other income sources. Prestige stars have earned artistic honor by winning symbolic capital such as awards and other forms of recognition' (McDonald 2015). The evaluation of the former type of celebrity relies on net asset value and the amount of personal gain they have obtained, while the evaluation system of the 'prestige star' obviously differs.

Just as 'big data' is impotent to solve the creative and narrative issues of film, statistics can't fully evaluate the value of stars. This is not only because the current film-related material generally has inaccuracies in statistical significance or other significances. More importantly, the data itself is more of a commercial measure of star-power, but the commercial value of a film does not solely rest with the star.

Though most stars can't be described as genius with either the noun or adjectival form as a professional identifier, getting cast as a character that fits their personality and presence to a tee does lend greater probability to the adjective 'genius' being used to describe their performances. Under such casting conventions, it is as if bringing to life a character they were born to play is, in and of itself, enough to engrave the actor's name on the wall of fame of great performances, such as Tang Wei as Wang Jiazhi, Hao Lei as Yu Hong and Zhang Ziyi as Gong Er. Thus, they are not as successful in all the films adorning their illustrious resume. The variables of this role make it difficult to rely on for information, but those more based on the artistic and aesthetic judgments of the director, the actors, the artistic achievements of the film, the commercial performance of the film, its placement in film festivals and its public influence.

To some extent, the popularity of 'little pretty boys' is an illusion, an 'ideological fantasy'. The 'little pretty boys' and his fans are the most active forces in the modern online sphere. Their undeniable popularity is more from the online world and so the Internet is, for all intents and purposes, the primary living space for this group, coupled with some 'cultural performance' forums. In the sense of 'film performance', there are not many cases that can be offered to us for discussion, leaving the most important identifier and context for stardom without a leg to stand on.

The relationship and tension between change and constant is, to some extent, a determiner of stardom, which is the basic form that is capitalized on and consumed. On an evaluation level, specialization and differentiation are the primary techniques and channels with which to achieve a goal. The referent of specialization is the 'famous face' that constitutes the 'movie face' in the signifier/signified and symbol/meaning constructs. Even at the height of his powers, crosstalk performer extraordinaire, Yue YunPeng's performances in *Revenge for Love* and *Top Funny Comedian* went over like a lead balloon. This shows there really is something called film sense. Meaning that, a certain shtick that may go over well in one artistic and cultural sphere may not actually be suitable for film. A star that is like a duck in water in a certain artistic or cultural sphere may also not necessarily be suited to film acting. Former Hunan Television, *Happy Camp* hosts highlighted by Northeast China sketch comedy superstar Xiao ShenYang and company almost became unwitting accessories to a 'Golden Turkey double billing spree'. So-called 'differentiation' emphasizes the different types of stars, and is related to the different levels of aesthetics in an era. It should be noted that the current level of recognition of today's stars is vastly inferior to that of Chinese stars who rose to fame in the 1980s or 1990s.

Conclusion

During the writing of this chapter, a TV series, *The Name of the People*, hosted by an 'old drama hand', whose asking price was far less than the 'little pretty boys', was a real ratings magnet. And the cast of the movie, *The Founding of an Army* was released. In the middle, it contains a lot of 'little divas' and 'little pretty boys', which forms a significant star phenomenon. The 'main-line film' surrounded by the mystique of the genre has attracted a bevy of A-listers to star in *The Founding of the People*. From a creative perspective, perhaps the combination of factors such as similarities in age, look and presence between the actors and their characters was the main reason for casting such 'special actors'. Similarity in look, similarity in spirit. The actor has to look the part and be right for the part. This has always been the audience expectation for the role of a famous historical character. The casting of so many superstars in an epic 'main-line film' may turn out to be a double-edged sword. Of course, it can also be understood as a strategy of actively targeting the youth demographic. However, whether these stars can be recognized in the 'look' and 'spirit' of the respective historical figures they play is certainly an open question, and it is one that can only be answered through the test of time.

REFERENCES

Balázs, Béla (2003), *Film Theory* (trans. H. Li), Beijing: China Film Press.

Dyer, Richard (2010), *Star* (trans. Y. Min), Beijing: Peking University Press.

Giannetti, Louise (2016), *Understanding Movies*, 12th ed. (trans. J. Xiongping), Beijing: Beijing United Publishing Co., Ltd.

McDonald, Paul (2015), *Hollywood Stardom* (trans. W. Ping), Beijing: World publishing Corporation.

Moran, Edgar (2014), *The Stars* (trans. W. Zhuya), Changchun: Jilin Publishing Group Co., Ltd.

Mujun, Shao (1982), *Essay on Western Film History*, Beijing: China Film Press.

Sadoul, Georges (1995), *Histoire générale du cinéma* (trans. X. Zhao and H. Chengwei), Beijing: China Film Press.

NOTES

1. As the iconic film phenomenon of the 17-year period, the '22 celebrities' are not in the sense of industry and star system, but more similar to the 'fighting heroes' or 'model workers' that prevailed as 'models' in that era.
2. In 1961, Premier Zhou proposed the selections of the stars of the Chinese film industry, and finally confirmed Zhao Dan, Bai Yang, Zhang Ruifang, Shangguan Yunzhu, Sun Daolin, Qin Yi, Wang Danfeng, Xie Tian, Cui Wei, Chen Qiang, Zhang Ping, Yu Lan, Yu Yang, Xie Fang, Li Yalin, Zhang Yuan, Pang Xueqin, Jin Di, Tian Hua, Wang Xingang, Wang Xiaotang, Zhu Xijuan and so on. They were named 'New Chinese People's Actors', commonly known as '22 great stars.'

10. Significance in Survival: On the Auteurial Visions in Lu Chuan's Films[1]

皇甫宜川/*Huangfu Yichuan*

Authorship in the System

Since the movie camera is no longer fixed in the 'theatrical conductor' position, point of view then becomes the most important means for the film director to be the author of his films. To a certain extent, with narrative development, the look of the film image is actually the ebb and flow of various points of view. This is the characteristic and core of the director's work. And once he authors his viewpoint through the creative process, he '[p]uts a personal point of view into his work and leaves a clear and identifiable mark on many or a large number of films' (Watson 2010: 9). It is possible for the so-called, film author, or 'auteur' to be spawned from this. Because from this point, often times we can get a glimpse of the viewpoints expressed in the film, and it is possible to peek behind the multiplicity of imagery, to perceive the director's attitudes, thoughts and artistic vision, most especially the 'personal view' hidden behind the authorially crafted pictures.

However, the status of auteur is a precarious one, especially in today's attention economy era. Even if the status and the System do not come to the point of mutual antagonism, at very least it will be subject to the system of absolutist discourse. Therefore, only two paths exist, either that of accepting a return to the System's sunny, well-lit, well-manicured and mainstream path, or continuing to walk the desolate path of the auteur's winding wooded wold. For the former, one may feel it to be ho-humly mediocre, yet glamorous and bounteous. And a good half or more of these opportunities have profound profit potential. Though for the latter, one may revel in that grandiloquent sense of individualist aplomb, while feeling that magniloquent sense of lamentable loneliness and penniless penury. Well, examples such as these are countless and timeless. Desolation implies an absolute attention vacuum, and in a perfect deficit of attention, value may cease to exist, and what is the significance in lost value?

How can artistry be established without significance? Although this inference sounds absolutely absurd, it is positively potent. Therefore, for those directors who have the ability or potential and are willing to pursue or maintain their own auteurial intent and identity but do not want to walk alone in the desolate wilderness, finding that middle-of-the-roadist approach may lead to the most desirable destination – respecting the demands of the System. At the same time, we respect our own inner pursuits and strive to achieve a meaningful survival in the dynamic balance between the two. Being the 'auteur in the System' may be such a path that can take both into consideration. There are some precedents that have been set by folks such as Francis Ford Coppola or Huang JianXin. So does Lu Chuan.

Lu Chuan's understanding of the 'auteur in the System' was crystalized in his master's thesis 'Regime of the author: A study of Coppola (1969–1979) in the context of the New Hollywood'. After studying a decade's worth of Coppola's films, Lu Chuan discovered that the System and the auteur can be harmoniously symbiotic. For example, in Coppola's auteurial 'growth', we see clearly the role of the System in his directorial success. As a happy combination of the film production mechanism and cinematic tradition, the System provides support for the Director both in terms of his survival and creativity. Survival within the System is the primary prerequisite of every auteur, and the sprawling system of life demands survival first, and development second. Auteurs who insist on extreme personal creativity tend to become mired down in a survival crisis within the 'System' (Chuan 1999: 62–63). Coppola is just such an example.

> He didn't have the same struggle as the pioneers of the new Hollywood movement who had to fight the System. He was not like the third echelon of New Hollywood, gradually assimilated in the process of struggle with the System and lost the expression of personality. In his creativity, Coppola maintained a relatively balanced dialectic with the System.
>
> (Chuan 1999: 62–63)

His 'work may be culturally or ideologically subversive but maintains a fundamental respect for the national film traditions (the core of Hollywood tradition is – respect for the audience) in his work. This has allowed his film to gain recognition within the System, and Coppola could survive in the System' (Chuan 1999: 62–63). Lu Chuan believes that these 'Auteurs in the System' are those who maintain respect for the System (audience) in the creative process, while simultaneously making full use of the resources (types and film mechanisms) provided in the System. The auteur in the System respects the System and internalizes it into his consciousness, while keeping focused on the cultural propositions in his obsessive expressiveness (Chuan 1999: 62–63). Lu Chuan ultimately extended his research on the relationship between directors from abroad and institutional relations to the prospects of the Chinese domestic film system. 'Though we are talking about the far-off place called America, and the Hollywood system that seems so incomparable to our Chinese *Hualiwood* system, I still believe that the core principles of the *Hualiwood* system in the future will gradually shift from the 'ideology principle' to the 'audience principle'. Young directors who create and survive in the new System will inevitably face the same or similar problems. For a young director who is just getting started and wants to be identified as an auteur during the dialectic with the System, a systemic/auteurial consciousness will benefit his life's work in the long run (Chuan 1999: 62–63).

Lu Chuan himself is the beneficiary of this very consciousness. When he graduated from the Beijing Film Academy as a graduate student in 1998, the Chinese film system was experiencing growing pains before its 'systemization'. Subsequently, the road to reform of *Hualiwood* has seemingly (at least in some respects) been moving in the direction that Lu Chuan hopes. Although today's *Hualiwood* system is not completely ideological – the 'audience principle' has become an important ethic in the current system – yet whether we are willing or unwilling participants within, it has become the driving principle of the Hualiwood system without stepping on ideology. We cannot know whether Lu Chuan's skosh of 'prophetic awareness' came from the film school's education or his own idiosyncratic thought. It nevertheless set a clear direction for Lu Chuan's own future development. Facts have subsequently proven that this 'small step' in Lu Chuan's theoretical understanding when he first sauntered out of graduate school really contributed to his 'giant leap' in his development as an artist. As stated during his interviews many years ago,

> The path of creating, '*The Missing Gun*,' including the creative road I'm going down at the moment, was grated during my study at the academy and paved during the writing of my thesis. I actually want to be a mainstream filmmaker, I want to make films that can be put into the cinema, not artsy-fartsy indies that only have midnight showings at the local art-house – yet at the same time have my own very personal voice within.
>
> (Chuan 2005: 58)

Obviously, becoming the 'auteur in the System' is not only Lu Chuan's experience studying at the film academy and the subject of his academic research, it is also the direction he has been working since he graduated. Fortunately, Lu Chuan's personal filmmaking path started almost simultaneously with the road of Chinese film systemization, which provided space and time for him to dare to finally obtain the authorship, or shall we say, *auteurship* in the process of dialectic with the System. He only needed to wait for the right opportunity to present itself. That opportunity was afforded to him by the 'Officer Ma Shan's lost gun'.

The Quest for Auteurship in the System

A film's narrative perspective is embodied in how the director develops the narrative. This is both the narrative model of the film and the narrative posture of the director. Most films use unrestricted narrative, which is the oldest practice in the film system. In this practice, the hypertext formed by the discourse between the film and the audience has always been the stablest and smoothest form of viewing in this system. But whether it is an unrestricted narrative or a restricted narrative, there is only one real narrative of the film, that is, the author of the film narrative – the director. Especially in the restricted variety, the purpose of this restriction is to hide the person standing behind the camera, so that the film looks more truthful and objective, and evokes the viewer's subconscious participation. Therefore, it is easier to manipulate the audience emotionally and psychologically with restricted narratives. Suspense films often prefer the use of restricted narratives to develop tension.

The Missing Gun took the limited narrative perspective and it provided excellent narrative support for the suspense of the film. The film tells the story of a policeman Ma Shan who inadvertently lost a pistol with three bullets in it. To retrieve this dangerous weapon in real time, Ma Shan attempted to crack the case by using himself as bait. In getting the thief to shoot with the stolen gun, Ma Shan himself took a bullet. Just at that moment, the police officers rush to arrest the gun thief. It is a detective story with no special characteristics, but Lu Chuan uses the limited narrative and the largely subjective point of view to make this ordinary detective story a gleeful, quirky and intriguing suspense film. Under the stewardship of the restricted narrative and Ma Shan's subjective point of view, 'who stole the gun' and 'how to find the gun' is not only a point of suspense in the film, there is also a chip that aggravates the gamble that is Ma Shan's destiny. Eventually, the manipulation of multiple viewpoints leads the film from the suspense structure of 'finding the missing gun' to revealing Ma Shan's inner world. By this time, the question of who stole the gun is no longer of any significance, and the film becomes a 'subjective movie' (Chuan 2005: 79). Meaning, the world of officer Ma and his lost gun. In this process, the coincidences of the film's limited narrative angle and the large number of Ma Shan's subjective viewpoints are the key to the formation of this subjective film narrative structure, visual logic and its potential meaning.

From the moment Ma Shan found that he had lost his gun, piercing anxiety, and physical and mental pressure instantly turned his living space into a world of self-consciousness. In this world, Ma Shan has only one logical relationship that needs to be considered and put into action, that is, 'Who stole my gun?' And therein a unique style of the film is created. For example, the town in the film looks so pristine – not only the natural environment is so clean, but the town that is supposed to be so busy and cluttered is actually clean and there is almost no extraneous people – because in Ma Shan's eyes, no one who is not directly related to the missing gun is present or meaningful. Therefore, the town in the film is not so much the real space of Ma Shan's life, it is better to say that it is a massive dream space in his eyes after the gun was lost, a space where he can 'seek the gun', a space where anyone could be the thief. And so, in this space, the characters he comes into contact with, and their connection with time and space can be very jagged and fragmented (such as the rapid changes of location in the conversations at Ma Shan sister's house, or the cross-cutting between the Lao ShuJing's house and a battlefield), the space can be filled with ideas (such as a table suddenly appearing and disappearing, and the visions of a family at night). The looks and behaviour of the characters are fairly quirky (such as Li XiaoMeng's odd expressions, or the wife's tracking), as long as it conforms to Ma Shan's, who-stole-my-gun logic. The starting point and penetration of Ma Shan's subjective viewpoint not only provides psychological rationality for stylized image rhythm, spatial processing, and relationship construction, but also guides the audience step by step to Ma Shan's heart, to experience the insanity of a man pushed to the edge by the loss of his gun. If it is not from the narrative logic of the restricted narrative and Ma Shan's subjective viewpoint, such a pristine town seemingly makes no sense at all. And if the setting for the film were a realistic, bustling town, the phantasm-like images of people appearing and disappearing suddenly, would seem illogical or impossible.

With the selection and application of these strategically planned points of view, Lu Chuan not only succeeded in creating a very interesting and meaningful stylized interpretation of a typical suspense film in his debut, but also through Ma Shan's inner stress, angst, nervousness, fear, confusion, depression and helplessness (Xueting and Qian 2007), the creative genius's personal understanding of the contemporary society in which he lived is expressed. Essentially, this inner feeling eating at Ma Shan's soul is:

> [a] kind of prevalent mentality in society, a kind of century disease. This illness is a psychological bent of people have doubts about real life. It is an anxiety of people who are insecure about their living conditions, relationships, livelihoods, and the like.
>
> (Xueting and Qian 2007: 55)

And so, the film touches on the sociological implications of the moment. However, if our understanding of *The Missing Gun* stops abruptly at this point and goes no further, it may not really touch on the deeper meaning behind the film. Lu Chuan is a director who tries to '[f]ocus attention on cultural propositions in his persistent expressiveness', through an auteurial identity. In his stunning and industrious debut, he wishes to express not only social angst, but also the root cause of a specific psychological structure transmitted by Ma Shan's anxiety. What situations and mental processes would make an ordinary policeman willing to give off his life for a lost gun? In this sense, the comedy of errors that results in the inadvertent loss of Ma Sha's gun is actually a reflection of the tortured state of mind of our Chinese nation. What is the cause of this psychological construct? Is it due to the inheritance of national genes or the sociohistorical environment? What is even more thought-provoking is the question, is this construct an isolated case or a collective unconsciousness? But no matter what, the cause of this construct is undoubtedly the rape of humanism, a tragedy at the individual and national level. The sublimation of this tragedy is hidden at the end of the film on the treatment of Ma Shan's death. When Ma Shan suddenly stands up after being shot to the ground, he passes by the crowd who was staring at his body on the ground and looks at them as if he were looking right through them, coming slowly towards the camera, and finally in a close-up frame, where we can see every emotional crease and crevasse on his face as cackles with laughter in equal parts joy and sorrow. In this long-range shift, the film has evolved from a type of psychological suspense to a tragedy of life. This poetic tragedy may be the true personal expression of Lu Chuan in his 'systemic dialectic' debut. In this sense, Ma Shan, once again standing up after death by his own gun at the end of the film, is undoubtedly the *coup de théâtre* of the film, and most certainly its *coup de maître*. Had Ma Shan been shot but not stand up or had not really died as a result of wearing a bulletproof vest, *The Missing Gun* would have been just a common film entry into 'the System' with a few nice little twists and surprises. However, the fact that Ma Shan stood up again after being shot and killed makes the auteurial masterpiece, *The Missing Gun* truly a Lu Chuan film, a symbol of the auteur in the System.

There are some residual flaws in the seemingly rigorous adherence to the psychological suspense formula in this film. The reasons may be as follows: first, some differences between Jiang Wen's concept and the Director's that necessitated certain compromises to compensate for these differences during the filming process. second, the increase of director's freedom made the desire for personal expression reignited while editing the film. For example, the second half of the film is scattered in terms of structure, pacing and motivations, as well as in the writing of the two essential characters, 'Stuttering' Liu and the thief. They are for all intents and purposes, the only two people in the film Ma Shan is unfamiliar with. The indispensable importance of these two characters in the logical chain of events of the film narrative should be derived from the logical structure of the original script. Stuttering Liu is the answer – the gun thief; the thief is the crux – the counterfeit gun provider. Without these two characters, Ma Shan's search for the missing gun cannot be established. Therefore, no matter how much the original script was modified during the filming and editing process, both of these characters must exist. Due to the fact that the film eventually moves fully towards Ma Shan's individualist 'subjective film', although the scene with the gun thief looked curious and interesting, it seemed suspiciously like the gravity 'pulling' the characters and plot towards the 'counterfeit gun' twist, thus yanking this sequence onto the screen. There is also a flaw in the Stuttering Liu character. In Ma Shan's psychological world, once he lost his gun, the street vendor whose name he cannot remember should not have stopped him to talk more. Even if the audience ignores the deliberate intentions of Ma Shan's first encounter due to Ma Shan's suspicions, then the second time the two meet, and Ma Shan is stopped again, the highly intentional nature of this plot device should be painfully obvious to the viewer. After Li XiaoMeng was shot by a man wearing a raincoat, Zhou XiaoGang, who had been following Ma Shan for protection, suddenly disappeared, and at this point there is a voice from offscreen calling out, 'mutton noodle soup for sale', which must have brought a smile to the faces of the cleverer folks in the audience. They must have already guessed that Liu Ba must be one in the raincoat, if not, a mutton soup vendor who Ma Shan is entirely unfamiliar suddenly appearing out-of-the-blue in a suspense genre film with an interlocking chain of events must confounded some out there. The fact of the matter is the unfamiliar vendor turning up again and again is quite strange. And at this point, there were still a full 20 minutes of screen time left. Be that as it may, *The Missing Gun* did win critical and audience recognition. Not bad for a debut film. This may be the best result of attempting to be the first 'auteur in the System'. Thus, capital, audience and critics alike can take something away from this film.

Obviously, *The Missing Gun* is a balanced dialectic between Lu Chuan and the System. The dialectic begins with the willingness of capital to invest in a genre script, and the cultural meaning reflected in this script promotes the association of Jiang Wen, which in turn strengthened the confidence and speed of capital investment in the script. Actually, 'The Huayi Brothers Media Corporation's decision to invest in this film took a total of three days' (Chuan 2002: 7). Here the audience principle in the System has popped its head out of its burrow. A generic director would be the least important element in this transaction. For capital, a script that has market promise and a bankable superstar are enough to fund a small-budget movie. And if the superstar is also a name director, then who the director is becomes inconsequential – maybe a nobody is even better. A good script is the foundation for a profitable project, then there is the addition of a superstar who is also a well-known director, so capital has reason to believe that at least making the film will not be a mistake. And that was the case. 'In the filmmaking process, Huayi Brothers and the Beijing Film Academy did not try to throw their weight around. They stayed completely out of the making of the film' (Xueting and Qian 2007: 55). What was fortunate about how it all played out was, Lu Chuan, who had just written the screenplay and also wanted to direct, was given the seal of approval to do so by Jiang Wen, and so Lu Chuan was given the director's megaphone, all the while 'backed' by the System. But behind this stroke of luck was his knack for the novel that helped him discover the novel, *The Missing Gun* and the ingenuity to adapt it to a script that gave both capital and Jiang Wen a pleasant surprise; as well as the stick-to-it-iveness to lobby for the script. More importantly, in the film production process, he strove under the pressure to 'adhere to the cultural proposition'.

If you understand that this was a young no-name director who was just given a seat in the director's chair at the face of a system that regarded him as insignificant, you may not call into question how much of *The Missing Gun* belong to the director's auteurship. To a certain extent, Jiang Wen was the embodiment of the System during the filming process. He represents the trust of capital and the imagination of the future market. The controversy, compromise and persistence of Lu Chuan and Jiang Wen are also the most difficult, important and most meaningful part of Lu Chu's initial dialectic with the System. Fortunately, however, Jiang Wen is also an 'auteur' to some extent, and Jiang Wen's position is even more obvious. He may also have tried to burn his personal brand onto the character of Ma Shan. That is actually how it was. It helped Lu Chuan and Jiang maintain 'consistency' in the ultimate meaning of *The Missing Gun* and aided the understanding of the character of Ma Shan, even though they had different ideas and proclivities in their collaboration (Chuan 2005).

So, from script to screen, some changes in the writing 'mainly in collaboration with Jiang Wen,' were bound to take place (Chuan 2005), yet those changes did not affect or change Lu Chuan's personal expression. On the contrary, he may have gained a lot of positive energy from the said collaboration. To a certain extent, it was that elder statesman with his own list of achievements and accolades who brought about the successful debut effort of a junior on his way to becoming an 'auteur' in the face of the System. But this success is probably difficult to duplicate, as it had a lot to do with chemistry. Another equally talented young director may have been completely obscured by Jiang Wen's powerful energy, or the two may have had creative differences and the project would have broken up halfway through. In this sense, this success also brought a bit of 'Lu Chuan-style' success. Philosophically speaking, this had something to do with the strategy and mindset of an 'auteur in the System'.

The Journey of an Auteur in the System

The Missing Gun gave confidence to the System, but even more so to Lu Chuan himself. Under the joint forces of the powerful faith, *Kekexili : Mountain Patrol* became the bona-fide journey of an 'auteur in the System'. With respect to the System, capital's interest in this subject lies in its good market promise. It is mainstream – it is in line with mainstream values and anchored in a modern environmentalist concept. It is genrefied – it tells the story of heroes chased by bad guys in the desolate wild west of China. It is spectacular – it is set in the mysterious environment of the Kekexili people. The script, which was finally greenlit by capital, is an attempt to depict, 'An anti-poaching story told through the desolate grasslands and shown through a genre film with a powerful story' (Chuan 2004: 24). The interesting thing is that Lu Chuan always manages to attract investment through a commercial script, then in the process of filming and editing process, makes changes to bring it in line with his own personal expression by relying on his artistic sensibilities and cultural respect present in the writing: not only in *The Missing Gun*, but also in *Mountain Patrol* and *City of Life and Death*. Whether intentional or unintentional, this is a microcosm of actions of the 'auteur in the System' within a macrocosm. It first introduces capital and then attempts to evolve. As for the degree of evolution, it depends on how the 'dialectic' is playing out. With respect to *Mountain Patrol*, the transformation is not unrelated to the selection and application of the film's viewpoints. Even during the filming process, the changes to the story and the presentation and interpretation of the final visual style are crucial. Or, to put it in another way, at least it offers the possibility of this change.

As with *The Missing Gun*, *Mountain Patrol* uses a limited narrative. A reporter from Beijing brings us into the mysterious Kekexili along with a patrol member. The difference is that the film does not use the subjective point of view of the reporter in the narrative. Instead, it focuses on the objective point of view with a little subjective point of view for the reports. The final form of the documentary style of the film is created under this combination of viewpoints. Due to the uniqueness of the natural environment of the Kekexili and the involvement of a large number of non-professional actors, such a combination of viewpoints makes the behaviour of the characters, and the development of the events, required the environment to be closed off during the shoot. In other words, in a special situation, the selection and use of such viewpoints clearly indicates the possibility of presenting the 'aboriginality' during the shoot. So, the choice becomes very important. If you had switched the director, even if this point of view strongly signals the 'aboriginality', during the shoot, the director may have continued according to the original script. So, Lu Chuan was changing by the situation.[2] This change not only altered the visual style, pacing and direction, but also led to the change of the last scene (Chuan 2004: 24). In a panoramic wide shot Ritai, who had finally caught up with the poachers, punched a poacher in anger and was suddenly gunned down by another poacher. When he was convulsing like a shot Tibetan antelope that he was struggling to protect, the poacher shot again, killing him. Ritai was put down by the poachers, just as if they were putting down Tibetan antelopes. Ritai and his comrades are actually just like the respectable and lovely 'endangered animals' in our society. Like the Tibetan antelopes, they are not protected.

In the original script, 'Ritai sacrificed himself in a fierce gun battle',[3] but in a more crueller and more realistic way was shot down, and he died on the Kekexili badlands. This change to how he died brought resolution to the story of vigilante justice. The patrolmen trying to find poachers ultimately catch none, and the story turns into a game of survival and death. The tragedy consciousness of the film thus re-emerges, not only humanizing the film to a greater level (Daxian 2005: 39), but also criticizing the status-quo of our society. The heroes' struggle turns tragic – to the sorrow of the patrolmen, and the sorrow of our society. Although Kekexili is in the no-man's land of the West, the story of this uninhabited area is related to the lack of the rule of law in our Chinese society. The sharp divide between the rich and the poor, the decline of morality and other 'fast-acting modern diseases'. It may also be related to the inequities of the world and to the women wearing apparel made of antelope fur halfway around the world. What is an auteur? Paul Watson said,

> The reason why the standard interpretation of Brokeback Mountain presumes Ang Lee to be its auteur, because, as a director, the authorship and meaning behind the text was controlled by him to a considerable extent. So, it is possible to attribute this work to him.
>
> (Watson 2010: 5)

By that measure, the name of the auteur of *Kekexili* can be attributed to Lu Chuan.

Mountain Patrol is certainly not a story about environmentalism, nor is it a vigilante hero's pursuit of a murderer. It is a story that should never have happened. Just like *The Missing Gun*, Ritai should not have died, and his comrades should not have died. The so-called accessories to the head poacher who were forced by life to help skin the antelope should not have died. Similarly, Ma Shan should not have died, Li XiaoMeng should not have died, and Stuttering Liu should not have died. Yet they are dead. The question that the film throws under the surface narrative is why these people died. Who was responsible for their death? From,

The Missing Gun to *Mountain Patrol*. From subjective films to documentary presentations. With such divergent differences in cinematic form, we find that the tragedy consciousness under the consideration of history, society and humanity has been deeply infused into Lu Chuan's films, which can also be said about Lu Chuan's third film, *City of Life and Death*.

The way the world works has always been discoverable through logic, even when it just gives us tiny traces and scant clues to find their relationship. And, so it is with Lu Chuan's three films. If there were no acknowledgement of the System in *The Missing Gun*, there would be no *Mountain Patrol* with its nearly complete 'auteur in the System' journey. And, of course, there would have been no *City of Life and Death*, as having a more powerful dialectic with the System afforded him the unconventional gambit that was *City of Life and Death*, which garnered equal helpings of praise and criticism. However, this text has no intentions of revisiting what has become historical controversy, but rather to explore the possible sources of such controversy from texts. In the opinion of this author, one of the important reasons is still related to the selection and application of the film's points of view.

Investigating the points of view in Lu Chuan work, you will find that his first three films come from an internal perspective, referring to the point of view of the characters in the film. In, *The Missing Gun* it is Ma Shan, in *Mountain Patrol* it is the reporter, in *City of Life and Death* it is Kadokawa Masao. The advantage of these points of view is that '[w]hen the point of view is subjective, we get more closely involved in the action, and our experience is stronger and more involved' (Bergs and Petrie 2010: 118). It is easier to get the viewer invested in the film, who feels as if he or she is a character in the movie. In, *The Missing Gun*, Ma Shan is the main character of the story. The movement and change of Ma Shan's subjective viewpoint and the narrative of the film form an organic whole. Through the extreme manipulation of subjective viewpoints, the film constructed a unique film world with which it artistically fleshed out Ma Shan's image. But in *Mountain Patrol*, the narrative logic does not focus on the subjective point of view of the reporter, but on the objective point of view, and the subjective point of view of the reporter syncs with it to complete the narrative. Because the film is edited through the perspective of the reporter, the core of the film is not to shape the image of the reporter, but to use the intervention of the reporter to complete the shaping of the mountain patrol team headed by Ritai. At this time, the 'objectivity principle' of the objective point of view makes the film form a palpable documentary style, and the interspersed subjective viewpoints of the reporter give the documentary style powerful emotional colouring. This alternating combination of subjective and the objective points of view serve to bring the audience into the film, who themselves become a character, to experience and feel the actions and emotions of the patrolmen, thus giving the film its power and impact. Nevertheless, it also turns out to be the bane of *Mountain Patrol's* existence. The characterizations are not 100 per cent successful. The reason for this is that the movie did not properly utilize certain key sequences, or scenes to match the subjective point of view of the reporter, to keep the camera more on the main character of Ritai, to reveal his inner world through the objective point of view through freedom of expression. The character of Ma Zhanlin on the other hand more successfully left his mark on the audience.

City of Life and Death obviously want to regain the unique and successful characterizations from *The Missing Gun*.

What's interesting is that, although *City of Life and Death* was made after *Mountain Patrol*, it is quite similar to *The Missing Gun* in many aspects. For example, the two films are all about 'one person'. *The Missing Gun* shows how a Chinese policeman went insane after losing his gun. *City of Life and Death* shows how a Japanese soldier has a mental breakdown during a war of aggression. Another example is the openings of the two films are nearly identical. *The Missing Gun* begins with Ma Shan lying on the bed for a beat or two, then he opens his eyes to find his irate wife complaining to him; after which things rapidly fall into an insane search for his gun.

City of Life and Death begins with Kadokawa lying on the edge of a trench for a beat or two, then he opens his eyes to find his comrades in the distance calling him forward, after which he is rapidly involved in a fascist atrocity that causes him to breakdown mentally. The ending of the two films play out in much the same fashion. In *City of Life and Death*, Kadokawa commits suicide, killing himself with his own gun. In, *The Missing Gun*, Ma Shan designed a trap that causes him to lose his gun, leading to his death. This is actually suicide. Comparing *The Missing Gun* to an embryo of an ordered sequence in the director's personal work, then after a few years, how much of *City of Life and Death* was affected by this embryo? In addition, the creative process of these two films was similar. *The Missing Gun* underwent great changes from script to screen. The same can be said about *City of Life and Death*. Is this not Lu Chuan's style? *Mountain Patrol* also went through the same process.

As with *The Missing Gun*, *City of Life and Death* sets a subjective point of view for Kadokawa and the journey of the film itself is an attempt to explore the inner world of Kadokawa through this subjective point of view. It proceeds to shape the image of a Japanese soldier who is slowly losing his mind as a result of the war of aggression. What is different from *The Missing Gun* is that the film loses Kadokawa's perspective in many of the film's most potent scenes of atrocities, such as the prisoner capture sequence, the rape sequence, Mr Tang's confession sequence, the scene with Mr Tang's children being killed by the Japanese army, the scene with Mr Tang's redemption and death by gunfire, and so on. In these atrocities, ever-present is Kadokawa's close friend the captain, whom Kadokawa once bathed in a relaxed, cheerful and warm scene, along with his comrades. Yet we barely even see Kadokawa. What is Kadokawa doing during those moments? Is he alone hiding somewhere to pray? Even though Kadokawa did finally appear in the Japanese army's operation to search and destroy mission in the refugee camps, in terms of visual expression, Kadokawa actually appears detached and aloof. He just broke into a specimen room and asked for a cross necklace from Mr Jiang. If this scene is not to pave the way for the 'Kadokawa-shoots-Mr-Jiang' sequence, is it possible that Kadokawa will still be missing in this military operation? In the inhuman and wholesale slaughter and rape shown in the film, the real narrator hidden behind the camera seems to be carefully guarding Kadokawa, trying not to let him see the spilling of innocent blood. Even in the church scene at the beginning of movie, Kadokawa was one of the soldiers who shot and killed the women in the secret room. It was also an act for which he made immediate apology and tried actually to remedy. He seems to have just fled directly from a classroom in a middle school in Japan to an invading army soldier in Nanjing. In the design of this sequence, it is difficult to prevent the audience from doubting the authenticity of this character. How did such a soldier fight all the way to Nanjing? What made him to be promoted in a short time?

As a war-themed film, there are two camps set up in *City of Life and Death*, the Japanese and the Chinese. The film sets up two viewpoints to expand the narrative. Besides Kadokawa's (personal) Japanese point of view, there is the Chinese point of view made up of Lu JianXiong, Mr Jiang and Mr Tang. Even though in is mind's eye Lu Chuan envisioned this group of Japanese characters and that group of Chinese characters completing a human world (Four-Person Dialogue 2009). However, due to Kadokawa not making an appearance in many sequences, the two narrative lines developed by these two viewpoints hardly form a powerful cross and organic fusion in the process of film narrative. The only intersection between the narrative lies with Kadokawa and the main characters in the Chinese narrative line is when Jiang asks for a cross necklace from Kadokawa and then requests him to shoot her as the Japanese military looks on. The shaping of the character of Kadokawa is somewhat flat, and weak in terms of realism in certain contexts. Thus, Kadokawa's suicide is not a necessary component of either dramatic or visual narrative. Due to the fact that the narrative does not offer up a convincing enough psychological basis and developed narrative logic that would lead to this conclusion. In a certain respect, compared with the continuity of Kadokawa's subjective viewpoint and the confusion of war that re-emphasizes this viewpoint, Lu Jianxiong's untimely death, Jiang's special identity and Mr Tang's act of betrayal not only makes the Chinese perspective seem too loose and fragmented, there is also not a powerful enough national ideological basis for overpowering Kadokawa's views. So, it is in the comparison of these two viewpoints, most especially with the disappearance of Lu JianXiong's viewpoint (this is the only Chinese point of view that can compete with the aggressor's point of view but is ended too early), that Kadokawa's point of view then begins to take over. It is also the imbalance of contrasts between the two viewpoints that leads to the emotional balance of the film. As the narrative developed, it slowly began to lean to side of the invader soldier Kadokawa. This is what leads to people's natural misunderstanding of the film. As a young Chinese director with great promise, and the true narrator of the film, it is natural that some may question the director's emotional tendency in the film.

City of Life and Death could have afforded Lu Chuan some stature in the modern cinema. Unfortunately, perhaps due to the success of the first two films, the 'auteurial' right to self-expression has spread like wildfire in his productions. The imbalanced manipulation of points of view that has caused some kind of dislocation and may have ultimately caused the film to lose out on this possibility. However, it must be pointed out that, although there is a difference between the willingness of the creator to be expressive and the final expression of the film, the setup of the Kadokawa's point of view is still of great significance in the Chinese war film. As far as capital in the System is concerned, obviously *City of Life and Death* is a well-targeted commercial film from the beginning, but since the auteur's creative foundation is based on the study of a large amount of historical content, this makes it very likely to move in the direction of a personal narrative. As Lu Chuan, who has been trying to become the 'auteur in the System', the discovery and reflection brought about by such a large amount of historical research, as well as the sentiment generated during the shooting and editing process, have not allowed him to establish such a film narrative model, which would definitely lead to some grievances and shortcomings in the final film under such a powerful appeal to personal expression. One may disagree with the film's point of view, the perspectives within it, and the performance style, but his personal expressiveness shows the spirit of independent thinking, which may be the value of this film. In fact, for this very particular film, the release and the discussions that emerged after its release may have allowed it to fully express what it intended. And the context of *City of Life and Death* has evolved into a more connotative and modern sense of the Nanjing Massacre super-textual works. So, like it or not, *City of Life and Death* might be a film that cannot be ignored in the succession of Lu Chuan's personal film and a series of Chinese war films.

Getting Lost in the System

City of Life and Death has afforded Lu Chuan, the auteur of system, the opportunity to ultimately become a member of the prestigious '100 million club'. Like it or not, the box office is fast becoming the pre-eminent determiner in the Chinese film evaluation system. Once a director makes it into the '100 million club', it means that a certain degree of success has brought about a sudden and very sharp increase in money and privilege. It also means the possibility of a higher budget for next film. Of course, this also means that the box office may become a magic formula for '100 million' director. But when all is said and done, is this a blessing or a curse?

The System is like a giant horse-drawn carriage. Although it is large and comfortable, once seated, especially clutching a '100 million' trophy in your hot little hand, some rules of the ride must be observed. Or perhaps it is better said that one will most certainly follow the rules subconsciously once seated upon the plush, luxuriant ride. Lu Chuan's new film *The Last Supper* was released before the end of the composition of this very text. Yes, there were the different controversies that surrounded the release of *City of Life and Death* three years prior, but now the viewers have a different controversy to the new film. As mentioned earlier, this controversy may in-and-of-itself be the value of a film, and to some extent, it is both the harbinger and purveyor of big box office. Regardless of whether it is the media, the experts or the audience, from day one of *The Last Supper*'s release, they all clamoured cacophonously to know the answer to the same burning question – what kind of box office number could *The Last Supper* possibly generate?

With the passage of time and tide, as Lu Chuan has donned the glorious '100 million' laurel upon his head and brought ancient celebrities such as Liu Bang back into the limelight, no one went to the theatre expecting to find Lu Chuan the auteur. All regarded this costume film inspired by the 'Banquet at Hong Gate' to be a super Spring Festival blockbuster – a king's 'feast' for the new spring's fest. Though the film rolled Lu Chuan's usual explorations of human nature into this sumptuous costume drama, and though the film is still full of allusions to history and metaphors about the present, and though the film is steeped in the usual pungent air of Lu Chuan style, at the end of the day does it all really matter? When Lu Chuan suited up in ancient armour and gear and commanded the presence of A-listers to join him in his grand 'supper', replete with sweeping vistas, grand action scenes and high-tech special effects, it should have been an instant home-run. Respect for market principles and the audience is the very heart of box office performance. But unfortunately, from the get-go, *The Last Supper* was not a 'respect-the-System-in-the-creative-process (the audience)', and a 'capitalize-on-the-System's-resources (genre and film mechanisms)', all the while 'transforming-respect-for-the-System-into-the-will-of-the-auteur', with a pinch of 'obsessively-holding-to-self-expression

-while-keeping-focused-on-the-cultural-proposition' recipe for movie-making. In making a large-scale commercial film, if you still try to hold too tightly to a healthy respect for the power of your own authorial expressiveness, it might just come across as an unhealthy disrespect for the power of the 'System'. It is a proposition that can so often put you in an awkward bind. After many years, Lu Chuan may have forgotten the words of his own master's thesis, which are, and I quote, 'The System, as a combination of film production mechanism and film tradition, provides support for the Director ensuring both his survival and creativity'. Survival in the System is the prerequisite of every auteur. Survival is primary, development is secondary. Auteurs who hold unflinchingly to their extreme personal creativity tend to fall into the crisis of survival within the System.

The emergence of the 'auteur in the System' is actually a phenomenon or result in the development of the film industry and art itself, because in a sense 'Every film is the brainchild of a dynamic marriage between merchants and artists' (Four-Person Dialogue 2009: 2). The auteurs in the System are trying to create a commercial product and work of art that both sides can recognize and benefit from. And there are also many successful directors out there. The reason why the middle-of-the-road approach can succeed is probably there is a certain genome in the genetic makeup of film as popular art.

If it floats your boat, you are welcome to revel in the joys of dancing with the System, within the System. You can also experience the pleasures of independence from the System. Of course, you can also choose to live in a meaningful way within the System. This path seems to be the best of both worlds, but it is still fraught with risk, because if you let your guard down for even a second, you may just get lost in the System.

That means, what one needs to be aware of is that, in today's unprecedented information age, business and information are so perfect that pure 'auteurs in the System' may have a tough time protecting themselves. Just like what is happening to the writer-directors outside the System, the director who lives within the System is also faced with the possibility of being transformed into an 'identifiable insignia' by the System. Even if this is the more palatable choice because of its close proximity to the finish line, when we are too busy focusing on – or applauding the 'meaningful survivalist' approach in this system, Capital, Auteurs and the Media will have themselves been commercialized. 'Auteurs in the System' is the conspiracy that is either explicit or implicit under the temptation of commercial interests. 'The commercialization of this concept has turned it into a business strategy that seeks to gain acceptance from the audience and becomes a concept that will certainly be conducive to the critiques of distributors and markets' (Watson 2010: 12). To some extent, *City of Life and Death* bears just this very portent: Who can say that Lu Chuan's rise to fame and admission into the exclusive '100 million club' did not benefit directly from the great controversial surrounding, *City of Life and Death*? Fortunately, for Lu Chuan, *City of Life and Death* is only an individual case, this phenomenon is a subconscious result of the spontaneous dialectic between the 'System' and the 'auteur'. But who can guarantee that this dialectic will not ultimately be transformed into a commercial sales concept down the road? At this time, the 'auteurs in the System' who have made a name for themselves may indeed be like bright, twinkling stars. When advertising, promoting and marketing their films, they try to sell their hard currency-like celebrity status. At which time, the auteur himself plays the role of a film's slick pitchman. In other words, the auteur is not trying to fight against the System to express his own ideas but is positioned as a natural extension of the System, recruited by the authority of the industry and accepting of his transformation according to the needs of the System (Watson 2010: 12). Thus, as the auteur in the System, the way of life is no longer full of 'meaning', but rather full of 'taste'. But this taste is sometimes sweet, and sometimes bitter, much like the grand *potpourri* of flavours in *The Last Supper*.

REFERENCES

Bergs, M. Joseph and Petrie, W. Dennis (2010), *The Art of Watching Films* (trans. Z. Jing and G. Yujun), Beijing: Peking University Press.

Chuan, Lu (1999), '"Auteurship in the system": Coppola study (1969–1979) in the context of the New Hollywood', *Journal of Beijing Film Academy*, 1, pp. 62–63.

—— (2004), interviewed by Ni Zhen, 'You're only young once', *Contemporary Cinema*, 6.

—— (2005), interviewed by Ni Zhen, 'Happily creating mainstream topics', *Contemporary Cinema*, 3.

Daxian, Liu (2005), 'The aesthetic of indifference, the weight of the soul and the rules and demands', *Art Panorama*, 1, p. 39.

Four-Person Dialogue (2009), 'City of life and death', *Contemporary Cinema*, 7, p. 44.

Watson, Paul (2010), *Cinematic Authorship and the Film Auteur*, 5th ed. (trans. L. Si), *World Cinema*, London: Routledge, pp.142–165.

Xueting, Zhang and Qian, Yu (2007), 'Unstoppable anxiety – Reading about the movie "The Missing Gun"', *China Literature and Art Criticism*, 2, p. 55.

NOTES

1. This text was completed in December 2012 at the request of the *Contemporary Cinema* editorial department. Due to the fact that the article and the accompanying dialogues with the director were completed in the past, but this article was not published until recently, the author chose not to make any changes to the original text to maintain a consistent style of academic observation. Let it be noted that director Lu Chuan's film, *Chronicles of the Ghostly Tribe* was released in 2015, after the original text was completed.

2. Lu Chuan: The more I filmed, the more I felt something was wrong. This is an act of idealism dedicated to devotion in the world. It is a deed of faithfulness of a group of real people in an extremely taxing environment, rather than a type of film in which the elements of drama are perfect, and the story develops seamlessly. I saw more and more severe poaching when we entered deeper plateaus and snow, and I felt that I had to do something about it. I had to tell a heroic story according to the real people of Hoh Xil. We must never continue to invent an affected 'seductive' story' (Chuan 2004: 25).
3. Lu Chuan: 'Halfway through filming I realized that I didn't want to shoot the original ending, but I had no idea how to change it. The countdown had already started, I only had two weeks. Then in the last two or three days, the idea suddenly came to me out of the blue' (Chuan 2004: 25).

SECTION III

HISTORY

11. Revisiting 1920s: Reflections on the Nationalism in Early Chinese Films

秦喜清/Qin XiQing

In 1920, the Commercial Press officially established the Living Film and Theatre Department, and in the same year licensed the establishment of film companies and film and theatre research societies, which included the *Shanghai Film Company* headed by Tan Tu-yü and the *New Asia Film Company* founded by the Yin Hsien-fu Brothers and Kuan Hai-feng. With the help of the technical wizardry of the Living Film and Theater Department, the three companies released three feature films, *Yen Jui-sheng*, *Swear by Oath* and *The Ten Sisters* in 1921, which formally kicked off the production of feature films in China. The founding of The Star Motion Picture Company in 1922 gave rise to an even stronger impetus for the development of Chinese filmmaking, especially with the enormous success of *An Orphan Rescues His Grandpa*, which was something of a boon for the Chinese people's confidence in their own film industry. Motion pictures became an increasingly alluring form of *nouveau* entertainment. By 1924, Chinese cinema was developing at blazing speed, with 31 production companies having been established in Shanghai (Po-ch'ang 1925). According to the statistics from the *China Cinema Yearbook* (1927) in 1925, there were 175 film companies in more than ten large and medium-sized cities such as Shanghai, Beijing and Tianjin, of which 141 companies had been established in Shanghai alone. Despite the fact that most of these companies disappeared without the release of even a single film and no one has seen hide or hair of them since, the clamour for the glamour of the industry at the time reflected a potent surge signalling to the world that Chinese cinema was beginning to emerge.[1] Accompanying said meteoric trend in production company openings was a swell in film production, from a mere 15 Chinese films produced in 1924 to 203 in 1928–29 (Bo 2005).

Under the powerful impetus of business and corporate interests, the scale of production reached a fever pitch, and amid the mumblings and rumblings the first golden age of Chinese costume drama and Kung Fu film was ushered in.

In the 1920s, Chinese cinema transformed from a landscape of shorts and genre-monotony to one of feature-length films and genre-variety, ranging from early crime films, detective pictures and romances, to morality plays and dramas, which refined the development of emotional themes until the shift towards traditional costume film and martial arts film narratives, which left behind clearly conspicuous developmental traces, and became the most important period for Chinese film to establish itself. In the historical and cultural context of the 1920s, national identity provided the impetus for the rise of Chinese film and played a central role in its development, while Chinese and Western co-existence became a one-way street down which Chinese film style marched on. Different film production houses made different choices on how to feature Chinese and Western cultures in their films and different schools-of-thought were formed. In a tightly interwoven pattern of Chinese and Western cultural fusion of tradition and modernity, common and elite, the modernization of Chinese culture showed through the seams and established the national identity in Chinese cinema.

Part 1: US vs Them

The English word 'nation' could mean ethnicity or state depending on usage. National identity is one of the important symbols of a nation-state. As a country of backward industry, the Chinese national identity in modern times has special connotations and challenges. After the 1840 Opium War defeat, China experienced 'Unprecedented change not seen in thousands of years (Li Hung-chang)'. The war with the Western countries and its subsequent series of unequal treaties fundamentally altered the relationship between China and the outside world. With attacks from both Europe and America, China's sovereignty took a huge hit, with territory being ceded and port treaties being established in the wake of the attacks. It was forced to transform itself from a powerful empire with a tributary system to a humble cog in the wheel of an emergent New World system. The Qing Dynasty was vanquished, and in the place where the ancient land of China once stood, a new nation-state was constructed following the model of the Western nation-state. 'Chinese national superiority' became the faded legacy of a lost empire, and the emerging nation-state was forced to cope with a more powerful and heterogeneous Western civilization. An 'us-vs-them' mentality arguably caused a once diverse Chinese nation rife with internal differences to assume a common identity to give way for the time being to the doctrine of a Sino-Xenic cultural gap. As a result, the various ethnic groups living on the vast expanse of land called China were united under the banner of 'the Chinese nation' within its own country.

Just as some scholars have pointed out, the nation-state's 'Definition of the self is always founded upon its relationship with the 'outside', bringing with it a powerful propensity towards internal homogeneity and external heterogeneity (Hui 2004: 686), thus forming a new Chinese national identity, goaded by Western civilization.

The word 'identity' is a concept that is as ambiguous as it is ineluctable. In the Chinese context, the English word for identity can be translated into 'identity', 'characteristics', 'unity' and 'identification' (Huntington 2005: 20). Samuel Huntington pointed out that, despite the incongruity in scholarly definitions, the core remains congruous: 'The central theme is thus: identity means self-awareness of a person or a group, it is product of self-awareness. Any special qualities that I or We have make us different from you, or different from 'them'. It expresses a self-image with personality and characteristics, is an image unique to the actor, formed in the process of interacting with others and occasionally changes (Huntington 2005: 20). Therefore, identification or identity is associative, and it always defines itself by comparisons with others. Simultaneously, this concept can be applied to both individuals and groups. As a result, national identification or national identity becomes the way a cultural community in a country defines itself and distinguishes itself from another nation. When Liang Ch'i-ch'ao, who advocated the concept of the 'Chinese nation', defined the concept of the ethnic group as nation, it was based on the relationship between China and the West, and the *We* and the *They*. In 1922, Liang Ch'i-Ch'ao pointed out when discussing ethnic issues:

> Blood, language and beliefs are powerful conditions for the establishment of a nation. However, we must not regard the division of the three as the division of the nation. The only element of the founding of the nation is the discovery and establishment of 'national consciousness'. What is national consciousness? It is, simply put, a conscious realization that you are Chinese when you relate to those who are not. They are Japanese and We are Chinese. Whenever you meet people of other nationalities, the concept that 'I am Chinese' should immediately come to mind. This person is a member of the Chinese nation. Our national consciousness has existed for countless years, and numerous people have worked together to make contribute to the 'cultural hub'. Conscious realization that you are Chinese in contact with other nationalities is the establishment of the national consciousness.
>
> (Ch'i-Ch'ao 1996: 604–05)

Although Liang Ch'i-Ch'ao recognized that blood, language and beliefs are all elements in the make-up of a nationality, taking into account the differences within the Chinese nation itself, he believes that, given the ethnic divisions within the country, there should not be a dividing line between these three elements. He emphasized the establishment of the Chinese nation from the perspective of national consciousness, the essence of which is, 'In contact with the people of other nations, consciously realize the I'. The 'I' here is nothing more than a visual representation of national identity. In addition to blood, language and beliefs, he emphasized the importance of 'the self' in the formation of national consciousness by means of a comparison of the 'heterogeneity' between Chinese and 'other ethnicities'. Liang Ch'i-Ch'ao's proposal and discussion of the concept of 'China' reflected the urgent need for the Chinese to establish a new sense of national identity and a new national consciousness after the demise of the Qing Dynasty and the emergence of the Republic of China.

Coincidentally, film was introduced into China at the end of the nineteenth century and happened to undergo a major social change in the 1920s with the transition from the abdication of the royal family in the Qing Dynasty and the rise of the early Republic of China. From the political system to common society, from lifestyle to culture and entertainment, change was omnipresent. In the sweeping social change that was taking place, '[t]he cutting of the queues and modernizing of clothing' an important event most directly related to the construction and clarification of national identity. At the beginning of the establishment of the Nanking Provisional Government in 1912, the revolutionaries introduced a series of decrees, demanding '[t]he cutting of the queues and changing to modern clothing' and bans on smoking, gambling and foot-binding. In addition to systematically sweeping away the old and replacing it with the new, Sun Yat-sen issued the 'Executive Order to the Ministry of Internal Affairs Regarding the Cutting of Queues', stipulating that queues be cut off within 20 days after issuing the edict and urged everyone to be a model new citizen in new China by abandoning Qing old policies and traditions, and keep up model appearances (Interim Government Gazette No. 29, China's Modern History Data Series, The Revolution of 1911 (8), Shanghai: Shanghai People's Publishing House, 1957, p. 25, quoted from Wei 2000). Here, the people of the new country were linked to the 'new appearance', and new image that corresponded to a new national identity. In addition to cutting queues, the dress styles and status symbols of the day began to change. Western suits and Chinese tunic suits, which later became known as the 'Mao suit' replaced the traditional Chinese robe and mandarin jacket, and the cheongsam became a symbol of the new women. Outward appearance had much to do with national identity. As a result, the screen image of Chinese that received widespread attention during the era has become a part of the construction of a national identity.

In the 1920s, China's social and historical change called for the establishment of a new nation, a new national identity and the image of the Chinese after the

'Cutting of the queues and modernizing of clothing' needed some sort of validation, and film provided just the means and the medium for such a validation of the new identity and image. However, due to the technological conditions of the day, the Chinese first saw their own screen image through the lens of the stereotyped Western conception. The national image they saw was unrecognizable and intertwined with colonialism. Chinese audiences, especially the intellectual class, were deeply frustrated. As researchers pointed out, the beginning of the Republic of China came from the top down. The first to accept these changes were the revolutionaries and the intellectuals who accepted and practised revolutionary ideas. And with the mandatory and irrevocable nature of government edicts, this top-down movement reverberated through the broad spectrum of social classes, resulting in the Westernized Chinese image from Western film (mainly American) being the first to bring discomfort to the audiences of the intellectual class, who identified with the growing social angst.

We are all aware that, due to the scourge of colonialism, the image of the non-Western, non-Anglo Chinese people in Western films are mostly stereotyped, with a homogenous image used as a symbol to blanket a heterogeneous Asian people. The cinematic image of the Chinese and Asians in general was mostly that of robbers or bandits. They were portrayed as low-class, ugly, timid, weak or violent and rude. Chinese thinkers couldn't disagree more with the image of Chinese in American films. They felt this distortion of their national image to be a horrendous and humiliating shame. So, endeavouring to break the stereotyped onscreen image of Chinese, and showing the true Chinese image to the world, became an all-important mission for Chinese production companies. Chou Chien-yün pointed out that, whenever there were Chinese characters featured in an American film, they were most certainly depicted as, 'Ignoble, dirty, barbaric and crude'. He called for 'strong public backlash' against what he called 'poor-quality films'. He advocated for a positive action, specifically, that the Chinese people start their own film companies, so as to 'Make films that depict the nobility and gracefulness of the Chinese nation and send them out to Europe and America, not only to protect the Chinese people's rights, but also show the great spirit of the Chinese nation' (Chien-yün 1922).

Chou Chien-yün's views were representative of the time. For example, the article, 'Vanguard voices: The industrialists and capitalists heralding the improvement of the Chinese film industry', stated the following:

> The films now showing in Shanghai cinemas all hail from abroad. The manner in which they characterize our social customs bears not even the slightest resemblance whatsoever to the reality of our national conditions. These films, inevitably teeming with ignominy and falsity, beshrew our great nation. A case

exemplar, Chinese actors are surely depicted upon the screen as thieves or marauders. In addition, these actors, yclept Chinese in these films, are by-and-large not Chinese. Thus, the knife of effrontery cuts deep into our bosom. Even when the actors in these films are Chinese by blood, they are nothing but long-time immigrants from far-off lands, sans the slightest inking of China's true conditions. They play in pictures according to the depictions of their countrymen learnt in the novels penned by foreigners. Seeing this manner of film, our people cannot but feel disgraced. There are some among us who curse such filmmakers and the movies they make, still others wish to establish film companies of their own in our nation – to produce their own films. Films which would shine a positive light upon China; films which may give others a glimpse of the truth by stories of the martial arts and the chivalrous swordsman; films which let them know the pith of our Chinese people; films which show them the singularity of our nation.

(Chien-yün 1922)

In 1920, the Great Wall Film Company was established in the United States on account of the prevailing dissatisfaction with the image of the Chinese people in American films. As Ku Chien-ch'en said,

In May of the same year (referring to the tenth year of the Republic of China), a Cantonese individual named Lam Hon-saang and others enrolled in acting workshops and film schools in the United States, as they had tired of the indignation they felt and the insults to their Motherland. They entered these academies determined to learn filmmaking techniques and master the use of filmmaking technology. In the 11th year of the Republic of China, the studio produced two shorts featuring Chinese Kung Fu and clothing styles, in the hopes of rehabilitating the reputation of Chinese people that had been lost through these unfair and inaccurate portrayals.

(Chien-ch'en 1996: 1362)

Ouyang Yü-ch'ien wrote the 'Star Motion Picture Company manifesto' that further stated,

China has its own superb ideas, pure ethics and straightforward customs that carry on its thousands of years of honorable history. If such a history can be introduced to Europe and America, the Western world will finally catch a good glimpse of the world's hitherto unfamiliar side, and new trends and thought can be birthed and thence be spread throughout the world.

(Yü-ch'ien 1926: 46)

Similar opinions were espoused in the reviews. The film *Yen Jui-sheng* was released at the San-san Cinema in Shek Tong Tsui, Hong Kong. Upon learning of the plot, some commentators remarked,

> This film, which should herald our national glorification, is terribly unsavory (Yen kills a harlot – author's note) with all manner of vile filth appearing upon the screen. Most of the Chinese characters assume the roles of knaves and rogues in American films. Our own nations' film producers should promote our virtue and culture, so that people who would otherwise view our Chinese people as something akin to an odious lag or a repugnant footpad shall have a change of heart about the matter, and perchance begin to think our race to be meek and benign. It is doubtless that this is the aspiration of the producers…
> (Hsing-sheng 1926: 136)

The hope for Chinese cinema was signified in the shaping of a new Chinese image to let the world see China in a new light. 'Appearances' in the eyes of others is an idea that is embedded right at the very core of the national-consciousness in Chinese film and played important role in their development and was seen repeatedly in early Chinese films. For example, in the film *For The Righteousness*,

> Scenes of freedom fighters battling against the police, in which both sides fight with courageous hardiment added considerable luster to the film and shall surely yerk the foreigners to admire our national fighting skill. However, the egregious misconduct in scenes of mallecho played against the Hu Ch'in character on the part of the police inspectors could have been done without, otherwise the foreigners shall think ill of our police detectives.
> (Hsien-tsang 1924)

Much of the content of *Soul of the Jade Pear*, which was adapted from a novel published ten years prior, was the object of critics' scorn at the time of its release for being terribly 'antiquated'. One review stated,

> A widow scruples not to parle with a man in the still of night, but when parley turns to remarriage, she believes pudency and sanctity to be paramount, therefore, in a world where the rational minds had long denied mercenary marriage, she thus found herself quelled, and quailed to be betrothed to her suitor or to shun that which her father bade of her. Such a pathetical show upon the screen makes it seem as if they were tarring on the archaic Oriental virtues of marital sanctity and mercenary marriage to be thrust yarely into the Westerners' gaze!
> ('Review of the death of Yuli' 1924)

These critiques pervaded reviews and permeated the visions of readers of the day.

Strongly competitive overtones were formed under the treatment of 'the Self' and of 'the Others'. After Chou Chien-yün called on China to set up a company and make films in the country, he immediately made a statement,

> After worldwide dealings began, it became apparent that anything previously held to never possibly happen had thus happened, and once it occurred, there must certainly be a reason and a value in its existence lest it cease to exist. Thus, we should never refuse to know the affairs of other nations. The film industry has been developing in the West for many years now, and it has achieved monumental innovation and progress. As for we Chinese, the requisite courage needed to alter the course of our destiny has been lacking until now, though it's better late than never.
>
> (Chien-yün 1922)

Consequently, just as with other Chinese national industries, there was a palpable ideological fervour in the country's early film industry, namely to catch up with all deliberate speed. Throughout the development of China's modern and contemporary history, 'catching up' has always been issue number one on the developmental agenda of modern Chinese society, which is exemplified by an early Chinese film market that was basically in the hands of the West and the Japanese. Chain cinemas such as the Apollo Theater, the Shanghai Grand Theatre, Ellen's Action Theater, the Republican Cinema and Ramos Entertainment are flagship cases. With the aid of these theatre chains, pre–World War I French films and post–World War I popular American films whose tickets were in high demand at the time had essentially monopolized Shanghai film market, making it a playground for foreign flicks and strange screendoms. So, at the time Chinese film producers often appealed to the idea of, 'Making the most perfect Oriental film to compete with Europe and the United States'. 'To compete against Europe and the United States, Chinese movies must go out to the world, they must receive worldwide distribution just like their European and American counterparts. Chinese cinematic exports should show the beauty of Chinese culture through film'. This was a popular view of the film industry at the time.

After more than a hundred years of development of the Chinese film industry, our heated discussion on the stiff competition in overseas market seems to be a response to the topic of the rise of Chinese cinema. International competitiveness for Chinese film is a long-term cultural mission.

Part 2: The East and the West

National identity choices in China and the West means the establishment of a national self-image that focuses on whether the on-screen imagery can be identified with, and also means focus on the pursuit of a 'Chinese' cinematic identity. Essentially, the pursuit of ethnicity in film, which touches on the ontology of film. The question of what kind of film is truly Chinese. In other words, the nature, content and form of Chinese film. When matching up with European and American movies and traditional Chinese and local entertainment, early Chinese films must be selected for both form and content.

As mentioned above, early Chinese films came out at the time of dramatic change in modern Chinese society, namely the transition from ancient empire to modern nation-state. In the process of this transformation, China gradually opened its doors to Western civilization and culture. Strictly speaking, the influence of Western culture on China can be traced back to the late Ming and early Qing dynasties. With the entry of Western missionaries into China, knowledge of Western geography, mathematics, astronomy and water conservancy, artillery manufacturing, philosophy, logic and art began to be introduced into China. Yet mere introduction of this knowledge did not bring about any particularly obvious shock to Chinese traditional society. That is, until the Opium War, when the severely wounded Qing Empire truly realized the sheer level of advancement of Western civilization and tried in vain to modernize. From the Westernization Movement, the Reform Movement of 1898, the Revolution of 1911 and the New Culture Movement, China's new transformation underwent an all-consuming process that ranged from technology to politics to thought. In this process, there has been unending controversy, screaming, wailing and gnashing of teeth, centred around the basic question of how to learn from the West and while protecting China's own indigenous culture. The Westernization Movement proposed 'Learning foreign technology to counter foreign invasion', and 'Retaining the essence of China while learning practical Western methodology' for the purposes of jump-starting industry, enriching the country, strengthening the military and developing modern education built upon the preservation of the prevailing political system. The failure of the Westernization Movement triggered the call for political reform in China. The failure of the Reform Movement of 1898, which advocated institutional reforms and upgrades, triggered the radical Revolution of 1911. At the beginning of the revolution, the seesaw battle of the New Republic and the restoration of the old dynasty reflected the fact that the traditional ideology and culture were still deeply-seated. The chaos of World War I in Europe aside, some intellectuals in China doubted the advanced nature of Western civilization in the process of introducing new Western learning. Consequently, at the beginning of the establishment of the Republic, after the system was firmly in place, next came the cultural-level debates. Which is to say, the transformation of China's modern state had graduated from the lower order of mechanization and productivity to the higher order of Chinese and Western cultural issues.

In 1915, *New Youth Magazine* and *Oriental Magazine* took the lead in discussing the cultural difficulties between the East and the West, which opened the floodgates of the debates about Chinese and Western cultures. The debates raged on for more than a decade, and hundreds of scholars centred their discussions on the characteristics of Chinese and Western civilization, culture and the direction of Chinese culture. The conservatives advocated for, 'Rooting China's new destiny in Confucianism', while the revolutionaries advocated for wholesale Westernization. As Chinese Communist Party co-founder, Ch'en Tu-hsiu once argued,

> Should we desire the construction of a new Westernized nation and organizing of a new Westernized society in the hopes of survival in this world, then we must first import the foundation of the Westernized society and state. Specifically, new beliefs in equality and human rights. Confucianism is fundamentally incompatible with this new society, new nation and new belief system. We must have complete awareness and fearless determination. The mistakes of the past must be swept away, and the prospects for a bright future must be ushered in! Otherwise, progress shall surely stagnate, and we shall undoubtedly be left once again with severe decline and certain doom!
>
> (Tu-hsiu 1916: 2)

This intense opposition between the old and the new became the feature of the cultural debate during the May 4th Movement.

Into the 1920s, due to witnessing the chaos of the war in Europe and learning more about European capitalist society, some intellectuals began doubting so-called 'scientific development' instead reverting to traditional Chinese culture and asserting that the losses of the West could be compensated for through Oriental civilization. Meanwhile, the expectations for China were high and it was believed that Chinese culture could create a new cultural system that could contribute mightily to the world after absorbing certain aspects of Western civilization. During this period, Liang Ch'i-Ch'ao's *Records of an Excursion Through the Heart of Europe* and Liang Shu-ming's *Eastern and Western Cultures, and Their Philosophy*, were most works at the forefront of this movement and produced a wide range of influences. Liang Ch'i-Ch'ao believed that China would have a great responsibility to its future, which was '[t]o further Chinese civilization through Western civilization, and to make up for shortcomings in Western civilization with aspects of Chinese civilization, thus merging them into a wholly new civilization'

(Chi-Ch'ao 1985: 371). Liang Shu-ming also supported Congruity Theory. In one breath, he acknowledged the advanced material life of Western civilization, believing that Western culture should be absorbed, and that fundamental transformation should take place. At the same time, he also advocated, 'Bringing back the China's former disposition', which he believed to be the fundamental spirit of the traditional Chinese 'The Chinese attitude as one of harmonization through adjustment' (Shu-ming 1985: 393–435).

At the beginning of 1920, when Chinese cinema had just embarked on a new path of exploration, it just so happened to coincide with the height of the debate between Chinese and Western cultures. Although to this day there is still a considerable distance between the two stances of the ideological and academic circles with respect to the popular entertainment industry, the relationship between the two is not clear at present, but the cultural debate is involved in many intellectuals. As a cultural symbol of the times, it undoubtedly has had universal impact. Actually, in the first half of the 1920s, the debate on 'Chinese style' versus 'European style' in Chinese film reviews could be regarded as a 'cultural debate' in the entertainment industry. It was the same as the cultural debate in ideological circles and poses the question of Western choices for Chinese films.

Movies were imported from the West, so the exploration of early Chinese films is based on the European and American films. The ultimate goal is to find the film style that the Chinese audience identified with, to establish the ethnic characteristics in Chinese movies and location of the 'Chinese' identification in the process. Similar to the process of Western film evolution, Chinese films were mainly intertwined with popular traditional Chinese entertainment, such as variety acts, opera, raree shows and the like. On the other hand, through the introduction of civilized drama and translated fiction, early Chinese films also absorbed Western literary and artistic works, including serious literature, such as Tolstoy's *Resurrection*; Alexandre Dumas' *The Lady of the Camellias*; Maupassant's *Necklace*; Oscar Wilde's *Lady Windermere's Fan*, as well as popular melodramas after the end of the nineteenth century, such as *East Lynne* and *Sans Famille*. During this period, the words 'Chinese style' and 'Europeanization' appeared frequently in film reviews, and there were whispers and rumblings of the evils of 'Europeanization'. Film is closely related to the psychology of national identity. During this period, 'Chinese style' and 'Europeanization' of the image style appeared repeatedly in the film reviews. To some extent, this echoed the greater cultural debate of the day. The early development of the film and the construction of a national identity for the Chinese nation moved together in stride. Film is closely related to the psychology of national identity. Because Chinese film shoulder the historical responsibility of establishing national identity, and Europeanization became a depreciating force and a pejorative in the cultural context of the time, one of the important topics of

China's film research in the 1920s is to explore, organize and analyse how Chinese films absorbed the influence of European and American films, and established themselves through Chinese and Western choices.

Japanese scholar Yamamoto Kikuo was the first to observe the establishment of early Chinese films through the lens of influence from European and American movies in *The History of Japanese, American and European Comparative Films: The Influence of Foreign Films on Japanese Films*. From the date of his birth in 1899 to the establishment of the Japanese film art system in 1935, Japanese cinema had undergone a lengthy process of imitation and pastiche of the Western influences for more than 30 years. French comedies, Western European art films, German Expressionism, French Impressionist cinema and early Soviet films successively influenced Japanese films at the budding stage. In the 1920s, with the establishment of Hollywood, American motion pictures grew in global popularity, and naturally became the primary model for Japanese motion pictures. The influence of European and American movies on Japan lasted until the first half of the 1930s. Yamamoto Kikuo explores all aspects of the influence of European and American movies on Japanese movies through a wealth of historical materials. His comparative research method has very important reference value for us in our research on the formation process of early Chinese film.

Of course, Chinese cinema and Japanese cinema are markedly different, both in terms of the number of productions turned out and in terms of the breadth and depth of the influence of European and American cinema. However, the above-mentioned comparative perspectives help us to understand anew the formation and evolution of early Chinese cinema from a novel perspective. The choices Chinese filmmakers make in imitating European and American films form two main aspects of similarity and difference, from which exactly how Chinese film creates an identity for its 'self' under the influence of foreign film culture while preserving its own cultural uniqueness is distinctly visible. These two levels together constitute film with Chinese characteristics. Yamamoto Hikuo said, 'Taking "comparison" into consideration is taking the essence of Japanese cinema into consideration'. Similarly, the influence of European and American cinema on China and the cultural choices that Chinese filmmakers made in choosing to put either Chinese and Western cultural elements into their films will be explored, which will help the reader to grasp the essence of Chinese film.

Part 3: Tradition and Modernity

In *The History of the Chinese Film Industry*, Ch'eng Shu-jen pointed out that the idea for film originated in China. Emperor Wu of Han's shadow puppet theatre was film's earliest known origin. It became popular after the Song Dynasty, and even in modern times there are old-style movies everywhere. He quoted the introduction article from the *Shen Pao Newspaper*. From Zhejiang, Hangzhou, West Lake to Gansu in the northwest, Luanzhou in the east of Hebei Province to Hu'nan in the South, there are different forms of these old-timely 'movie' performances. Though it may be different in form, the basic principles are very similar. They are all made of thick paper or sheepskin, controlled by lifting lines placed behind the paper curtain, and projecting the image by oil lamps so that the viewers can see the shadow of the activity. Working with the shadow performers of these performances are singers; therefore, there were usually opera troupes in these old-time movies, which sing the stories, bang gongs and handle the minutiae of the performance. Most of the material of the old film plays comes from historical novels and ghost stories, such as *Romance of the Three Kingdoms, The East Zhou Dynasty, Book of the Kingdoms, Biographies of Fengshen, Journey to the West, Legend Of The General Who Never Was, Expedition to the West* and *Madame White Snake*. There were also descriptions of family, social and political customs. The audience for these performances was rural folk (Shu-jen 1926: 1321–22).

Ch'eng Shu-jen traced the origin of the movie back to the shadow puppet theatre that began in the Han Dynasty in China and revealed the idea that became a national habit. Yet upon careful scrutiny, the similarities between the old movie and the new movies, essentially a screen and a moving image, notwithstanding, the basic principles are fundamentally distinct. The Western movie is rooted in modern science such as chemistry, optics, electrical engineering, electrical power and so forth. It transforms reality into an on-screen image, while the image of ancient Chinese movie is a crude simulation. Most importantly, there is only an approximation of the effect between old movies and what we call movies nowadays, but there is no technical continuity. They two are nearly as different as night and day. Therefore, Chinese shadow puppet theatre as the origin of the movie is more of an exercise in self-esteem and national cultural respect than an academically persuasive argument.

Nevertheless, Ch'eng Shu-jen's historical narrative provides an inspiration for us to understand the early Chinese cinema. In other words, although the old shadow theatre differs greatly from film in technology and form, there is a latent consistency or continuity in material and aesthetic acceptance. The shadow of early Chinese film is apparent in the old shadow puppet theatre, which is the combination of image and traditional historical novels and ghost stories. Ancient shadow puppet theatre arguably has given birth to the projection technology that was eventually used in movies. While the technology may have changed, the basic materials and narratives have remained unchanged. Traditional entertainment content has transformed into new forms of modern entertainment, which became an important way for early Chinese films to establish themselves. The fact of the matter is, this fits perfectly with common patterns of world film development. Early movies constantly drew from traditional forms of entertainment, such as Vaudeville acts and stage plays in the United States, and gradually transformed them from traditional entertainment consumer products into pure filmed entertainment consumption products. For early Chinese movies, this transformation is manifested by the localization of foreign entertainment. From the shorts filmed in Beijing at the beginning of the twentieth century to the short film of Asia proper to early 'commercial' film productions, to the costume films made in the middle of the twentieth century, the indispensable role of traditional resources in early Chinese movies is vividly apparent.

Among the short films produced by the Asia Films Company, *The Filicide Case*, *The Long Slope* and *The Sacrifice to the Yangtze River* were all adapted from Chinese traditional opera repertoire. In 1920, Mei Lanfang's *Ch'un Hsiang Disturbs the Class* and *Heavenly Maidens Shower the Earth in Blossoms* were produced by The Commercial Press, which had just made its bid to enter the film market, and the greater film business proper, continuing down the path of drawing inspiration for new productions from traditional resources. In 1921, the Chinese Film Production Company made the opera film *Four Heroes Village*. Beijing Opera adapted *Four Heroes Villages* from the chivalrous novel *The Green Peony* published in the Daoguang period of the Qing Dynasty. The story is about Lo Hung-hsün, the son of a famous general, who was falsely accused of stealing and therefore imprisoned in Beijing. On the way, he is abducted by his enemy, Chu to the Four Great Villages. The servant reports to him in written correspondence, and the heroes such as Hsiao Chi, Pao Shih-an and Hua Chen-fang rescue Lo Hung-hsün. In the first few years of the 1920s, quite a few films produced by the Commercial Press were taken from traditional dramas and novels, such as *The Lotus Flower* (1922), adapted from *Cheng Yüan-ho Singing Folk Stories*, *A Pious Wife's Stew* and *The Dream of a Taoist Priest*, adapted from the short amazing *The Stales Coral* and *The Laoshan Taoist* in Pu Songling's *Strange Stories from a Chinese Studio*. In 1925, The Star Motion Picture Company brought Pu Songling's *Carmine* from *Strange Stories from a Chinese Studio* to the screen.

By the mid and late 1920s, this kind of creative thinking that benefited from producing traditional-style Chinese entertainment adapted from Chinese operas and novels gradually came to prominence. Costume films, swordplay films and ghost stories taken from traditional content formed the first creative peak in the history of Chinese cinema. Despite the fact that the good, the bad and the ugly had all been represented as a group within this cinematic smorgasbord, the general quality of the film was on a steady decline, and waves of chiding criticism and biting backlash came pouring in from critical media circles. Be that as it may, a number of costume films and swordplay films had stirred the heart of the Chinese and ignited their sense of national identity through these traditional narratives, which enabled audiences to gain national identity through stories of history, while the power of the national sport of Chinese martial arts was a physical inertia that served as a foil for the Western technical power, greatly satisfying the Chinese people's proud sense of national identity. So, from the perspective of the genesis of the costume and swordplay film production trend in the 1920s, it turns out that commercial demand is only one piece of the greater puzzle. From the perspective of a deep-seated national psychology, these films captured the Chinese people's imagination and tickled their fancy by telling stories of defeating the enemy which appealed to need for an idealized Self. They enjoyed the pleasure of freedom through images of transcending the limitations of physical potential and exploring the potential of their own imagination, while at the same time expressing the joys of being Chinese. And so, this was arguably the only way for Chinese films to find their own national identity.

At the same time, the modernity aspect of early Chinese film cannot be overlooked. After the mid-1980s, American scholars Tom Gunning and Miriam Hansen introduced various aspects of the concept of modernity into early film studies. Hansen proposed 'Vernacular Modernism' and holds that cinema adds to the various contradictions of modernity from different emotional levels and projects the profound influence of modern technology on the human experience at a sensory level. Hansen expressed,

> While the spread of urban-industrial technology, the large-scale disembedding of social (and gender) relations, and the shift to mass consumption entailed processes of real destruction and loss, there also emerged new modes of organizing vision and sensory perception, a new relationship with 'things', different forms of mimetic experience and expression, of affectivity, temporality, and reflexivity, a changing fabric of everyday life, sociability, and leisure. From this perspective, I take the study of modernist aesthetics to encompass cultural practices that both articulated and mediated the experience of modernity, such as the mass-produced and mass-consumed phenomena of fashion, design, advertising, architecture and urban environment, of photography, radio, and cinema. I am referring to this kind of modernism as 'vernacular'.
>
> (Hansen 2009)

This vernacular 'Combines the dimension of the quotidian, of everyday usage, with connotations of discourse, idiom, and dialect' (Hansen 2009). Like Hansen, Tom Gunning re-interpreted early movies from the perspective of the modernity experience. He named the movies made before 1906 'Cinema of Attractions', which connotates that film does not rely on narrative to connect with the audience. It is not by creating a realistic illusion to passively immerse the audience, but by revealing the visual characteristics of the film, breaking a self-encased anecdotal world, and grabbing the attention of the audience as much as possible. The 'Cinema of Attractions' directly solicits spectator attention and incites visual curiosity, which is interesting in and of itself (Gunning 2009). No matter whether it's a close-up, a Méliès-style fantasy, a slow motion shot, a flashback, a body double, multiple exposures or some other means of cinematization, all served to strengthen the novelty of the film. Simply put, visual impact and landscape are the most important elements of Cinema of Attractions. Therefore, the 'Cinema of Attractions' is linked with the shock experience of modernity. Newly produced movies are seen as a concrete presentation of novel modern experiences. Gunning emphasized,

> No matter how we understand it, in modern culture, film is not only a practical activity, but also a decisive innovation force. In view of its great charm of the public mood, its mechanical strength and working style, its vigorous and contradictory tension between the picture and the movement, the film can be regarded as a metaphor of modernity.
>
> (Gunning 2010)

In fact, as Gunning said, when narrative film became the mainstream, the Cinema of Attractions existed in some way, such as avant-garde film practices, and it was also a component of narrative film. Looking back on Chinese films of the 1920s, we find that spectacle played an important role in the film of the era. In the 1920s, when the Commercial Press Movie Theatre produced, *Heavenly Maidens Shower the Earth in Blossoms*, some moving clouds were superimposed over the scenes of flying heavenly maidens in order to liven up the atmosphere and improve the aesthetics of the film (Jihua et al. 1963: 34). The multiple exposure technique became a common special effect in 1920s films. Pu Wan-tsang said in 'The Photography of Phantom',

> The film camera is really the most important piece of film-making equipment. Because it can often surprise the audience, such as the actor talking to himself; or the actor has a dream or as a ghost in the story, the person he dreamed of suddenly emerges from the same picture, or sees his body slowly disappear. And the general audience doesn't know how it was done. When the audience sees this kind of illusion, they aren't interested in the technical hows, so, the photographer can perform one or two kinds

of novel tricks in each production, which adds tremendous excitement to the film.

(Wan-tsang 1924)

It can be seen that early Chinese filmmakers had a clear conscious of the attraction of special effects pictures. Pu Wan-tsang then introduced in detail the shooting methods of double exposure and dissolve, including how to fade in and fade out (Wan-tsang 1924). Ch'eng Pu-gao wrote in *The Theory of Film Production*: 'In addition to introducing the general photographic methods, he also introduced the techniques of double exposure, iris-in, two kinds of stop camera techniques, stop-motion, and stop-action' (Pu-gao 1924). At that time, these techniques were real novelties to the audience.

Using double exposure effect to make the same actor appear in the picture at the same time, the early American films *The Prisoner of Zenda* and *Little Lord Fauntleroy* employed this technique, which was widely imitated in early Chinese movies, such as *Good Brother, The Gong of Warfare, The Children* and *Valley Orchid* and *Sister Flowers* in 1933. The use of this technique to create special effects provided viewing pleasure to eager Chinese audience thirsty for hipness in cinema. Influenced by the European and American movies, *Die Nibelungen* (1924) and *The Thief of Baghdad* (1925), in the mid and late 1920s, the enthusiasm for Chinese movies with special effects imagery and quality cinematography was funnelled into swordplay films, costume dramas and fantasy movies.

As a result, like many other backward modernizing countries, the modernity implied in Chinese cinema also shows ambiguous cultural characteristics due to the inextricable connection with tradition. It is embodied not only in the telling of traditional stories and display of national skills with the spectacular imagery, but also in the adaptation and localization of Western literary and dramatic works. Chinese films have attempted to integrate different cultures and values into their film narratives, and in the 1920s tried to integrate heterogeneous cultures and values into the film narrative. In this way Chinese film fed into and promoted the modern transformation of Chinese culture, thus realizing the construction of national identity.

REFERENCES

Bo, Chen (2005), *The Age of Chinese Film Editors: General Outline*, vol. 1, Beijing: Central Party Literature Press.

Chi-Ch'ao, Liang (1985), 'Journey through the heart of Europe (Extract)', in C. SongBian (ed.), *Selected Readings on the Pre- and Post-'May Fourth Movement' Cultural Debates*, Beijing: China Social Sciences Press, p. 371.

—— (1996), 'On the ethnicity in Chinese history', in C. QiTai, L. ShuQing and X. Shu (eds), *Selections of Liang Ch'i-Ch'ao Theory*, Guangzhou: Guangdong People's Publishing House, pp. 604–05.

Chien-ch'en, Ku (1996), *History of the Development of Chinese Films: China Silent Films* (ed. China Film Archives), Beijing: China Film Press.

Chien-yün, Chou (1922), 'Shadow opera chat', *Shen Pao Newspaper*, 15 March.

Gunning, Tom (2009), 'The cinema of attraction[s]: Early film, its spectator and the avant-garde' (trans. F. Bei), *Film Art*, 2.

—— (2010), 'Modernity and cinema: A culture of shocks and flows' (trans. L. YuQing), *Film Art*, 2.

Hansen, Miriam B. (2009), 'The mass production of the senses: Classical cinema as vernacular modernism' (trans. L. YuQing and Y. JingLin), *Film Art*, 5, London: Springer.

Hsien-tsang, Yen (1924), 'Comments on *For The Righteousness*', *Shen Pao Newspaper*, 1 April.

Hsing-sheng, Hsing (1926), 'Spring and Autumn on the screen', *Silver Light*, 1&2, *Chinese Silent Film*.

Hui, Wang (2004), *The Rise of Modern Chinese Thought: Empire and Nation*, vol. 2, Beijing: SDX Joint Publishing Company.

Huntington, Samuel P. (2005), *Who Are We? The Challenges to America's National Identity* (trans. C. KeXiong), Beijing: Xinhua Press.

Jihua, Cheng, ShaoBai, Li and ZuWen, Xing (1963), *A History of the Development of Chinese Films*, vol. 1, Beijing.

Po-ch'ang, Chou (1925), 'A review of Shanghai film industry in one year', *Shen Pao Newspaper*, 1 January.

Pu-gao, Ch'eng (1924), 'On film production', *Cinema Magazine*, 1–2, cited from *Chinese Silent Film*, pp. 952–58.

'Review of the death of Yuli' (1924), *Shen Pao Newspaper*, 12 May.

Shu-jen, Ch'eng (1926), 'The history of the Chinese film industry', *Chinese Silent Film*, pp. 1321–22.

Shu-ming, Liang (1985), 'Eastern and western culture and their philosophies (Extract)', in C. SongBian (ed.), *Selected Readings on the Pre- and Post-'May Fourth Movement' Cultural Debates*, Guangzhou: Guangdong People's Publishing House, pp. 393–435.

Tu-hsiu, Ch'en (1916), 'Constitution and Confucianism', *New Youth*, Item 3, November.

Wan-tsang, Pu (1924), 'Photography of Phantom', *Film Magazine*, 1, cited from *Chinese Silent Film*, pp. 950–51.

Wei, Qiu (2000), 'The trend toward queue shaving and clothing modernization after the Revolution of 1911', *Historical Review*, 2.

Yü-ch'ien, Ouyang (1926), Manifesto of Star Motion Picture Company, 1, Yü chieh Ping-ch'ing, *Chinese Silent Film*.

NOTE

1. In 1926, there were about 40 companies in Shanghai that had filmed films (see Volume I, Page 54, *The History of Chinese Film Development*, 1998). Compared with Chou Po-ch'ang's statistics of 1924, the actual scale and development speed of Shanghai Film Production Company in the mid-1920s can be seen more accurately.

12. The Optimistic Tradition in Early Chinese Films: A Perspective of Intellectual History

安燕/An Yan

The popularization of optimism in the Chinese cinema of the 1930s and 1940s not only spawned a major creative paradigm, but also gave way to an ethical idealism complex in Chinese films. Granted, in today's twenty-first-century Chinese films, very surprisingly, the ethical idealism paradigm and optimism principle of a large corpus of stories and endings lie in the infinite and incomparable vitality of its cultural constructs and cultural subconsciousness. The esteemed Gao RuiQuan pointed out that optimism is a powerful theme in spiritual mainstream of modern Chinese society:

> Chinese spirit is highly optimistic these days, due to the fact that modern China has experienced a historical transformation from a pre-modern to modern society. The premise of the modernity concept is, faith in progress and the triumph of progressivism, which has destined the banner of optimism to fly its colors high over the entire era. First of all, China's modern optimism is both world-view and history. It is also expressed as both epistemology and human nature. Chinese-style optimism can be described as the spiritual temperament of the natural needs of China's social revolution, which has existed for more than one hundred years. It also has an intrinsic connection with Utopian tradition, scientism, metaphysical voluntarism and utilitarianism of modern China.
>
> (RuiQuan 2011: 149)

The progressive films in the 1930s epitomized optimistic Meliorism, Salvationism, Moral Monism and the creation of an ideological path that set up a certain ideology with which to solve all problems that reflected typical Utopian characteristics at a time when ethnic conflicts had intensified, and Optimism had gained a self-evident rationality. This was oriented around the longing for a successful revolution, the yearning for an ideal life and a better future, as well as the anticipation of establishing a new social formation, and the desire for a modern society with independence, freedom and equality. The narrative choices of emerging films and national security cinema of the 1930s were either about the suffering of the lower classes, forcing them to revolt, defending the state against aggression, or the disclosure and criticism of the unacceptable dark side of society. Regardless of the theme, they are full of descriptions of poverty, suffering, indignity and oppression. But no matter how tragic the story was, the film had to end on a cheery note, to indicate a way out, to find an answer to the problem or to clearly point out prospects for resistance.

Raging Waves won critical acclaim for strengthening the theme of peasant struggle, for showing the way out of trouble, it '[e]xposed the ills and evils of the still extant embers of feudal society, portrayed the plight of the peasant struggle, and showed he way out for the masses'. 'This type of cinematic anti-feudal expose is very necessary in China today. The enlightenment movement in cinema shows us a very straightforward way out' (Nai-fang 1993: 414–16). Fang Yan praised *Goddess of Freedom* for showing the escape route for China's rebel girls.

> In real life, China needs an entire group of rebel girls to run after the original 'runaway rebel girl', in order to show the way for the next crop of rebel girls. In this respect, *The Goddess of Freedom* has provided answers for a generation of women who are terrified, tremulous, confused and wary.
> (Yan 1993: 56)

In *Soaring Aspiration*

> [o]ne may assume the transformation of this group of characters, to be overly optimistic, but the fact of the matter is, so long as you are unwilling to be a slave to a dead, colonized state, this transformation is inevitable. There are no mournful lamentations or gnashing of teeth in *Soaring Aspiration*. What everyone believes is that the power of the masses is the only real power. And so, the film is filled with the magic of youthful energy throughout, which is exciting.
> (Di 1937)

Wu Yung-kang's *Soaring Aspiration* is bursting with optimistic energy. It is worlds apart from his previous melancholy films, *The Goddess* and *Waves Washing the Sand*, and in it the reshaping and transformation of character of the intelligentsia in the Republican Era shone forth before our eyes. For those watered-down, aimless, ambiguous films, left-wing criticism was unrelenting.

Conscienceless is relentlessly sombre and bleak, especially the scene in which Chao Min-ch'ieh falls to the ground on his knees with his arms stretched to heaven after returning home, his life turned to black, unable to see the light, which contrasts sharply with the ending of Ding Ling's, At Daybreak, where everyone rushes to the center of town like torrential waves just at the first light of daybreak.

(Ch'en 1932)

Nowadays, the impetuous appeal to Consciencism in the bloody scenes in *Conscienceless* in the wake of the reign of terror of the Republican Era seems extremely dated. What our current era needs is not the conscience that has to be 'discovered through ethical exhortation and moral education'. What it needs is a 'conscience' that keeps pace with the times and fights the good fight. The traditional Confucian 'doctrine of the conscience' must be changed and transformed in light of a new era, to become a new morality accepted by the times. The inconclusive, irrelevant morality of the past is not only unhelpful, but actually harmful to progress in this era. No matter how dark reality seems, every intellectual with a conscience needs a pair of eyes to see the light at the end of the tunnel. They all need to have confidence and belief in the future, to be able to think optimistically and positively to fight on till the end. Based on this criteria, Chen Wu and Ling Ho once decried the ending of Oppression as, 'nothing but distorted nescience' (Ling Ho 1933). Likewise, Shu Yan held that *Oppression* concertedly skirted serious social problems in the hifalutin name of 'law and order' and was just an expression of preening, namby-pamby dogmatism. '*Oppression* is definitely not China's way out of darkness. It not only fails to find a correct path for the country, but itself leads to a dead-end. I found the solutions offered up in the film to be highly questionable. I thought that this film couldn't depict the negative social life of the declining people; it should have had a more positive meaning' (Yan 1933). *Cry of Women* is similarly wandoughty.

The directions to the way out of our collective quagmire are so vague and inane as to be disconcerting. For a film to be called Cry of Women, but be devoid of 'shouts' in actuality is something of a travesty, and a glaring flaw in the film.

(Feng 1933)

In *Night in the City*,

Strong social reform policies make the scenes of drag out the 'to the countryside' message at the end of the film, and actually confuse the cause and effect of social phenomena, causing the expose of the dark side of city life depicted in the film lose its meaning entirely!

(Xuan 1933)

Therefore, the 'realizations' in *Night in the City* are entirely 'off base'. The daughter in the film goes off to marry a young aristocrat on account of her father's illness. Her compromise is a result of the fact that she is not able to 'truly understand' class antagonisms: 'We need a new female warrior who is capable of sacrificing and never compromising' (Chen 1933). Refusal to compromise is a fighting stance. Only through battle can a new future ideal be won. This is an central connotation of optimism. Tsai Chu-sheng's, *The Pink Dream*, thus lacks a 'correct position' and 'realism'; *The Pink Dream* can be merely an empty and trivial pink dream. The screenwriter Mr Tsai Chu-sheng, 'Should be standing on the bottom rung of an oppressed weak minority hierarchy and disallowed from hiding away in his ivory tower singing the praises peace and joy, or singing odes to heaven, 'Oh blossoms, oh moon, oh my love! Remember, thou shalt never treat art as jest; we wish it to become a movement that hastens the ushering in of the new golden era'.[1] Although, *Plunder of Peach and Plum* is an excellent and exquisite film that adequately exposes the darkness of reality, the ending tragically offers neither an escape route nor an adequate solution. 'It does not show an obvious way out to the audience seeing its own decline unfold before its eyes! Perhaps this is the film's fatal flaw!' (Kang 1935). Such an excellent film as *Plunder of Peach and Plum* that shows the darkness of reality and the tragedy of life actually has increased critical depth and power in its tragic ending. However, this point is difficult to understand for the left-wing commentary at that time, but it has become the biggest failure of the entire film. Suffice it to say that this signifies the optimistic musings of left-wing thought.

Even though the film was accused of being powerless to 'hasten the realization of a golden new era' it did more or less unconsciously signify progressive intentions. Although Shen His-ling's *Cry of Women* did not actually 'cry out' and was a 'work of vaguery', it did depict an ideal in the heroine Yeh Lien's 'independence' and 'struggle' of resistance. With the sound of the first whistle of the morning at the end of the film, and the words of the revolution ranging in Shaoying the revolutionary heroine's ears, 'The individual struggle is futile, be strong and fight', the beautiful prospects of the revolution are suddenly revealed In front of her very eyes. Shen Hsi-ling's other film, *Homesick*, also tells the tragic experience of the heroine Yang Lan's exile in Shanghai and her resistance (Bing 1935). At the end of the film, Mei Hua, Yang Ying and a group of individuals who escaped from the war to their hometown commit themselves to a rescue. With blazing hues of firelight dancing across his face, Yang Lan's lover and spiritual teacher Mei Hua cries out, 'Where is the national spirit of China?' 'Where is China's youth?' It definitely sent out the cries of the War of Resistance, ending the author's pain in its tragic sentiments (Ho 1993: 313). Mei Hua and Yang Ying's cries, 'Made every member of the audience feel that it was time to take up the fight'. The screenwriter's tragic message was that everyone's hometown was in danger of perishing. In other words, the entire Chinese nation was about to perish. Where was the Chinese youth? Everyone had a responsibility for the future of the country. Although in the film, Mei Hua and Yang Ying have to face the tremendous pain of the demise of their home country, the cries for 'China's new youth! China needs you!' has repeatedly and powerfully expressed the strong optimistic theme that the 'New youth should be responsible for the country's future', and that 'The new youth was the hope of national salvation'. *The Boatman's Daughter* tells of a boatman's innocent daughter who turns to a life of prostitution under the pressures of a black-hearted society. Although at the end T'ieh-erh was once again imprisoned for smashing the brothel, 'Mr. Shen Hsi-ling is trying get to the essence of the issue, to let everyone know eliminating prostitution can't be solved by reformism' (Gang 1935). Only resistance and revolution like that of T'ieh-erh can win the day. Even if resistance comes at a huge price, it is the 'fundamental solution' to the problem. *The Crossroads* tells a story of the different encounters and choices of four unemployed college students. Brother Liu joined the anti-Japanese efforts. Hsiao Hsu committed suicide due to depression. Lao Chao and Ah-T'ang lose their jobs. At the end of the film, Lao Chao, Ah-T'ang and the same unemployed Yang Chih-ying and Sister Yao go forward unhesitatingly, indicating that the only way is living like Brother Liu.

Tsai Chu-sheng's *New Women* attempted to show three different types of woman in a transitionary period, Chang Hsiu-ch'i, a bourgeoisie female who indulges in pleasure, Wei Ming, a weak and less determined 'Chinese rebel girl' and enlightener of the working class, Li Ah-ying. Even if the image of the character is ambiguous and inadequate in the film, the director's intention is obvious: Li Ah-ying, a woman of beauty, will-power and bravery is the true New Women. Li Ah-ying is highlighted through symbolism in the film. In the light of early dawn, Wei Ming returns from the dance floor to Li Ah-ying, who is busily teaching the workers to sing the battle hymn, 'On the Huangpu River'. The shadow of a departing Li Ah-ying on the wall becomes deeper and more pronounced until it completely enshrouds Wei Ming's shadow. As the factory whistle blows, a group of female workers neatly dressed as combatants sing high-spirited marching songs. These women serve as the screen incarnation of millions of real-life Li Ah-ying in China, who became fully awakened 'New Women' marching on to the new life. Even Wei Ming's death does not stop Li Ah-ying's progress. Obviously, they were heading towards the new world that Wei Ming anticipated. As Cheng Jihua noted in the *The History of Chinese Cinematic Development*,

At the end of the film, the auteur beckons scores of woman workers to march forward, trampling on the newspapers reporting the news of Wei Ming's death, filled of optimism and inspiration, suggesting the struggle for human liberation. The prospects suggest that only the working class can shoulder the historical mission of overthrowing the old society.

(Jihua 1963: 339)

The image of the female roly-poly, who gets knocked down but gets up again, was featured several times in the film, and the hues of encouragement and the significance of optimism vividly colour every frame. Wang Ah-da in *The Beauty of Perfumed Grass* finally goes on to revolution after life deals him a knock-out blow. In prison, he tells his younger brother Lao 'erh, who was arrested and imprisoned for 'instigating a strike', 'I believe what you said, but what about the future?' To which his brother replies, 'There are poor people in every country, but as long as we all work together, we can go on to live in prosperity'. Despite the two of them being hurt by life, they nevertheless look forward to the future realization of the Utopia, regardless of their suffering. This is an example of the deep-rooted optimistic worldview in Chinese culture. It is difficult for any external suffering to shake the steely calm of their inner spirit. In *Three Modern Ladies*, written by Tien Han and directed by Bu Wan-tsang, the film affirms Chou Shu-chen's progress and struggles by contrasting the lives of three women, giving the character positive qualities. At the end, Chou Shu-chen is ousted from the telephone company for participating in a strike against the pay cuts and the unfair dismissal of workers. She poses the question to her mother, 'What is there to be afraid of, when we both have two hands?' Hearing what they say, the visiting Chang Yü realizes their lofty aspirations, and positive and optimistic attitude. Chang Yü is tremendously moved by their resolve and holds them by the hand for a long time. *Children of the Times*, written by Hsia Yan and directed by Li Ping-ch'ien, shows the power of the progressive worldview to overcome adversity. Dissatisfied with an arranged marriage, the male protagonist Chao Shih-ming leaves home, and gets involved in the 'May Thirtieth' anti-imperialist movement along with his fiancée Hsiu Lin. In the face of brutal repression, Hsiu Lin, who was born into a wealthy capitalist family, relented and returned to the comfort and safety of her family home, an act that only serves to strengthen Shih-ming's resolve. He tells Hsiu Lin, 'I have experienced a new awakening! My consciousness is now opposed to you. I live to fight a bloody battle against the old world, and to do that I must embark on a new path!' As the two divorce, Shih-ming says resolutely, 'The cruelty of history has led you down a regressive path. I know now that there more important things in life than love'. The harshness of survival in a cruel world and bitter struggle crushes the spirit of many but makes Chao Shih-ming all the more diligent. Next to a wheel in the machining room sits a beaming Chao Shih-ming, wiping away sweat as he waves to people. An ending of typical high-spirited optimism.

The air of optimism is one of the distinguishing features of 1930s progressive cinema. It is neither coincidental nor humanistic, but a universally ubiquitous influential ideology. Even if *Night in the City*, directed by Fei Mu, did '[m]ake great reformist and utopian socialist mistakes', it at least was attempting to '[p]ull back the curtain of the city enshrouded by night's darkness to find the light'. In *Dawn Over the Metropolis*, after Ch'i Ling rescues his miserable and tormented little sister from the hands of his nomadic half-brother, Hui Ling, 'They began to walk down the path to prosperity silhouetted against the backdrop of a blazing orb just peaking its head into the golden sky'. At the end of *The Wind*, Hsiao Ming is reunited with her family just as, 'The last remnants of night give way to the glowing embers of the morning shimmer over the skyline as the frenzied roar of the wind whips across a newly modernizing metropolis'. When the horn sounds at the end of *Existence of the Nation*, weapons are raised, and sudden and pounding waves of freedom fighters rush the anti-Japanese forces together in the spirit of solidarity. At the end of *Struggle*, a seriously injured Ken Fa dies with the smile of victory on his face after blowing up the enemy's armoured vehicles. At the end of *The Dawn*, Ah-Hsiang, who has engaged the enemy in close combat dies. The brilliant streaks of white blades set off against spurts of bright red blood somehow endows him with a certain subtle magnetism. The white rays of the morning sun ascending the crest of the mountain illuminate a banner waving against a liquid sky. At the end of *The Children of Troubled Times*, a poet Hsin Pai-hua, who is newly converted to the cause of revolution, meets with Ah-Feng amidst swarms of refugees in a wasteland decimated by gun and cannon fire. Their friendship, their feelings melt together into a white-hot magma of fervour for national self-defence. Fires burn, guns ring out, bugles rally the troops to charge, and quick as spitfire from a sub-machine gun, young and old, men and women, poets, farmers and soldiers alike bravely rush the enemy, their hearts aglow with the flames of patriotism in their heroic last-stand for their nation. At the end of *The Refugees* is a band of homeless refugees that has been awakened under the guidance of Hsiao Ying, 'At a stark and tenuous dawn, a tragic song fills the air. They carry their guns, raise their feet together in a march, and tread away stepping in time to the rhythm of the anthem'. In *Victory Song*, 'Soldiers relying on the power of their own solidarity and united efforts, press on tirelessly into the grey of dusk. They finally pass through the torrents of a rushing river and cheer in unison to the sound of a heroic victory song. At the end of *New Peach Blossom Fan*, the couple Fang Yü-min and Su Fang reunite, they suddenly heard that imperial troops have been sent to Chinan. Su Fang encourages Fang-yü min by saying, 'Our happiness is in the fight!' Fang-yü min bids farewell to Su Fang and rides to the front lines to fight against imperialism. At the end of *Life and Death*, Li T'ao, who was seriously injured in battle, encourages Chao Yü-hua and Liu Yuan-chieh to continue their work. 'As they mourn over his remains, it is as if they are seeing the great guiding light of Li T'ao's holy and great soul still leading the army forward with a smile!' (Bing 1993: 229–345). Whether it is 'step forward at the morning dawn' or 'step out of humiliation, and step into a new life' or 'be awakened and step into the light', or 'walk hand-in-hand and step together toward progress' or 'victory or death, step out from under oppression', these optimistic paradigms explored and developed in the progressive realist films of the 1930s were not only inflammatory at the time, but also belonged to any of the main-line films, such as hero films, revolutionary historical films, war films and even non-main-line films. The ideologies presented within produced a sweeping, reverberating impact, which not only passed on a certain set of artistic concepts, but also an embodied, a strong and a stable sense of identity in the spiritual world that passed on artistic value, as well as a stable worldview and ideology.

In the crop of directors from the 1930s, Sun Yü was recognized as most representative of Optimism and Romanticism. In an article entitled, 'Director, Blood of Love', Yü described his style, 'Just like in the film *Wild Rose*, I have always advocated for vitality of youth and life, a sound body, and a progressive spirit'. He went on to say,

> To the greatest extent possible, I have just wanted to depict as much of the pain of the lower classes as I can. I am not however a pessimist. I want those who are oppressed to realize the power in their pain, and that they need not be frustrated.
> (Yü 1932)

Ling Ho described Sun Yü as an 'optimistic, innocent, romantic, progressive, revolutionary poet' (Ho 1996: 1281–84). He believed that,

> From *Wild Rose*, and most especially in *The Little Toys*, the great Sun Yü was the very definition of a poet who has fully demonstrated his own unique style. He portrays 'youthful vigour' in a relaxed and vivid manner. He believes modern society to be dark, ugly and cruel, but he also believes the world itself to be beautiful. He has great hope for a brilliant future, and that the world is trending in a positive direction, because, after all, the lovely sunshine after the dark night is an inevitability. Most especially for the intellectuals who have

suffered greatly from the harshness of our reality. They expect an even better future than the rest of us.

(Ho 1934)

The Big Road was criticized in its day because of its leisurely and light treatment of an emotional subject, and for the interweaving of gimmicks into the plot and for distortion of the characters. However, in the film, 'In the screenwriter's passion and anticipation for change, he advocates for the battle cry of the anti-imperialist spirit', which is for the purposes of 'playing on our deepest sympathies' (Chou 1935). The optimism of the film is ubiquitous. When Chang Yi is unemployed and feeling dispirited, Chin Ko lifts his head, smiles and says, 'Unemployment is just a fact of life. Why should we feel bad?' And encourages everyone, 'Brother Chin's friends are all positive and optimistic!' At the end of the eighth scene, Brother Chin and other five people lead an alliance of more than fifty workers, marching happily to the countryside as the sun rises overhead, casting a silver lining around the clouds, symbolizing a bright future. Stepping forward at steady pace into the future is exactly the same as in the film, *Wild Rose*. The last shot of *The Big Road* was in the vision of Di Hsiang's who had luckily survived, standing up again with Brother Chin, Mo Li, Hsiao Lo, and the four of them pulling an iron roller forward, superimposed over the face of Ding Hsiang with the road song resounding through the sky. It is the sublimation of Brother Chin's death, which, on one hand implies an undying spirit and eventual resurrection. And on the other hand, implies that more people will be summoned to join the torrents of revolution until the revolution ultimately wins its final victory.

Sublimation is an extremely common aesthetic strategy in revolutionary films, which indicates the spiritual ascension and enhancement of a character, event, behaviour and some specific pattern through symbolic forms, making it the standard and demand of mainstream ideology. Sublimation embodies the most prototypical optimistic connotations. An optimistic longing for life and the revolutionary success, and an expectation of 'a truly human society' is the driving force behind Brother Chin and the other revolutionaries. At the end of *Daybreak*, Ling Ling was sentenced to death for setting free her revolutionary cousin, 'Please ask those soldiers who shot her if it happened at the moment that there was a beautiful smile on her face'. She said,

> The revolution will not break, one fell before it, and one came again. She died with a smile of victory, it was as if she could see her cousin and the revolutionary fighters were singing a military anthem and continuing to work hard in the darkness and onto a brilliant future!

(Chou 1935)

With the death of Ling Ling being sublimated, the film once again magnified the optimistic theme of bravery. Although Sun Yü's works contain scenes of great sorrow, such as the fatalistic understanding of human evil in the film *Going to Nature*, the terrifying memories of historical nightmares in the film of *The Little Toys*, he is optimistic and positive in general. Even though Aunt Yeh in *The Little Toys* experienced many painful experiences in life, at the end of film, she cries out, 'The enemy is coming! Let's go out and fight! Wake up, don't be dreamers!' It's not a nightmare of a madman, but a cry of an awakened individual. Sun Yü may be more willing to express his thoughts by Aunt Yeh. Some have criticized Sun Yü's blind allegiance to, 'the doctrine of diligence' and 'unshakable optimism'. (Wei, 1936) In fact, this 'doctrine of diligence' and 'optimism' were not unique to Sun Yü but was a common trend that had come into vogue in the progressive films in the 1930s and 1940s. However, Su Yü's romantic spirit and poetic temperament reinforced the escapist fantasy that is 'optimism', causing it to split into rigorous realism or critical realism. Progressive optimism is the inevitable evolution in the whole of the twentieth century.

Part 2

After the war in the 1940s, progressive films took a step forward in expanding the depth and breadth of critical realism. In the expression of optimism, it was no longer as superficial and direct as in the 1930s. Some excellent films such as *The Spring River Flows East, Eight Thousand Miles of Cloud and Sky, Myriad of Lights, Sorrows of a Bride, Long Live the Wife, Unending Love,* and others are even tragedies or full of scenes of tragedy, seemingly the polar opposite from optimism, but these films either have optimistic circumstances within the plot or hint at optimism; the former are the films *The Spring River Flows East, Eight Thousand Miles of Cloud and Sky,* the latter is *Myriad of Lights.* One of the three threads running through *The Spring River Flows East* is the positive anti-Japanese thread represented by Chang Chung-min and Wan Hua. This thread is repeatedly repressed due to the threat of political persecution and is relatively obscure. But the director's desire to use this thread to hint at the bright side of China is rather obvious. This thread is what the hope in the film rests on. The first half of *Eight Thousand Miles of Cloud and Sky* depicts a group of progressive patriotic youths represented by Chiang Ling-yü and Kao Li-pin, who enthusiastically embarks on the journey and promote the anti-Japanese war, 'Arise! All those who don't want to be slaves!' calling out zealous anti-Japanese slogans are rife with evocative messages trumpeting the call of war.

Although, *Myriad of Lights* tells a tragic tale of the life, livelihood, family disputes and unemployment of the plagued protagonist Hu Chi-ch'ing, after experiencing a great many trials and tribulations, he is ultimately awakened. When he comes home from the hospital, he wakes up from a coma and hears his mother say that he should not trust the capitalist Chien Chien-ju. He should instead learn from the progressive Hsiao Chao and Ah-Chen. He remarks, 'This is what I should be doing'. The film clearly indicates that, after Hu Chi-ch'ing's awakening, only being like Hsiao Chao and Ah-Chen, a person of solidarity and fraternity, optimism and confidence, will he be granted a remarkable future. Most of the progressive films of the 1940s showed a clear optimistic intention, which also affirmed the continuation of Chinese film lineage.

In 1947, Chen Li-t'ing directed *Far Away Love* at the Second China Film Workshop, and tells the story of Yü Chen, a maid from the countryside. Under the encouragement and enthusiasm of the national anti-Japanese, she left her husband Hsiao Yüan-his, an intellectual who was alienated from the era and disregarded the national interests of the country, and firmly committed herself to the anti-Japanese war. Hsiao Yüan-hsi found Yü Chen on the way to escape and asked to remarry. Yü Chen asked him to discuss this topic after the victory of the anti-Japanese war. The last shot of the film is that of Hsiao Yüan-hsi, stunned and helplessly watching Yü Chen, vital and shining like the sun, heading into the sunset. *Along the Sungari River*, directed by Chin Shan, is a film that overtly depicts the struggle of the Northeasterners in Manchuria and their fight against the Japanese Empire. A youth and a granddaughter in the film grow up in the shadow of the decimation of the Japanese army. The kind and naïve young guy who used to live a simple peasant's life becomes an awakened warrior who combines personal destiny with national destiny. The granddaughter hones herself to become strong. The development model of the film follows the typical optimistic path: from weak to strong, from spontaneous to conscientious, from the individual to the nation. *Spring Couldn't Be Locked Away*, directed by Kun Lun, Wang Wei-I and Hsu Wei, tells the story of a petty-bourgeois intellectual female Mei Chun-li who recaptures her youth out of the clutches of frailty. Her husband Wu Ching regards her as a plaything there for his own amusement, wilfully forcing her into bondage. With the help of progressive intellectuals such as Lin Erh-wen and Ch'en Yün-ch'i, she begins to resist and grows determined to divorce Wu. One stormy night, she flees the gilded prison that is their villa and goes to her sister-in-law, Lin Erh-wen's farm. When Wu Ching tries to raise a mob to take her back and terrorizes her with a gun, a crowd comes out from all directions to support Mei Chun-li. They take up arms in preparation for a battle. Wu Ching puts down the gun in fear, and fleas the scene like a scared dog without its master. Chun Li falls to her knees and weeps in a fit of emotional catharsis, and the crowd lifts her and walks forward. The film depicts Lin Erh-wen's farm as a bright, desirable place, a spiritually vibrant domicile. The film attempts to depict it as an unreal utopia, but the moral ideal expressed throughout the film is the spirit of experimentation and 'in unity there is power', with connotations such as spiritual rebirth, which colours the film with a dab of optimism.

Three Women, written by T'ien Han and directed by Ch'en Li-t'ing, is also about growth and progress, but there are slight differences between the film and *Three Modern Ladies*. Yü Yü, a character in 'Three Modern Ladies', has completely degenerated. Chen Jo-ying dies of illness. In the film *Three Women*, Liang Jo-ying is weak-willed and is given over to life's pleasure and creature comforts. Chin Mei who makes a living by selling her body wants to commit suicide, but they both become strong and turn their lives around with the help of a young progressive, Li Hsin-ch'ün. Liang Jo-ying, who is weak-willed, pleasure-seeking, and Chin Mei, who sells her body to desires her own death, become strong and go on to a new life. The 'new life' connotations in *Three Women* are clearer and stronger than in *Three Modern Ladies*, and its sense of optimism is stronger. *Hope in the World*, directed by Shen Fu, portrays archetypical imagery in the character of Teng Keng-pai, a university professor of revolutionary heroism. He actively resists Japan and sacrifices himself to save others. At the end of the film, 'He is taken prisoner at dawn when the crow of the cock breaks the morning silence'. It goes without saying that there is optimistic significance in the cock crowing at dawn.

> These characters in the film show that people like Teng Keng-pai are not only one or few but are many. They are being refined and tempered by the pressure of reality and moving towards a revolutionary path, where thousands of revolutionaries will stand together in solidarity. This is an inevitable truth.
> (Jihua 1963: 236–38)

Winter of Three Hairs, written by Yang Han-sheng and directed by Chao Ming and Yan Kung, is story based on Chang Le-ping's comics. Through the encounter of San Mao, it reconstructs the unfortunate fate of homeless children and satirizes and exposes the darkness of the feudal society of old China. Although the film depicts the suffering of San Mao, and at the film's end has him leave the opulence of a wealthy manor and return to the homeless children, the director gives San Mao an indomitable, fearless tenacity, fully convincing people that 'San Mao and other countless homeless children like him are destined for a brilliant future'. They are aware that a bright, beautiful world must exist. The cold and bitter rambling for countless scores of homeless children must come to an end and they can go on to live a life of warmth and dignity fit for every human being (Jihua 1963: 241). The optimism of *Winter of Three Hairs* is apparent through its stylings.

Crow and Sparrow, written by Ch'en Pai-lu, and directed by Cheng Chün-li, tells the story of a group of characters that truly and profoundly presents the darkness and disintegration of the KMT-controlled areas on the eve of liberation. Citizens under pressure are awakened and depict a society on the edge of enlightenment.

At the end of the film, K'ung Yu-wen returns home as people are gathering there for the New Year's Eve dinner. He puts a pair of Spring Festival couplets on the door. It is 'The booming of firecrackers outside that can clear out the old, while Spring Festival couplets can bring a new life'. A new year, a new climate and a new life are on the way. *The Dawning*, written by Hung Shen and directed by Ying Yün-wei, adopted a cross-sectional structure, which was rare in early Chinese motion pictures. The film shows a wide variety of people gathered in a small hotel on account of a car breakdown. The film tells of a selfish and bossy hotel owner, Wu Wen-mo, an aggressive and cruel Mr Lin, and a group of young people who are positive and progressive. As stated in *The History of Chinese Cinematic Development*, the screenplay was written in anticipation of the victory of the anti-Japanese war. Ying Ju, Tsung-chün, et al. 'Represent the new blood, who rush to the vanguard, this shows that the author had a great goal in mind when he wrote the piece, which was to persuade the people to turn away from the dark past and look toward the brilliant future'. At the end of the film, 'The moment the cock crows at dawn, Ying-ju, Tsung-chün, Lan-yan, Wen-hui, Wen-yü, an elderly woman, and Wang K'uei-fang all riding in chauffeur Yang's car, driving forward onto the great expanse of open road ahead!' (Jihua 1963: 301–02). *Wild Fire and Spring Wind*, written by Yi Ch'ün and directed by Ouyang Yü-chien, was completed in 1948, and tells the story of a demure female artist, Fang Hua and her journey from weakness to awakening. Ultimately, as Fang Hua hears the song of the wildfire being sung by youths outside, she herself is ravaged and feeble but seems to be heeding some kind of call. She climbs out from bed and walks dodderingly towards the fire. She falls to the ground and begins crawling with all her might towards the light. Although she is on the ground in a subdued state, the sublimation of her spirit is clear to see, and eternal life is hers. Outside, the songs of the youth become louder and brighter, gradually enveloping everything. At the end of the story, there is a voice-over that highlights the main theme, 'What is destroyed leave to the fire, what is fallen leave at the funeral pyre; like a wildfire in spring breeze is rebirth, shining its glory down upon the good earth'. There is twofold optimism of, *Wild Fire and Spring Wind*: one is that Fang Hua's body is dead, but her soul is eternal; the other is that the winds of change and the fires of refinement sweeping across the land would surely usher in a bright future.

Optimism did not appear solely in Mandarin film, but the optimistic leanings in the Cantonese films from the era are quite obvious. *The Dawn Must Come*, produced by the Naam Gwok Film Company was written by Chan Caan-wat, directed by Wong Wai-yat, and is a story of class struggle. It was highly praised at the time and was deemed a 'revolutionary masterpiece of Cantonese film'. At the end of the film, 'The group of people who have been through painful experiences together finally board a ship bound for their liberated hometown' (Jihua 1963: 323–32). If the main goal of the optimistic paradigm of 1930s progressive film was mainly to show the journey down a bright road of continuing the fight, it can be summarized as, 'the light is down the road ahead, don't give up the fight'. The optimistic paradigm of 1940s progressive film was mainly centred around rebirth, or that the light was not far away, and can be summarized as 'The light is just up ahead, raise your head and run to it'. This is because the victory of the national revolutionary war in the 1930s was the main social goal. It was a long and winding road destined to be fraught with blood, pain and battle, but the revolution was the right path to the light; the beautiful prospects of the war of liberation in the 1940s were in sight, and national change and forward momentum were the main forms of optimism.

Part 3

The prevailing optimism in the progressive films in the 1930s and 1940s was no coincidence. It found its roots in the profundity of Chinese cultural traditions and intellectual history. The esteemed Gao RuiQuan believes that,

> [A]s western science and technology begin to spread in China, the enthusiasm for progressiveness brought about by scientism generated the radical development of optimism in epistemology, only the optimism in scientism had gained unprecedented status in Modern China. More importantly, it planted the seeds of optimism in the fertile soil of Chinese philosophical traditions – the theory of original goodness of human nature. When it was combined with progressivist trends, which were popular in modern China, it gave rise to a burning fervour for optimism of China in the early 20th century. In the overall context of progressivism, optimism not only made the prospect of good deeds to attain moral perfection very attractive, but also lent credibility to the idea of the beautiful society that had been presumed and visualized by the Chinese people. It became the basic premise of all Utopian structures of China in the 20th century. From Confucius and Mencius to Cheng Zhu, the theory of the original goodness of human nature has become the mainstream of Confucianism's theory of human nature and can be said to be the theoretical premise of Confucian affirmation of life, formation of the idealistic sage soul and moral idealism.
>
> (RuiQuan 2011: 148–50)

As a matter of fact, in the practice of Confucianism's ultimate pursuit of perfection, 'happiness' is not only regarded as a form of work, but also as a spiritual realm.

> From Kong Yan's happiness, the journey of Two Yan to find Kong Yan's happiness and Zhu Zi's views on happiness and pleasure, to Yang Ming's 'Happiness is nature' and on to post-Yangming, especially the Taizhou School, 'the pursuit of happiness' always runs through In the course of the development of Confucianism, becoming a symbol of the spirituality of Confucianism
> (Chunhui 2012: 120)

When Zhu Xi distinguishes 'pleasure' from 'happiness', he maintained the belief that 'pleasure' was a kind of joyful emotion that is held inside and never exposed. 'Happiness' is the exposure of this kind of joy and emotion, so-called 'showing up'. Zhu Zi also said, 'If referring to yourself, happiness finds its significance in sharing with others, if you are filled with pleasure, you will find happiness' (Chingde 1986: 452). From the development of pleasure, happiness to gentlemen's personality is a 'secondary advancement' process of moral ascension. This process implies the gradual progress of Zhu Zi. 'Pleasure', because it is necessary to 'show up' and share with the public, naturally has the meaning of work in practice, Wang Xinqi and Wang Longxi regard 'happiness' as 'the nature of the heart', distinguishing spiritual 'happiness' from secular enjoyment, and giving it the noble meaning of 'the work in practice of happiness': 'happy' is not only spiritual, internal, but also practical and transcendent. Xi Qi has the most profound, the deepest and the closest to China's modern times optimism of all of Wang's students. He emphasized that 'happiness' should be 'true'. 'Happiness' is regarded as the premise of 'gentlemanly good deeds'; 'happiness' is 'the unity of all things' and shows his optimistic and heroic spirit of taking the world as his own responsibility. The positive minds as well as the behavioural values that are implemented in practice. The distinguished Mr Chen Lai believes that, in fact, the integration of 'the benevolence and allness of things' as the internal foundation of humanitarianism to 'provide liberal relief to the masses'. It is to be implemented as social care to the miserable. While 'the unity of all things' is an expression of the spirituality of Confucianism, it is necessary to cultivate and pursue a spiritual realm. It is to be implemented in inner life (Lai 1995: 258).

Therefore, as with the 'the unity of all things', 'pleasure' contains the dual spiritual realm of the external environment and the understanding of the inner world. Without cultivation of the inner self and enlightenment, a state of being without inner worries and sorrows, it is impossible to create courage, specific actions and practices to break the web. Sometimes, we are awe-stricken at why the modern Chinese intellectuals have shown a collective yearning for progressivism and optimism when the country was in danger, why we can give up or partially abandon our individual world-view, aesthetic tastes or modern rationality, then why intellectuals self-marginalized universally in modern times. Actually, we find a deep ideological basis in this idea of, 'the unity of all things'. The ultimate value of 'the unity of all things' has long been deeply immersed in the soul of Chinese intellectuals, a lingering cultural subconsciousness that, when encountering any kind of dramatic change though the ages, is very easy to comprehend, as it radiates the unstoppable true passion of the original. Apprehending the knowledge of the world, providing better service to the people, diligently studying the quintessence of previous knowledge, and supporting peace.

Some scholars believe that a paradox existed in the beginning twentieth-century China. On one hand, the intelligentsia and those with lofty ideals were deeply concerned about the survival of the nation and culture. On the other hand, there was a curious optimistic spirit that accompanied the worry and angst. This superficial paradox hid the inevitability of thought, which is precisely the dual spiritual realm of the inner and outer worlds contained in the 'happiness' of 'all things in one'. The inner environment is the state of worry about the nation and culture. The external situation is the action and responsibility for saving the nation and culture in danger. If worry exists, there will be revolutionary action. This is the decisive role of epistemology in action theory. So, it can be seen that optimism in modern China can find profound roots in China's ideological tradition. K'ang Yu-wei's, *Book of Great Harmony*, Liang Ch'i-ch'ao's, *On the Young China*, Sun Yat-sen's, *Accomplish a Task in One Stroke*, Li Ta-chao's, *Youth China*, the political blueprint for political democracy and economic democracy built by free intellectuals in the 1940s, new Confucian moral ideals, Mao Zedong's agricultural socialism, the utopian history of this twentieth-century Chinese society has repeatedly confirmed the continuity of cultural traditions.

In the famous essay, *On The Young China* written by Liang Ch'i-ch'ao, he expressed with fervour and conviction the optimistic picture of 'Young China', 'Prospects for the future are like the sea', 'Be like the sky who will never die' and 'be borderless like the country'. That Utopian blueprint showed that China will 'become great in the future' (T'ai-yan 1906.). His teacher, Kang Youwei's, *Book of Great Harmony,* which was completed in the early twentieth century, puts forth a convincing argument that human development is a process of getting rid of barbarism and getting close to civility, finally reaching a perfect ideal kingdom. T'an Szu-tung affirmed that the development of science and technology will bring great benefits to mankind in *The Doctrine of Benevolence*. Ch'en Tu-hsiu, Ch'ü Ch'iu-pai and other Marxists believed in scientism and social progress, and anti-scientific cultural conservatives, such as the new Confucianism, Tsung Tsung-san, Hsiung Shih-li, Liang Shu-ming and others, believed that traditional culture is the eternal source of spiritual truth. Although they are different, their theoretical presuppositions are based on the future, the development of culture and the development of human optimism. Li Ta-chao regards personal self-cultivation and the establishment of a proactive and optimistic outlook on life as the foundation for creating *Youth China* (Yu 2000: 426). The famous line, 'The youth of me, created the family of youth, the country of youth, the nation of youth, the humanity of youth, the earth of youth and the universe of youth', which has been recited and imprinted on the hearts of generation after generation of Chinese.

> After more than a century of history, 'progress' has become a self-evident public consciousness, even a premise that is not observable. Contemporary Chinese basically live in the conceptual framework of progressive theory. Although there are very few philosophers such as Zhang Taiyan who criticize this, they do not affect the belief of Chinese progressivism.
>
> (RuiQuan 2011: 158)

When optimistic progress theory becomes a public consciousness, and commonsense rationality becomes the uber-stable structure of modern Chinese society, it is perfectly evident that, optimistic progress theory influenced Chinese filmmakers in the 1930s and 1940s in terms of their outlook on life, the world and art. To this very day, it still influences the creation of contemporary Chinese films with its powerful ideology that is especially thought-provoking. The trend of optimism in the film of the 1930s and 1940s is a reflection of the zeitgeists in this era. Whether the film exhibits 'the correctness of consciousness' depends on its progress, optimism and the courage to face the reality of suffering and the visionary, 'basic solution' thoughts and the antithesis to its thesis in the form of its backward, reactionary, 'incorrect consciousness'. Fei Mu's, *Night in the City*, was accused of 'incorrect consciousness' due to the fact that he finally escaped to the countryside. *Spring in a Small Town* of the 1940s was considered to be 'so pale and morbid', and 'he moment that time forgot'. It is representative of 'culture' 'negative tendencies', as it represents a duality and the weakness of the character of Fei Mu who was a petty bourgeois artist. Wu Yung-gang's, *Waves Washing the Sand* was severely criticized as 'devious', 'ludicrous' and 'reactionary'. This criticism pained him greatly and shook his artistic views to the core, which put him on the path of true 'progress' and 'optimism' during the national defence film era. The holism of early Chinese progressive film is the result of the joint actions and cultural trends of the times they belonged to, as well as the historical fact of national peril. It is understandable that the era itself was validated as being supreme and exclusive, and brought in with it epistemological dogmatism, which killed the diversification of artistic works and viewpoints in film and, to a certain extent, killed the spirituality and vitality of film as art. This epistemological dogmatism is also a point of vigilance in today's film against the backdrop of 'economic determinism'.

REFERENCES

Bing, Chen (ed.) (1993a), *Selected Works of Chinese Film Critics in the 1930s*, Beijing: China Film Press.

Bing, Liu (1935), 'Homesick', *Morning News: Daily Movies*, 6.

Ch'en, Wu (1932), 'The meaning of "Conscienceless"', *The Times*, 23 July.

Ch'en, Wu (1933), 'Night in the city', *Morning News: Daily Movies*, 10 March.

Chingde, Li (1986), *Zhu Ziyu Volume 20*, Beijing: Zhonghua Book Company.

Chou, Guang (1935), 'The big road (Review 1)', *Morning News: Daily Film*, 1.

Chunhui, Ruan (2012), *Study on the Thought of Conscience: Post Yangming Study*, Changsha: Hunan University, Ph.D. thesis of Chinese Philosophy.

Di, Ye (1937), 'Review of "Soaring Aspiration"', *Xinhua Pictorial*, 2.

Feng, Su (1933), 'About Mr. Shen XiLing and cry of women', *Morning News: Daily Movies*, 15 April.

Gang, Pian (1935), 'The boatman's daughter' (Comment 1), *The Morning News: The Daily Movies*, 11.

Ho, Ling (1993), 'Shen Liling paradox', in C. Bing (ed.), *Selected Works of Chinese Film Critics in the 1930s*, Beijing: China Film Press, p. 313.

—— (1934), 'The queen of sports (Review 2)', *Morning News: Daily Movies*, 4.

—— (1996), *The World's Famous Director's Biography: Sun Yü's Theory*, in *China Silent Film*, Beijing: China Film Press.

Jihua, Cheng (ed.) (1963), *The History of Chinese Cinematic Development*, vol. I, Beijing: China Film Press, p. 339.

Kang, Lu (1935), 'The film that exposes reality: On the content of plunder of peach and plum', *China Daily*, 9 January.

Lai, Chen (1995), *The Realm of Nothing: The Spirit of Wang Yangming's Philosophy*, Beijing: People's Publishing House.

Mo'erh, Ling Ho (1933), *Comment on Oppression*, 'Shen Newspaper of 'Benedict Supplements Film Special Issues', 17 August.

Nai-fang, Hsi (1993), 'The evaluation of raging waves', in C. Bing (ed.), *China Left-Wing Film Movement*, Beijing: China Film Press, pp. 414–16.

RuiQuan, Gao (2011), 'Progress and optimism', in X. Jilin and S. Hong (eds), *The Core Concept of Modern Chinese Thought*, Shanghai: Shanghai People's Publishing House, p. 149.

T'ai-yan, Chang (1906), 'The theory of evolution', *The People's Daily*, 7, September.

Xuan (1933), 'Raging waves and "Night in the City"', *Shen Pao Newspaper*, Freedom Talk, 24 March.

Yan, Fang (1993), '*Goddess of Freedom* and Chinese women', in C. Bing (ed.), *China Left-Wing Film Movement*, Beijing: China Film Press, p. 56.

Yan, Shu (1933), 'The way out of oppression', *Morning News: Daily Movies*, 14 August.

Yu, Gu (2000), 'The anarchism and the origin of Chinese marxism', in X. Jilin (ed.), *On the History of Chinese Thought in the 20th Century (II)*, Shanghai: Oriental Publishing Center, p. 426.

Yü, Sun (1932), 'Director, Blood of Love', *The Times: The Movie Times*, 15 September.

Yu, Wei (1936), 'Going to Nature' (comment 4)', *Film & Theater*, 10.

NOTE

1. Hsi Nai-fang's, *The Pink Dream*, Su Feng's *Just a Dream*, Lu Szu's *When Can We Wake Up?* in Bing (1993: 324–32).

SECTION IV

INTERVIEWS

13. Interview with Director Guo Ke: Whispers through a Crinkle in Time

Date: 21 September 2017
Location: China Film Archives Conference Room
Interviewee: 郭柯/Guo Ke (Director of *Twenty-Two*)
Interviewer: 孙红云/Sun HongYun (Associate Professor of Film Studies at Beijing Film Academy)
Compiled by Liu YiLun

Beginning with Twenty-Two

Sun HongYun (hereinafter referred to as Sun): Let's start with the creative process of *Twenty-Two*. I think I remember seeing the documentary about 'comfort women' when I was in school getting my master's degree. I was very impressed by the Korean director Min Yingzhu's 'whispering'. Later, I found the tape. The content is not clear, but I remember deeply. The title of the film. When did you first learn about 'comfort women?'

Guo Ke (hereinafter referred to as Guo): I really don't remember when I first heard the word. In 2012, I saw an article on Weibo about the story of a comfort woman and her Japanese son. I was deeply touched by that story, and I came up with the idea of filming a movie about comfort women.

Sun: I know that you were raised by your grandmother, and so you feel close to the elderly, but feeling close to a comfort woman is different than your grandmother.

Guo: Let me show you the picture in the article that gave me the impetus to make the film – the old woman is Wei ShaoLan and her son. The foreground of the photo is a very old person, the camera is totally focused on her face and the son is behind her. When I saw these two old people, I thought there must be a lot of stories behind them. Everyone knows how the comfort women were victimized. She also gave birth to a Japanese child, who's now 68 years old. I really wanted to get to know their story on a deep level.

Sun: Who did you get in contact with besides old lady Wei ShaoLan?

Guo: After seeing the article, I went looking for Professor Su ZhiLiang on Weibo. Professor Su trusted us enough to give us Wei ShaoLan's address. As it just so happens, I wasn't filming any projects at the time. I travelled to Guangxi and got an audience with her. Actually, everything went very well over the next six months. It was because I didn't have any other projects in the works that I had the time to concentrate on doing this. And investment money was easy at the time. So, after preparing for about a half a year, in December 2012, we started filming the short film *Thirty-Two*.

Sun: There are many coincidences in the success of the documentary. I think I had already conceptualized *Thirty-Two* when you started shooting. The research was already done at that point if I'm not mistaken. Did you know that there were only 32 comfort women left in China when you got a hold of the list? For *Thirty-Two* did you pick the subjects out from a large-scale group photograph or was it just the mother and son?

Guo: I was just going with my gut. When I decided to make the film, Professor Su told me that there were only thirty-two comfort women left, and it was then that I decided on the name for the project. After making the short film I wondered if I should put the names of the thirty-two women in the end credits, and so I compiled the list of their names. While I was making the ending, Professor Su was texting or e-mailing me the names of the ones who had just passed away. It really hit me like a ton of bricks. I wondered how they were leaving us so quickly? In the space of less than two years, the number thirty-two had been reduced to twenty-two. And in the process *Thirty-Two* won some awards, which fed my ego I guess, and kept me moving forward. At the same time, the group of women kept on dwindling, exacerbating that feeling I had of living with my grandma when I was a boy. It gave me the feeling that I should keep going.

Sun: *Thirty-Two* had gotten an investment of more than thirty-thousand RMB, which was from a television station, right?

Guo: It was the owner of a private company who invested the money. A television station would never invest in a project like this.

Sun: Where was *Thirty-Two* shown after it was finished?

Guo: Online. On 11 November 2014, during Phoenix Television's Third Annual 'Double Eleventh Celebration'. After it won the award, the film was played on TV for the first time, and it gradually started getting some attention.

Sun: The crew you used for the film was the same you used when you were making narrative films right? Wasn't it pretty much this same crew?

Guo: I piecemealed together a crew made up of people I had known for more than a decade. The people you use on every production may be different, but every time we do put together a team of people we've gotten to know and trust who really want to be there.

Sun: *Thirty-Two* mostly focuses on the lives of the comfort women at the time. How accepting they were about the things that had happened to them in life, their toughness and tenacity touch the audience on the deepest level. You are a narrative film director with a feature film crew, who puts a lot of effort into shooting refined poetic imagery. Feature films and documentaries use two different kinds of aesthetics. How did you approach the relationship between them?

Guo: Actually, I was just trying to find my way right along with the creator. Neither of us really knew how a documentary should be made. Much of film expression is veiled and implicit, which is something that we wanted to get right. We didn't want to preach, we just wanted to put the comfort women up there on the screen. We definitely wanted to let everyone know that we were filming a person, an elderly person, so that's the way we presented *Thirty-Two*. But there were a number of personal habits that I couldn't quit, for example the use of a piece of filmmaking equipment called a 'crane'. At the time we also used a dolly, but the ladies were just sitting there while we were pushing-pulling shot on the track. I took one look at the footage and thought it looked really fake, so I just got rid of it. But as far as the use of the 'crane' is concerned, I had a much stingier attitude about it, what I mean by that is, I just couldn't bring myself to cut out the footage we took with it, because it'd cost me an arm and a leg paying the guy to operate it.

Sun: How long did you guys shoot there?

Guo: Our team stayed there for eight days but couldn't stay longer as it was too costly. I personally went there often over the course of about six months and stayed there every time for around three to five days.

Sun: Could you understand much of what those ladies were saying when they spoke their local dialect?

Guo: Pretty much, yeah. But while we were filming we still had an interpreter on set.

From Research to Filming

Sun: *Thirty-Two* completely turned your mindset from a feature film director to a documentary filmmaker. Did you shoot *Twenty-Two* at the same time?

Guo: No. During the interim I worked on other projects. I didn't decide to make *Twenty-Two* until the end of 2013. I was doing the project on a shoestring then, because I didn't have time to go and fight with the investors. So, I went looking for some of the comfort women myself to see if I could pick up where I'd left off.

Sun: Did you do all of the research yourself, or did you have a team?

Guo: I still did it the way we do in feature filmmaking, which is that the producer will help make all the arrangements for you. You know I actually really admire documentary directors, they have to shoot the thing themselves, with the camera on their shoulder, but I have to hire someone to help me shoot it, because what I get out of running the camera myself cannot match the imagery I see in my head.

Sun: How many people went to do research for the film?

Guo: Four. Two producers, a screenwriter and myself.

Sun: How long did the research process take?

Guo: About twelve days. Professor Su provided me with the information of twenty-two former comfort women and found them pretty quickly with my phone. After I had gotten to know them, I prepared to start filming. We decided which ones would be featured prominently in the film. I also prepared an outline of the things I wanted to ask, which I didn't use after shooting actually began.

Sun: You didn't use the questions you'd prepared due to practical constraints.

Guo: They weren't sufficient; they were too narrow in scope. There's plenty of suspense in real life.

Sun: You didn't take any footage while on preliminary visits or during the research process?

Guo: No.

Sun: During preliminary visits you talked face-to-face, but during filming, twenty-some-odd crew members went with you, didn't the women feel uneasy about it?

Guo: It wasn't a problem. Because I trusted in the fact that I had a pretty close relationship with them. And besides, I always have all my ducks in a row first.

Sun: Judging from the shots you took, the camera crew must have stayed pretty far away from the subjects and not intruded on their lives. How did you accomplish that?

Guo: I would have the film crew stationed outside the gates of the women's compounds. I wouldn't let them get anywhere that they could be seen, and if any of the ladies went out for some sun, we would have to park pretty far away. Actually, for the first day of filming we were like we were feature filmmakers: the lighting and equipment, cases and c-stands had been moved into that elderly lady's house, just like it was a real film set and everybody was swarming her house like 'locusts'. It was like her home was our turf. I think it really disturbed the ladies' lives having us there, so I let the producers know that I only wanted the camera and sound crew there, and anybody not directly involved in the day-to-day production to leave the set.

Sun: You had a team of around twenty to thirty production personnel on set, yet I couldn't see even the slightest hint of bother, especially that elderly mother from Shanxi and her daughter-in-law discussing the thing about the kitty. The candid moments of the scene were very vivid, with big, sweeping shots, yet you couldn't see even the slightest trace of the production crew's interference. How long did you shoot each day? From what time to what time?

Guo: It was like going to a regular job. We'd go to the location at about 7:00 AM and wrap shooting at about 5:00 or 6:00 PM.

Sun: To give the women time to relax and unwind.

Guo: I still had to ask the old lady and her family, out of respect for their lifestyle. For example, if she was used to sweeping the floor in the afternoon, I wouldn't make her sweep it in the morning. Whenever she would do it, that's when I would film it. Even if it wasn't a big change, even if the lighting was a little better at a certain time, I wouldn't shoot because the lighting at that time didn't add any value to the production. We just sincerely wanted to show respect for our elders. Maybe no one can even see it, but I can feel it inside. Let's just say that one of those elderly women passed away right now and I were shameless enough to go stand on her grave and take pictures of her gravestone and didn't feel the least bit bad about it even though we Chinese have some pretty big taboos about it. In those elderly women's eyes, I would be seen as someone with no conscience whatsoever.

Sun: *Twenty-Two* took place over a full four seasons. There were shots of the heavy snow at both the beginning and end of the film, which left a deep impression on many people. Did you deliberately read the weather forecast, or did you just get lucky in the weather department?

Guo: On February 4, 2014, I received a text message from Professor Su. He told me that two of the comfort women had passed away and their funerals would be held on February 6th and 9th. I just finished up the research and gotten in touch with them. I hadn't even started shooting yet and yet two of them had passed away. When I heard the news of the deaths I didn't overthink it, because intuition told me that we were still going to shoot the movie. I immediately greeted the cinematographer and the sound engineer. The next day, the three of us came from Chengdu, Xi'an and Beijing and met in Xi'an. On the evening of the 5th, we went to a city called Yangquan in Shanxi Province, and gathered together for a meeting. It snowed all night long. When I got up on the morning of the sixth, the cinematographer commented that God was lending us a helping hand. So, we fired up the camera and the first thing we shot this funeral from on top of the roof.

Sun: Some say that snowfall can set the scene, but for such a grand shot, I wondered if it could have been fake.

Guo: There's no point in making a documentary if you're going to fake it. Absolutely pointless. Scenes in narrative films need to be designed, but when you make a documentary, you take what God gives you. That day, we just quietly set the camera there on the tripod and let it roll. The people and things that appeared in the frame and all that snow fluttering down are the stuff you couldn't even think up if you tried. It has such richness and emotion to it. Consequently, our own emotions were running high that day, which just strengthened my commitment to take on the film. The appeal of making a documentary is very strong, and the power that life itself gives you something you could never imagine in a million years. Why didn't it not snow on February 4th or 5th? If it had snowed prior to filming, we wouldn't have even been able to get up the mountain, because all of roads would have been closed. Wouldn't you say that the hand of God was helping us along? And then it wasn't until it got dark at night that it started snowing again.

Sun: If the snowfall was the hand of God reaching out to help, then what about the rainfall in Hainan?

Guo: I never check the weather forecast. If it rains, then I shoot in the rain. It just happened to be raining on the day I was filming. We can actually connect these two events together and attribute them both to the hand of God.

Sun: You didn't take long time to shoot in each scene. How long did the troops stay in Hainan before you had that heavy rain?

Guo: Seven days. But I personally had been in Hainan for more than 20 days, because there were two comfort women I was busy filming, which took fourteen days altogether. But filming the others only took a day or two.

Sun: There is a Japanese girl in the film who was the caretaker for the comfort woman in Hainan. Did you happen to meet her, or did you specifically ask her to come?

Guo: When talking with her family, someone mentioned this Japanese girl the lady had known when she was in Haikou. So, we invited her to come. Of course, we also had to use some photojournalistic techniques like having the camera set up beforehand, letting her enter the set first, and making sure when the care picked her up that the camera was shooting from a distance.

Sun: The shots were really well-composed. The one where her back was facing the camera and sitting in the old man's room. She began narrating all the emotional things from her past, and began crying, which felt very natural to me. I know that the part was probably shot sequentially. Is a similar scene in the film the one at the gravesite?

Guo: Yes, people were asking us to go.

Sun: Did you make that decision after finishing your research?

Guo: Yes.

Sun: That shot is packed full of meaning, and there's none of that phony, contrived feeling to it. If it were shot in the narrative film style of shot-reverse-shot, then it would have felt too dramatized.

Guo: I am just learning to feel my way through this stuff. This documentary truly brought me a lifetime's worth of benefit. Just like you said, life is never what you imagine it will be, but it is always what's most real. In my previous films, all the actors had to wear their heart on their sleeve, with big in-your-face emotions, but actually, what's behind that is also highly emotional. Besides making people feel happy, documentaries can do so much more.

Ethical Issues of the Documentary

Sun: You probably encountered some opposition in the process of directing the subject on camera, but besides them did you ever encounter opposition from family members as well? What did you do in that case? Did you give up, or rethink your ideas and then resume shooting?

Guo: Professor Su was like a god in the hearts and minds of those women. I just took the letters of introduction he gave me and that was it. No opposition from anyone – and the families were very supportive too.

Sun: Some subtitles appeared in the film, superimposed over an image which said that one of the comfort women from Shanxi declined appearing in the movie. Shouldn't the producers have had a heart-to-heart with her before filming commenced?

Guo: We talked about it all very thoroughly before filming, and everything was set to go. But she probably wasn't feeling very well that day, she said, 'Could you please not put me on camera today? It probably wouldn't be very good for me afterwards'. She was very sweet about it. Very soft. I mean, it's moments like this that really test the director's mettle and his creativity! If she wouldn't let me put her on camera, then how could I possibly tell this story? Should I film a little or secretly set up a telephoto lens on a tripod and hope I can get something usable in the can? I would never film her if she didn't want me to. That's ethics 101. So, what we did was film a pillow shot while we chatted with her. You know she's actually left this world already. And if I'd secretly filmed her at the time and put her in the movie just to serve my own selfish purposes, I wouldn't be able to sleep at night. I'd be worried that she might come looking for me from beyond the grave. I know that sounds pretty silly, but you really have to believe what goes around comes around. Karma won't let you get away with anything.

Sun: How long did the production crew stay at her house?

Guo: For more than two hours. After she decided not to let us put her on camera, we just wrapped for the day and talked about the next shooting location. We talked about things for a while and that's when I came up with the idea of cutting away to a pillow shot. A colleague of mine went with me to talk to her and see if she was in a different frame of mind. The producers set up a shooting schedule, while I took it upon myself to pacify her. We delineated everyone's jobs and responsibilities, which is why you have to have such a big crew.

Sun: In the process of setting up who would be filmed and when and how, and all the communications that took place before shooting, even with the consent of most of the former comfort women and their families, over the course of the interviews, there were numerous occasions when they were right in the middle of talking about events from the past and the mood suddenly did a one-eighty. They would tense up and say, 'I can't say it. I can't talk about this. I have nothing more to say'. Actually, the things you asked them in the interview were extremely difficult to talk about. How did you start the interview? Shouldn't they have understood what it means when a film crew shows up on your doorstep?

Guo: She knew. But we never talked openly about it. I don't want to reopen old wounds. So, when the camera was set up, I just completed the interview all in one fell swoop. Whatever she could talk about she would say, and whatever she couldn't talk about she would keep to herself. And that was fine.

Sun: Did you interview them all yourself?

Guo: No, all of the twenty-two we invited were interviewed by area locals. Some of them would wear headphones, and I will talk to them from the distance. There was also a native of the area who could speak the local dialect on the monitor. I wore a headset and he told me what she was saying.

Sun: It was very difficult to get the interviewer to start talking. I noticed that the film shows one of the interviewees talking about her family, one being her foster daughter and the other her daughter-in-law. I don't know if it was just a coincidence, but none of her own biological children said anything on camera. I wonder how you managed to get them so deeply involved.

Guo: I really didn't want to delve that deeply into their relationship. Old Mao YinMei only has a daughter. And Li AiLian's son is very shy. It was just a lot easier to get her daughter-in-law to talking. So that was the way it went. We will be more forthcoming when our family members are the ones asking the questions. But when it was our turn to ask the questions, we just followed her lead. For example, talking about the things that made her happy or unhappy when she was a child. Just between you, me and the wall, she was actually pretty gullible. She was very naïve that way, but the thing is, it depends on whether you actually have the guts to go ahead and try to trick her. Listen, I grew up with my grandmother, I know this very well. I believe that you should never try to trick the elderly. My grandmother passed away in 1996, and I don't have the chance to be good to her anymore. And now I've gotten to know these elderly women who were in my film. The fact that I am a director doesn't really amount to a hill of beans. It doesn't matter at all. What matters first and foremost is that I am a person. So, what would happen if the film didn't turn out well? I never thought that *Twenty-Two* was going to be a really great film, but at least I can say with the utmost certainty that I can face these women – these elderly women – with a clear conscience. That's how I really feel.

Sun: I can feel the goodwill that you showed in dealing with these elderly women in the film. So, when they didn't want to talk about something, you didn't push them. Some directors wouldn't do that. They would just keep pushing and probing from behind the lens trying to peer inside like a voyeur. But you treated them with respect and goodwill; and I can feel the love.

Guo: It's a very polarizing film.

Sun: Nowadays practically any film you made would polarize audiences. Film aesthetics are diverse, and that's normal. This discussion is rather timely. Some people might say that you are exploiting the 'comfort women' theme for your own personal gain. Two years ago, after reading about the film for the first time, I didn't write any reviews, although I said that I would always support you, because at the time I considered the theoretical ethics of the documentary. This should have been done at the national level. To take these women and their stories, seal them up as important records, and wait until the right time to unveil them to the public. This is the theoretical ideal, because some of these women are still unwilling to be noticed by others while they are still alive.

Guo: Do you have an appropriate time frame in mind?

Sun: This would allow us to skirt certain ethical questions. Some of these women do not want to be mentioned as a 'comfort woman'. As long as these women are alive. It's humiliating. After all, it is the deepest trauma in their lives. Although the documentary has healing properties, there is also the possibility of being hurt more. Before its release this year, it seems that only eight of them are still alive. There are actually different definitions of 'comfort women', mainly referring to the military sex slaves who are forced to be used, but the comfort women in *Twenty-Two* are the ones the Japanese soldiers would rape as they took the land but weren't taken away when the troops moved on. Then the Japanese went to the next place to engage in the same thing all over again, causing even more pain, and torment with this despicable act. The film as a whole, the questions were posed tactfully to the subject being photographed. At the end of the film the professor said that he had been doing research on the comfort women for more than a decade, which caused trouble for the women involved. He admitted, had he known the result, he would never have done it in the first place. Crystalizing this into words in the film makes you can feel that you are answering some of the tough questions hanging over your heart along with those of the audience. As these women pass away your need for concern will lessen. It is not that you have changed anything, but that you have been left with the final voices and images of these women, as they are immortalized.

Guo: I didn't delve too deeply into the comfort women's private lives in the film. On a surface level, I took everyone to their home and then took them on a tour. The teacher you talked about, Mr Zhang ShuangBing, actually did many years of investigation and wrote a book of oral history on the subject. I have read the book, and more specifically, the oral transmissions about the rape, which are really bloody. They even go into detailed descriptions of it all. I was wondering why Professor Zhang said that he had 'stun' them. He said that he was 'stunning' those women, and that I was 'disturbing' them. From the depths of my soul I feel it's no problem. The only way that Professor Zhang could continue on with his work was to ask those who were still alive among the group to give their testimony in exchange for his word. Professor Zhang has done so much work over the past decade and he has strong opinions about it all. I saw one of the comfort women brought to him today, so, I included her testimony, along with the Japanese girl's as well as a teacher, Mrs Chen HouZhi, all of whom had had contact with these comfort women at different points in time and for different lengths of time. They all have their own thoughts and feelings on the matter as well. The only one who doesn't really have an opinion is me, because I have only been in touch with them for a couple of years now.

Sun: And so, you never reopened old wounds, with *Twenty-Two* you exercised a good deal of restraint.

Guo: Whatever I see in my head is what I tried to put on screen. I'm a member of the 80's generation. I trust that it can lend the 90's generation some different perspectives, once they get a chance to see it. Being that my predecessors you talked about have an age advantage – their own experiences growing up, which lends them different perspectives from what I can see. These women are aged, and it is not good to compromise their happiness. I remember like it was yesterday, after viewing the film an audience member in Chengdu said to me, 'Thank you guys for not allowing those women to be hurt again before they leave this world'. I think that just about says it all. And that's exactly what I did. When these women do leave this world, they will still be happy. We also tried to preserve their beauty in the film for all posterity. We don't want for them start talking and then be and to see nothing but pain and anguish.

Versions and Marketing

Sun: Two years ago, the version of *Twenty-Two* I saw at the Beijing Film Academy was very different from the official release I watched in the theatre a few days ago. The changes made in editing were very extensive. The original version focused on documenting the present-day lives of the comfort women. Now the theme of this edition is particularly clear and concise. It focuses on the anti-Japan War and concentrates on their experience as comfort women. The overlaps between the original version of *Twenty-Two* and *Thirty-Two* are more numerous. What was your approach to editing the new version?

Guo: The version of the film that premiered at the Beijing Film Academy in 2015 was longer than the theatrical version and was very slow-paced. In 2016, we screened it at some festivals. We made some changes to it after seeing the reactions we got from audiences here in Mainland China as well as in other countries, and after my own repeated viewings of the film. There was too much emphasis on self-expression in the previous version. Now the film has to go out to the whole of society. If you want to communicate emotionally with everyone, you can't overindulge in your own emotions. So, on that basis I made some trade-offs and cut out certain parts.

Sun: The sheer scale of the cuts you made was massive. It must have been quite a process.

Guo: I guess. In 2016, I showed it in South Korea and then in Moscow, and then again in Xi'an. After watching it on the jumbo screen so many times, I went into the edit bay and spent about half an hour reediting it. I cut it very decisively, because I just couldn't hold back anymore, these things had been building up inside me for too long.

Sun: There are a lot of pillow shots in the current theatrical version. For example, the comfort woman from Hainan just finishing her story of taking a pair of guns to fight against Japan, when you immediately cutaway to a man cutting coconuts and jackfruit with a knife thereby manipulating time and space. Are you hesitant to use this type of rhetorical pillow shot?

Guo: No not at all. I just hope that the audience is more accepting, they'll gain some perspective that way. If you want to enter the commercial market, you'd darn well better take the audience into consideration. If the work is too ego-centric, how could it possibly take others into account? Since it is a product, it must be pleasing to the eye. This version is 'Dragon Logo', certified by the Chinese Film Bureau, which means that I can't add any content. I'll get in trouble if I do. I can't add, I can only cut.

Sun: After making cuts, the film doesn't need to be reviewed by the board again?

Guo: I still have to repeat the process. If I want make cuts, whether it's in a few minutes here or a few seconds there; regardless of how long the deletion is, it's all reported. The process goes pretty fast. But, if I add any content, it will be necessary to apply for another special review.

Sun: Did a narrative film director help you with the final editing and direction?

Guo: No, I did it all myself. The 2015 version was a fine cut made by Mr Liao QingSong. This version – the one that plays in theatres – was all my work. I mean, cutting it down from the original 112 minutes to 99 minutes.

Sun: In the first version of *Twenty-Two*, I remember that there is no final song. When did you come up with the idea of putting a song over the ending?

Guo: It was the distribution company's idea. They asked me to listen to the voice of a young girl named Yan Chi and said that Wei ShaoLan, one of the women featured in the film, could have a theme song, and this young girl could do her own interpretation. I agreed. Just singing a theme song for one of the people in the film wouldn't interfere with anything. At first I didn't have any particular expectations about it, but when I put her song to the end of the film, the effect was really good. As soon as I heard her voice, I knew how to end the film. After the music was recorded, I made new changes to the ending.

Sun: The song at the end coupled with the film's content work together to form a taut moment of tension. It has great flair. While the ending is restrained but dynamic. As far as the editing is concerned, the theatrical version of *Twenty-Two* flows really well, which is due to your understanding that this film is to be seen by the general audience, not just professional documentary researchers. The films aimed at the general public should move quick and look good and have strong visuals. This is the biggest difference between your two versions. The theatrical version is very compact and more clearly oriented around a single subject. I have to give you a big thumbs up for two reasons. First, I have to compliment you on your courage. It takes a lot for a young director from the 80s generation to make a documentary about Chinese comfort women. And then for you to continue to polish and re-edit the film two or three years after it was completed and do all the promotion following its release. I applaud your tenacity! Is all of this work because of the comfort women and their story or does it have to do with anything else?

Guo: These women have become part of my life. I can't say that they are my whole life, but a really big part of it. When any of them pass away, it pains me greatly. In the past two or three years, I have tried to make the film even more successful, like finding ways to get it out there and entering it into the film festival circuit. I don't have any other resources at my disposal. The only thing my professor and I can do at the moment is just enter it into film festivals one at a time. I am responsible for getting the film into film festivals in the mainland. But I can handle it, because they are all in Chinese. My associate Long Qing's English is good and has been helping me get it into the foreign film festivals. All this stuff just takes time. Case in point, I once thought about making another trailer and poster, but then, who has the time?

Sun: Doing all this work must feel like taking care of a newborn baby.

Guo: The film is my baby. A parent's responsibility is to the child. And as long as the child is healthy, then your heart will be there for it every day. The same is true of the film. If you can do things for your child, then that's the happiness there is. You asked me how could I make other movies? Wouldn't that be like abandoning my child and going to have a child with someone else? That's just impossible. So, if I don't try my hardest to finish this film, I won't do any other projects. Because I wouldn't have the energy. During filming I was called upon to make another film, but the film was the kind that takes a lot out of a guy, it's exhausting to make. And anyway, I don't have the aspirations to be a famous director.

Sun: From the application for the dragon logo license permit to the selection of today's theatrical release, is this time-frame based on the issue of the dragon logo, or is based on the theatre's plan? Because in China, documentaries are largely box office poison. The highest grossing documentaries were *Mr. Deng Goes to Washington* and Himalaya, *Ladder to Paradise* released in 2016, and the total box office grosses were only 16 million Yuan. '22' was selected for this year's Anti-Japanese Victory Day. Is that according to your marketing plan?

Guo: There are some things that you just can't plan. For example, the August 14th release date, which is the date of the donation of the film to the Nanjing Massacre Memorial Hall in 2016. The director of the memorial suggested it be released on August 14th, 2017. So, it ended up being August 14th this year.

Sun: When did you receive your dragon logo license?

Guo: On October 10th, 2015, which was the only way to get it shown at the Beijing Film Academy on December 11th. Without the dragon logo, I wouldn't dare to show it publicly. The director of the Nanjing Memorial Hall suggested that on August 14th, the Nanjing Museum of the Site of the Liji Lane Comfort Stations in Nanjing help us to do crowdfunding, and as a result we raised a million renminbi for publicity and distribution. But it took a long time. In December, there was opposition from the distributor. Their head was spinning when they realized it had to be released eight months later. It was nothing but a headache to them. Eight months was a very pressing time-frame for me, because a lot of things weren't ready, so we were running around like chickens without a head. Then the distribution company had some ideas, for example, doing an advance screening. August 14th is a Monday instead of the traditional Friday or Saturday. Normally, this is not a good time to screen a film, but August 14th is more significant, being that it is the 'comfort women's anniversary'. This film was never shot for great box office, it was shot for great meaning.

Sun: What was your initial box office expectation? Were you emotionally prepared for the result?

Guo: The box office thing never even entered into my mind, if it had, it would make me look like a real amateur. It's a huge breakthrough for a documentary to just get into the theatres. For it even to make it to the end of the first week is an amazing feat.

Sun: Documentaries in Mainland Chinese theatres are generally sentenced to the day-one-and-done kind of fate. But *Mr. Deng Goes to Washington*, *The Verse of Us* and *Himalaya: Ladder to Paradise* all fared a little better, and there are those that do sell out their limited theatrical run. In 2016, I went to the theatre to see Chen WeiJun's *This Is Life*, and there were only three or four people in the theatre at the time, counting myself. You practically couldn't see the poster as it was stuck way off in the corner somewhere. But over the past few years, it's made a comeback and we're starting to make the rounds in theatres again. With the box office receipts for *Twenty-Two* on the rise, I'm sure he you have a lot on your plate.

Guo: Yes, I do. I'm very grateful to my prior experience as an assistant director over the past decade. It has really given me an anchor. If I was in my twenties, it would have a really swelled head right now, but I can take it all in stride at this age. I do whatever I need to do however it needs to get done. And, however I need to be I'll be. Without the support of society and the public, *Twenty-Two* wouldn't have the box office it has today. That's clear as a bell. But I don't deserve the credit for this. There are too many directors much more capable than me. Why can't their films perform this well at the box office? I understand very clearly why *Twenty-Two* can elicit this kind of reaction today.

Sun: That's great. Chinese movie-going audiences don't care much about documentaries and are not really very cognizant of them. *Twenty-Two* allows Chinese audiences to enter the theatre to understand history, learn history and focus on the present, which is a positive for a Chinese documentary. 'Systemization' is a new buzzword in the Chinese documentary world. I'm sceptical. What do you think?

Guo: Do not systemize it. Systemization will strip away the most honest aspects of the documentary. As long as the documentary solves the ethical problems, then it can go mano-y-mano with feature films any day of the week.

Sun: Its connection to real life and its value as a historical record is a testament to the tenacious spirit of the documentary.

After Twenty-Two

Sun: This humble documentary made on an investment of ¥3 million CNY has now earned box office receipts exceeding ¥170 million CNY. How do you gauge your creative future? Is it going to be in feature filmmaking or a documentary filmmaking?

Guo: I figure it will be in feature filmmaking. I am not a professional documentary filmmaker by any stretch of the imagination. I mean, you accept the good things that come your way, but everyone knows that *Twenty-Two* is by no means my personal accomplishment. It is a product made because I was in the right place at the right time and I knew the right people. That's something that can never be duplicated. Seeing how things have worked out, I know now that not getting into the capital market sooner has actually given me the chance to find myself and to find my life at a slower pace. Whether it's in narrative films or documentaries, I will continue to go at my own pace into the future.

Sun: I believe that the experience of making this documentary will have a tremendous impact on your future feature filmmaking career.

Guo: It's definitely had a huge impact. At this point, if someone had me go off and make some documentaries about animals, I would be very interested. If they put me somewhere for two or three months or a year to make a film, I would grin and bear it, but I'd need to have a big team working with me, not just two or three people. Just shooting two- or three-minutes' worth of film a day would be fine. Speaking of animals, I don't know if I have the opportunity to make a documentary like it in the future. *The Travelling Birds* is really good.

Sun: You raise the same birds as the ones in *The Travelling Birds* don't you?

Guo: I have been raising them since childhood. If you want to take a lot of close-ups, then the relationship between the bird and the photographer must be very good. I've seen the film and wondered how the director would cohabitate with these animals in the future? Birds also have their own emotions. They follow you every day. You can't just take a few snapshots pat them on the head and leave. Before I saw *Wolf Totem*, I had the same feeling. It's really hard to make a documentary, no matter if the subject is a person or an animal, how do you get along with them after you have finished shooting?

Sun: This is the most difficult problem facing the documentary director, and it's been that way for ages. Although you said that your achievements with *Twenty-Two* were all about being in the right place at the right time and working with the right people, I think you must have had regrets during the filming process. Could you tell me one or two?

Guo: I regretted it when that comfort woman passed away, but I didn't have the chance to get her on camera. I really feel awful about that! Our team went to her house before the shoot in May and learned some things about her and agreed that we'd come back the following month to film. As a result, we just went along according to the shooting schedule. Then I was shooting somewhere in Hainan, I was preparing to go to her house three days later, but then I got word that she'd passed away just a few days before and would never appear in *Twenty-Two*. Not getting her on camera. That's my biggest regret.

Sun: You have been an assistant director in a dramatic series, and you made two documentaries. So next thing up is your return to making narrative films?

Guo: Yes, I probably will. Time for dipping my toe in the documentary water is over, now it's time to hit the feature film pool. Although my career may go downhill after this, I have to man up and do venture up to the feature film Director's chair. I have been an assistant director for so long, and I have been working on documentaries for a few years now. I believe the time has come for me to have some feature filmmaking experience. So, it's time to step up to the plate. To come out of my shell. I've already told the next investor. 'If you're willing to take the risk, then let's play the game. I'll invest too. Let's not think about things like ROI right now, just let me put my heart and soul into it. This is the right way to play. Don't worry, don't worry, let's just take it slow, even if it takes three or four years to make it'.

Sun: How many did it take to make *Thirty-Two* and *Twenty-Two*?

Guo: Five years. From June of 2012, when I first met Wei ShaoLan, to August 14th, 2018 when *Thirty-Two* premiered. A full five years. This is probably having just a one-time thing. Because the trajectory of my life will definitely not keep going like this. I'm ready to go on to the next phase. I want to have a family, to have children of my own. I can't throw that by the wayside to do other things. So, I think maybe it really was mean to be. Everything just lined up so perfectly and allowed me to spend five years working on these projects. But that doesn't mean that you'll be granted another five years, does it?

Sun: Maybe, maybe not. No one knows what the future holds. It looks like sometimes documentaries have a certain magic. They hold on to you and never let go.

Guo: Which is something I never thought possible in a million years.

14. Interview with Director Mei Feng: The Aesthetic Compass of Classic Films

Date: 31 March 2017
Location: China Film Archive Conference Room
Interviewee: 梅峰/Mei Feng (Associate Professor, Department of Literature at the Beijing Film Academy, Film Screenwriter, Director) of *Mr. No Problem*
Interviewer: 徐枫/Xu Feng (Professor and Producer, Department of Film and Television, Central Academy of Drama)
Compiled by Liu YiLun

Upbringing and Memories

Xu Feng (Hereinafter referred to as, Xu): You were born at the end of the 60s in Inner Mongolia, but by all intents and purposes you are a native of Zhejiang.

Mei Feng (Hereinafter referred to as, Mei): Right. My father went to Inner Mongolia in 1965 and I was born there in 1968.

Xu: So, you pretty much have the air of a Zhejiangese.

Mei: My family has always kind of kept the Southern thing going. The timbre of my parents' voices is still the same, but life in the North has given me a cheerful outlook and character. As it turns out, environment does have a pretty big effect on a person's psychological and spiritual self.

Xu: What place did literature have in your life when you were young and what role does it play in your work?

Mei: Back in my teens it was movies that had a huge impact on me. My father worked for a construction company and later left that job for a management position at a production company in Ulanqab. I know it sounds counter-intuitive, but I actually didn't watch many movies when I was young. In the late 1970s and early 1980s, a number of classic Chinese films had another run at the box office. They were all in black-and-white, and that black-and-white imagery left a huge impression on me, especially the ones made before 1949, like *The Spring River Flows*

East and *Eight-thousand Miles of Cloud and Moon*. Of course, I also watched foreign movies like, *Pépé le Moko* and *Zorro* in the cinema, but it was that feeling of Chinese films that caused the real epiphany. I came to the realization that movies are so different from real life. As far as reading goes, I didn't consciously start to have an interest in literature from a certain period of time; but I was kind of subconsciously influenced by my father's hobby of going to Xinhua Bookstore to buy books whenever he got a paycheck. Which is why our house was full of foreign literature. I was most interested in Dickens.

Xu: The films of China in the 30s and 40s, especially the leftist movies, obviously imprinted themselves deeply on your upbringing.

Mei: Correct. Besides, *The Spring River Flows East* and *Eight-thousand Miles of Cloud and Moon*, I also watched *Crow and Sparrow*. The world the characters movies inhabited was completely different from my own world. I don't know why those people appear under the same roof. Although I couldn't understand it at the time, I was very impressed. Later on, learning the history of film, I realized the status of those works in history.

Xu: Did you borrow from any of these classic 30s or 40s films in the creative process of *Mr. No Problem*?

Mei: In the visual design process, I gave the staff the task of watching lots of movies from that time. I personally watched, *Spring in a Small Town* and *Myriads of Lights*. *Myriads of Lights* especially gave me a lot of ideas for aesthetics and stylistic techniques. Later, I watched *Crow and Sparrow* twice.

Xu: It seems that these three films actually make up a kind of trifecta, a group of references that helped scaffold you up and prepare you for your directorial debut. Is that the case?

Mei: Yes, it is. These three films were made in the style of a stage play, so there's that palpable theatrical feeling of everything taking place completely indoors. In the films, they did a tremendous job with staging in the indoor space.

Xu: Apparently literature, especially modern European literature, has had a great influence on you.

Mei: I started reading Western literature from when I was in high school, and Emily Brontë's *Wuthering Heights* left impacted me greatly. In contrast, *Jane Eyre* wasn't impactful enough.

Xu: Then in your heart of hearts, how does Balzac and Dickens' work stack up next to *Wuthering Heights*?

Mei: Balzac and Dickens' novels are basically social documents, which tell of the fates of its characters within the torrents of social change and the tides of the times. Their work will always put people right smack dab in the centre of nineteenth-century Europe, serving as a sort of compass the reader can use to observe and characterize the era. *Wuthering Heights* is a world of spiritual, emotional and highly personal experiences. The *Wuthering Heights* I read back in the day was a woodcut illustrated version of the Foreign Literature Press (a subsidiary of: The People's Literature Publishing House). The evocative descriptions in the book are very ethereal, very detailed and very terrifying. The Hollywood film adaptation is very different from what I visualized when I read the novel.

Xu: You wrote your first screenplay during your college days, called 'A Deserted Island for Two', which is a kind of homage to Ingmar Bergman's *Persona*. In your time in university you were big on the literature of Fyodor Dostoevsky and Eileen Chang, and the films of Ingmar Bergman. These three people, in particular, played a critical role in the development of your artistic sensibilities. Can you tell us about their influence on your creative vision and style?

Mei: The biggest influence on me is *Dostoevsky*. It doesn't matter if you look at it from a literary history perspective, or a sociological, psychological perspective or even the philosophy of religion, the positions he takes in his novels are irrefutable. When I read *Crime and Punishment*, *The Idiot* and his first famous novel *Poor Folk*, I was immediately sucked into their world. After reading *The Brothers Karamozov*, I felt that it had done what literature is best at – helping shape the spirit. Some of his more difficult works that I understand now, I didn't actually fully understand at the time of reading, like *Demons* for example, because I didn't know much about the eras, the radical political groups or social movements outlined in the novels. But they were the most important part of my literary collection in college.

Back then, I often went to the National Library to watch videos. At the time, I didn't know Bergman's status in the history of film. I was sitting in the screening room watching one of his movies and I was floored. If you don't study film history, it's not easy to get that kind of special introduction to Bergman, but after watching the film, I started to going to the library to read *World Cinema* magazine. I read the scripts that best represented each of his periods in this magazine, and the whole experience impacted me greatly.

I didn't really read much of Eileen Chang's work at the time. The earliest exposure to her work was not *The Golden Cangue* or *The Legend Collection*, but *Gaze*. I found out that there was an incredibly talented female writer who had such unique powers of observation and great appreciation of the details of life who lived and wrote in the Republican Era and became obsessed with her. Then, I read *Legend*, which is a lot like *Wuthering Heights*, the strong nightmarish quality to it immediately brings me into a world of visual imagination, spirituality and eccentricity.

There was a great perk of studying at the University of International Relations – all the materials used in foreign language classes were scripts – even our speaking and listening textbooks were scripts from *The Sound of Music*. Plus, on Mondays and Tuesday nights, the school began to hold half an hour of CNN and ABC international news viewing sessions from 6:30 and began showing American TV series or movies at 7:00. I watched a ton of Hollywood classics at the time, such as Brian De Palma's, *Dressed to Kill* and Francis Ford Coppola's, *The Conversation*. I couldn't even understand some of them because there were no subtitles. Later, I went to the Beijing Film Academy to learn about their status in the history of world cinema and began to learn their creative techniques.

Xu: So, now that we've talked about Dostoevsky, Bergman and Eileen Chang, let's talk about Lao She. How did you come into contact with his work?

Mei: I learned about Lao She's work from the history of literature, and I did not make any special efforts to read it. In fact, in my four years of college, I paid more closer attention to the contemporary Chinese literature of today than to modern Chinese literature of the Republican Era. Even to this day, I have yet to get to know the works of Ba Chin, Mao Dun and Shen Ts'ung-wen in their fullness; I've only read their masterworks. The same is true of Lao She. Professor Guo XiaoCong, who gave us a modern literature class back in the day, had some particularly captivating lectures; and he himself was an amazing student at Peking University. When he told us about the history of modern literature, he didn't just make it all about the naked text, but about the author's life and the most important aesthetic parts of the work. He even brought some noteworthy excerpts into the classroom, which made for some pretty interesting and diverse class discussions.

Xu: You have had some civil service experience. What is the impact of civil servant life on your understanding of society and creativity?

Mei: After graduation, I became a civil servant, which means I officially entered 'the system'. My impression of being a part of the system was that you are like a statue or a nameplate on your desk, it's just fixed there, and you can't move. But once you are in it, you find that there is a sense of freedom, like there is a little niche carved out just for you to move around in. Right after I graduated I had the jitters big-time, I was full of worries, angst and uneasiness about my future. I had no idea what my future was going to be like. But after starting my job, I found there was nothing that didn't set well with me. One thing at the time was very important to me – I was sent to work in Hailar for boot camp, and I was supposed to stay there for a year. It was then that the vastness of the world suddenly became vivid – from the office buildings are the vast prairies, the blue skies and white clouds on the grasslands. There was the Yimin River that flows directly north to Russia. We stayed there for a long time. From the geospatial coordinates we always got the impression that the river flowed from the west to the east, but the vast Yimin River actually flows from north to south – it always threw my internal compass off. It was a bit like my own misplaced fate at the time. I had gone from Beijing to Hailar; I might as well have been in Timbuktu. We all say that art imitates life and so I had to get close to life. In that sense, we can understand the works of European romantic writers such as George Sand and Emily Brontë, and they will understand that living life is food for the soul to these artists and is the fodder for spiritual growth.

One year later, I went to Hohhot and started living that metropolitan way of life. I lived the nine-to-five life of a civil servant. In the fourth year on the job, I say first-hand the turning point an era – Deng XiaoPing's southern tour speech. After his speech, the floodgates were opened, and waves of people poured out of the state organizations to do business. In the social environment of 1993 and 1994, the people were on a high, they suddenly started seeing the possibility of a new life. In 1994, with a copy of *Popular Movies* journal in hand, one of my classmates told me that the Literature Department at the Beijing Film Academy was enrolling graduate students. I felt that life had new possibilities. And so, in 1995, I was admitted to the Beijing Film Academy.

A Man of Many Hats

Xu: You are a man who wears many hats – the first is a history teacher and researcher at the Beijing Film Academy, the second is a screenwriter and the third is a director. What kind of relationship is these three sides of yourself? Especially as a screenwriter and director, what is the difference when looking at your own work as opposed to the work of others?

Mei: In my heart of hearts, the ME who is a university professor is the ME like the best. People traditionally have to stick to one career path for their lives. In retrospect, I think that being a professor was my university dream. The university campus is the safest possible environment, and people are the freest there. The life they live every day is reading, studying, exercising or pow-wowing with friends and classmates in their same age group in the same environment. For me, being a screenwriter is pretty worry-free, because the life of a writer mainly centres around a person's work. It's mostly discussing ideas with the Director at certain points in the creative process. I've had the pleasure of working with director Lou Ye, who has excellent work methods. After filming starts he never calls me up to go on-set to do rewrites. That's just the way he works. It's related to how he forms his aesthetic ideas. I only have one directorial experience. Actually, it was just me trying my hand at directing. My greatest feeling about it is that there were too many things to worry about. So many things need to be coordinated and so many decisions need to be made. The Director must have enough courage to withstand the stresses of the job and need to overcome both physical and mental pressure. So, I stress about the critic's arbitrary evaluation of my work.

Xu: As a screenwriter, do you have any regrets about any of your four collaborations with the director Lou Ye?

Mei: I have different feelings about different stages of life. When we first started working together, we would tit-for-tat with each other how much the film belongs to the screenwriter and to how much it belongs to the Director. Lou Ye is not the kind of director who is terribly loyal to the words on the page. To him the script is only the basis and framework of the movie blueprint already in his head. As a director, he brings different elements into play that jive better with his own personal tastes and style. For that reason, the script is just a loose collection of text that serves as the basis for the final cut of a Lou Ye film. At this point, I don't really elaborate on the difference between movies and scripts. There is actually only one kind of movie, that is, the one that the Director worked his fingers to the bone making. As for the script, just like it said in the introduction of that French screenwriting textbook we had translated back in the day – when the film is in the can, the script should be filed away neatly in the round file back behind the studio.

Xu: So, in the making of the film, the Director is always the guy who has the final say?

Mei: Right!

Xu: The reason why so many screenwriters become directors is that the final draft that they typed their soul into is too far from the final cut. Is this one of the driving motivations that made you turn to directing?

Mei: You're on to something there, and in truth, that's basically how it is. If you're passionate about movies, and fate smiles at you and gives you the chance to make one, then you should go all out to express what came from your soul, because your soul types your meaning into the text. Your meaning has linguistic, aesthetic and philosophical significance. I try to focus all this into a spirit or an energy that I imbue into the film.

Xu: So, when did you start thinking about directing your own stuff?

Mei: At the end of 2014, when the Beijing Film Academy proposed the 'Neo Beaux-Arts' program.

Xu: Then you didn't actually think about to direct your own scripts before that?

Mei: Right. My personality or, shall we say, my personal methodology doesn't exactly jive with today's Chinese film market. The Youth Film Studio (note: affiliated with the Beijing Film Academy) has a program in place that lends support to young teachers who want to make own film projects, which gave me a truly fantastic opportunity. At the Shanghai International Film Festival in 2015, the Youth Film Studio held a formal press conference and officially released eight films, six of which were made by teachers of the Beijing Film Academy and *Mr.*

No Problem is one of them. Professors Cao BaoPing and Wang Jing's projects are included in that, and two films were produced by Mr Xie Fei, and the film was directed by his students who are M.F.A.'s.

Xu: Is the 'Neo Beaux-Arts' program going to sync up with today's Chinese market or is the goal to try and do something different than we are seeing in today's Chinese film market or is the goal to contribute to the differentiation and enrichment of the current Chinese market? Because there are examples of films from the program that sync up nicely with the market, like Cao BaoPing's, *The Dead End* and Xue XiaoLu's *Finding Mr. Right* series.

Mei: The diversity seen in *Mr. No Problem*, for example Lao She's writing, the art film aspects, and things like that, have validated the 'Neo Beaux-Arts' as a system, including diversity, complexity, stylistic variety and aesthetic appeal. For example, Wang Jing's *Feng Shui* is basically done in the style of a social documentary art film, which is a totally different approach from Cao BaoPing's focus on commercialism, genre and celebrity. So, in the 'Neo Beaux-Arts' program, there are films done in Cao BaoPing's signature commercial style, then there are those with genre-film stylings, and sensitive emotionality of Xue XiaoLu, and others with the social documentary stylings of Wang Jing, which are made with humanism and ethics in mind. In this sense, the works of these distinguished filmmakers are extremely diverse, each person has his or her own style, and is looking for a space for personal expression. This is the basic framework of the 'Neo Beaux-Arts'. It tries to approximate the movie industry, so that it can maintain a diversity of possibilities, and form a unique voice for the Beijing Film Academy professors who each have their own respective professional creative background.

Xu: You announced the *Mr. No Problem* project at the end of 2014. Why did you choose to adapt Lao She's work?

Mei: A movie channel came to me wanting to do a TV movie to commemorate the 50th anniversary of Lao She's passing, but ran into funding issues, plus at the time I didn't know which one of Lao She's works to adapt, so I didn't spend any time on it and we never moved forward with the project. But later, the Beijing Film Academy launched the 'Neo Beaux-Arts' project, and I put the idea out there for the project to be made at Youth Film Studio. So, actually, after I first made up my mind to do the project, I began actively looking for novels to adapt.

Xu: I systematically read all of Lao She's work?

Mei: Yes, I bought the whole collection lock, stock and barrel.

Xu: When did you start work writing the script? How many redrafts did it go through before getting to the final draft?

Mei: I started writing the script for the project after I got it at the end of 2014. I worked on it until October 2015. It went through about five or six drafts before we had a shooting script.

Xu: Did the distinguished Shu Yi – son of Lao She – lend any advice during the adaptation process?

Mei: Actually no, Mr Shu Yi was very nice. He told me that the movie rights for his father's other literary works had been purchased long ago, but the rights to *Mr. No Problem* had been available for many years and no one seemed even remotely interested. He was very curious about why I was interested in this story. I told him about my intentions for it going forward, and then he let me have the movie rights. Basically, for free. I didn't have to pay any licensing fees.

Xu: Could you talk about the investment structure for the film?

Mei: As a project supported by the Youth Film Studio, there were start-up costs involved. Three or four other production companies took a look at the script and were familiar with the amazing work of actor Fan Wei – who was attached to the project. Total costs after the whole pre-production were about six million RMB.

Xu: So, the main creative staff on the project was basically comprised of professors from the Beijing Film Academy?

Mei: Yes, the principal creative staff were all professors from the Beijing Film Academy and the old graduates from the Youth Film Studio. The sound designer was Zheng JiaQing, professor of the Sound School of the Beijing Film Academy. The art directors were Wang Hao and Zhang DanQing from the Academy's Fine Arts School. The director of photography was Zhu JinJing, a graduate of our cinematography department. Scenery, props and make-up were all supervised by graduates of the Youth Film Studio, who previously worked with Zheng DongTian, Xie Fei and Zhang ShangYu, and worked on Youth Film Studio projects. The graduates had a real soft spot in their hearts for the Youth Film Studio. They heard that it was a project of a Youth Film Studio and an adaptation of a work of the distinguished Mr Lao She and they wouldn't even talk about compensation. They did all the work for free. It really touched my heart.

Casting and Performances

Xu: What was the casting process like?

Mei: We first submitted the script to Fan Wei's agent, we did not tell him who wrote it. Fan Wei was really excited after seeing it and told his agent he'd take the role. We met face-to-face and took to each other real well. Once Fan Wei was attached to the project, the other actors were all in.

Xu: When reading the novel, did you have the Fan Wei in mind for the lead role?

Mei: I generally don't have any particular actors in mind when I write a script.

Xu: You once told me a very interesting thought you had, that there was no good-looking character in this particular project. Were there any conscious casting decisions made?

Mei: That is how I felt at that point in the writing, but when it came to the point of discussing the characters with the actors, I just felt differently. I thought that Lao She must not like any of those characters, they were especially eccentric, over-the-top, dumb and detestable. But when I was actually doing read-throughs with the actors, I found that their creativity breathed life into the characters. The real cast was a great fit for the characters in the novel, which really put my mind at ease.

Xu: Commercial cinema is so eager for eye-candy, especially when it comes to the actors, always looking for the 'objects of desire'. There is a discrepancy between your work and audience demand. You don't emphasize this, which lends even more of an air of realism than what's seen in Lao She's original novel, but the characters still had a that exaggerated, cartoonish kind of feeling to them, similar to what was described in the novel.

Mei: Right. When the novel is to be transformed into a real, tangible, physical and persuasive reality, I try to pick some actors who can draw a bit of distance between the original characters in their appearance, temperament and the way they carry themselves.

Xu: Considering the fact that you have worked as a screenwriter for four films, but never worked as a director, did you have any difficulties in directing the actors?

Mei: I ran into practically every conceivable situation on-set, and it was mainly the rapport between the actors and their and concerted efforts that allowed us to get through it all. Due to the production expenses and actors' scheduling issues, the actors had never gotten together for a table reading and no one had actually even met each other before we rolled cameras in Chongqing. So, mistakes happened with the acting in terms of the rhythm, mood and timing of the performances, and even little things like blocking and movement. They kept on breaking concentration and breaking character. In the face of this situation the only thing I could do was to convince myself over and over again to let the logic of life be my guide. Looking back on it, I do have a few regrets. There were a few scenes where I could've directed the actors a little more accurately. For example, there is a scene where Ding WuYuan and Qin MiaoZhai meet for the first time in the office hall, I kept feeling like it was a little off, but I didn't know what technique I could have used to make it any better.

Xu: At the end of the day, these two characters give off fairly cartoonish and satirical quality, but your directions during the shoot were for them to be played very true-to-life. There was actually a conflict between the two sides idea-wise.

Mei: Yes definitely. I penned the script based on the mood of the novel, but what I filmed was reality. This was a big challenge for the actors.

Xu: When Fan Wei was working on his role, was it more doing his own thing, or did he work closely with you?

Mei: Both actually. Fan Wei's pre-work on the character was really great. He had come up with different ways to perform different scenes and different ways to attack the dramatics of the phrasing in the piece. So, when it came time to shoot the scene, he basically just acted out what was written in the script. Besides being completely faithful to the spirit of the script, Fan Wei ad-libbed a bit and improvised some lines. As long as it seemed comfortable and natural, I was cool with it.

Xu: Oh, so you left things wide-open for improvisation. Besides Fan Wei, did any other actors improvise during filming?

Mei: Everyone else basically stuck to the script.

Xu: The character of the third concubine speaks Shanghainese, a soft-sounding dialect. Did that come from the actress herself?

Mei: Yes. After deciding to give the part of the Third Concubine to Shi YiHong, I figured her husband, Xu Bo, should also be Shanghainese. I read a lot of information on the subject that said lots of showbusiness icons and capitalist tycoons from Shanghai ran off to Chengdu to avoid the war. Boss Xu and the third concubine speak Mandarin on social occasions or in public places, but behind closed doors they speak Shanghainese. We did this, more to create some kind of imaginary idea of what it was like during that era.

Xu: Was the selection from the famous opera, 'The Drunken Concubine' the Third Concubine sang from the script itself, or was it done impromptu?

Mei: It was totally on the spur of the moment. Shi YiHong is tremendously influential in the Peking opera world, and also happens to be the heir-apparent of the Mei School of Chinese opera. The lyrics of 'The Drunken Concubine' are also very relevant to our story.

Themes and Spaces

Xu: Out of so many great books by Lao She, what made you choose *Mr. No Problem*?

Mei: I was looking for a story to set to the screen, there was definitely a method to my madness. I didn't read any of Lao She's novels, novellas or short stories that were familiar to audiences or had been adapted for film and television. For me, it's a really difficult choice to make a film about the Republican Era, because no matter whether you film on the backlot at Chedun Studios or Hengdian World Studios, it would still feel like running off to make some lame serial drama set in the Republican Era. So, the choice of *Mr. No Problem* for adaptation is based on purely visual considerations. Geography-wise, the story is set in a mountain farm near Chongqing, far removed from the modern city, so the place would conjure up an ethereal, heavenly sort of feeling. I thought the confined space and limited scope would lend itself to some pretty cool, cinematic visuals.

Xu: So, first and foremost it was the setting of the novel that attracted you, not the theme?

Mei: The theme attracted me right from the get-go. That said, *Mr. No Problem* has some really unique surprises in store for the reader when taken within the context of *The Complete Works of Lao She*, whose works were basically stories told against the backdrop of Beijing. Then suddenly you get this story set in Chongqing during the Republican era. Lao She created a short work with a super special tone, technique and style. I was really curious about what kind of mood he was in at the time he wrote it, and what the deep meaning behind the story was.

Xu: What is the deep meaning of the novel in your opinion?

Mei: In my humble opinion, the piece is a fascinating 'observation' of the deep structure of Chinese culture – the worldly social culture. Lao She's behavioural logic for Chinese people to live their lives – how they react in the face of problems. He has his own observations on all this stuff, it's not just the surface of the dramatic turns of events.

Xu: So, do you think it is a novel of manners?

Mei: Definitely!

Xu: What is the biggest problem you faced in adaptation it? Or, what did you think needed to be highlighted when the novel was adapted for the screen? What kind of media transformations needed to be made to the text of the novel?

Mei: The first thing that should strike anyone when they read Lao She's novels is the cartoonish, serio-comic tone. Lao She's description of the actions, appearance, air and manners of the three heroes in the book are totally over-the-top. So, the biggest problem for me is how to transform the imaginary world evoked by the author's abstractly transmogrified serio-comic stylings into a tangibly physical world. I could only use the clumsiest way possible, to extract the most important things from the novel and implant them directly into the script. In other words, we first had to write the actions, characters, and lines based precisely on the model and framework of the novel, and then turn it into a more objective narrative tone that is faithful to the physical feelings of life. As time went by though, we found that the sumptuous flavours of the novel were gone. In the script, the tantalizing delicacies produced by the author's novel use of language had turned bland and stale – it just told the story of three men and one woman. So, armed with some new perspective, I started to write the second and third drafts. Down the line, I felt that a two-hour feature length story that takes place entirely on a farm would lead to some aesthetic fatigue and flat-out boredom on the part of the audience. So, to bring some diversity of setting, I created a great family compound for the film that doesn't exist in the novel. Master Xu, Third Concubine and the rich people live in the courtyard. Ding WuYuan manages the farm. He goes to Chongqing and escorts the lords of the manor around helping them live well and be happy. The scenes that were taken in the novel that have no specific setting have been given a 'physical reality'. With the addition of the family compound, the use of space in the film is much more pleasing. Otherwise, the whole movie would just be like one long stage play that shows farm life.

Speaking of sense of space, I'd like to say a bit more about it. The space in *Myriads of Lights* and *Spring in a Small Town* is very natural and does not deliberately emphasize the characteristics of the space itself, it just gives us a feeling – that's where the characters should be. For example, several characters in *Spring in a Small Town*, whether they are walking to the city, going to the river to row a boat or drinking wine in the house, just make you feel good inside. In my opinion, the sense of space in many movies makes me feel real uncomfortable. It seems to be deliberately put together in a certain configuration and feels like it's got that heavy imprint of human design on it. It feels oversaturated. That's why asked for the spaces the Ding WuYuan appeared in to make sense. He plays Mahjong with his wife and some girls and did everything he had to do through the natural course of personal convenience. In this way it feels completely spontaneous when other people and another special configuration present themselves.

Xu: I discovered something, on one hand the film is looking for visual characteristics given a sense of the era; on the other hand, in the completed film the visual features of the era are watered down to some degree. In other words, you spent a lot of effort to find a space that is visually closer to the times, and at the same time you had to handle this space more abstractly.

Mei: The art director Wang Wei and I had had long discussions about that. I told him that, visually speaking, less is more. Like putting a flower stand or a pot of orchids in the room. I watched *Spring in a Small Town* over and over again, so I suggested that he see it, and that really helped clarify his ideas. In the farm set, the props he prepared from the Republican Era were extremely well done. But then I told him to remove certain things. Xu Manor is an extremely opulent place, the furnishings of the house have to be very luxurious – carved beams, tablets, large porcelain bottles; but the masters and ladies usually do not come to the farm, they will not spend money. Ding WuYuan likes this little kingdom. His little room is well arranged – a recliner, a tea set and a fish tank that are absolutely exquisite.

There is also a happy Buddha statue set next to the fish pond. Valuables are locked in the closet and need a key to be opened. But in the common, ordinary setting of the farm, everything had to be taken away, that's where less is more really comes in. The three rooms on the farm are completely different styles – Ding WuYuan's rooms are more traditional and classical, very elegant, close to his own low-key, comfortable state. Qin MiaoZhai's rooms are more artsy, the cabinets are all crooked; the room is totally helter-skelter, with two busted bed boards set up in an ad-hoc manner alongside two totally different benches sitting there. It all looks totally makeshift. No kettle or mirror on the table, and nothing on the wall.

Xu: Which is more important for setting the tone of the film? The locations or the black-and-white imagery?

Mei: The locations. We started to scout for locations in Chongqing before the Spring Festival in 2015. The farm in the novel is very elaborate. Lao She uses a lot of beautiful prose to describe the farm's abundant produce and its otherworldly Xanadu-like beauty, but there is a definite gap between reality and the farm depicted in the novel. No matter where an ancient town is located geographically, the moment it becomes a tourist attraction, it becomes a stereotype. It's like, you've seen one tourist attraction and you've seen them all – it's really sad actually. There was no place in the lush ravines of the southwestern mountain ranges that is just as beautiful as what we saw in the mind's eye. So, we had a whale of a time scouting locations. We went to Red Sand Dyke in Wuxi, where there was a farm located way up at the top of a mountain, more than 3,000 metres in elevation. It was a gorgeous wide-open space. There were cows, horses, sheep, pigs, chickens and ducks all over the place. We photographed everything, but in pictures the place felt more like the northern grasslands than anything else. I was kind of on-the-fence about what to do. The winter's snow hadn't melted yet, and I felt like I was right back on the grasslands of Inner Mongolia in the dead of winter all over again.

Xu: So what kind of farm did you guys finally settle on?

Mei: We finally settled on a farm in Beibei district of Chongqing. The location manager drove us to the location up a mountain road. Several key members of the creative team sat by a window and looked out over a small, flat valley surrounded by tranquil, green mountains. There was just a river and some houses dotted amongst the lush greenery. While we were making our way back down the mountain road, I discussed the whole thing with the cinematographer and the art director, who both felt that the place was a real gem.

Xu: Which place did you guys decide on for Master Xu's residence?

Mei: Old Town Longxing, about one and a half to two hours' drive from downtown Chongqing. Lots of TV dramas that take place in the Republican Era are shot there.

Xu: What factored into your decision to shoot the film in black-and-white?

Mei: I have seen tons of movies set in the Republican Era. Those with high budgets look more beautiful, and the vibrant colour of *Lust, Caution* looks really great. The thing is, we were making the film on a shoestring and shooting in colour would have lost the physical quality of life of the Republican Era. That and the fact that movies from China in the 1940s are all black-and-white, which gives the film a classical vibe, and at the end of the day we were making a film from a book by Lao She. So, the producers thought that making the film in black-and-white was a pretty good idea.

Structure and Characters

Xu: The structure of the great Lao She's original novel was internally divided into a certain number of acts, but actually it does have its own latent structure. You can divide it into three segments. Did this appear at the scripting stage, or was it only made clear when the film was finished?

Mei: The first draft of the script had a three-act structure. When we clarified the book's narrative and adapted it into a narrative of the script, the outline of the structure presented itself. The novel itself is written very clearly as a three-act drama, and later retains its own identifiable characteristics, once we identified them, the script kind of wrote itself.

Xu: From the novel to script to screen, which characters retained the original concept of the novel to the greatest extent, and which characters' screen incarnation ended up being different from that of the original novel?

Mei: Ding WuYuan and Qin MiaoZhai's screen incarnations play as close as possible to their incarnations in the novel. The ones that are really different are You Daxing and Ming Xia. They are depicted in the novel being very dark and negative people. You Daxing is an intellectual who has just returned from studying abroad in the UK. Most of his hair has fallen out, with only a few wisps left in the back, and his clothes are just plain ugly. Ming Xia was never wooed by a gentleman caller when she was young. After You Daxing comes back from England, she starts clinging to the guy and won't let go. She wears You Daxing's love like a badge of honour to show off to her cohorts. She follows him wherever he goes like a little puppy dog. The Ming Xia in the novel is a short, unsightly and frustrated girl who wraps herself in so many layers of clothing that she looks like a little ball. As far as looks are concerned, Third Concubine and Ms Tong as described in the novel, are very beautiful. Although Ming Xia is not good-looking, she is however a well-disciplined, proper and simple woman who really knows her place. When we cast Yin Tao to play Ming Xia, I told the makeup and costume designers not to make her look too bloated, which also brought decisive changes to the ending of the film. Ming Xia in the novel, as the wife of You Daxing, goes with the workers to steal eggs for her husband's welfare. I talked with Yin Tao and we changed her stealing eggs into taking bribes, but even if she accepted bribes, she wouldn't have the heart to tell her husband that. We made some reversals and changes to play up the drama.

Xu: This novel highlights the tragic nature of two people. Of course, tragedy is not absent in the original, but the irony of the original is more obvious, and the tragic hero motif in your film is clearer. As a person who wants to reform Chinese society in some small way, You Daxing actually has a skosh of heroic temperament and lofty tragic sentiment. Ming Xia is true blue to her husband and wants to do whatever it takes for him. She actually believes that what she does should be reasonable in the grand scheme of Chinese society. Whether it is the consciousness of a heroic reformer or a woman who tries to fit in with the ways and the mores of China in a specific historical period, both ultimately fail. This raises the tragic stakes. Ding WuYuan exhibits a clearer understanding of how the game is played in Chinese society according to its firmly embedded rules than You Daxing does. These two characters were completely different from their incarnations in the novel. That said, there are also some middle-of-the-road characters who seem to have retained some of the flavour of the original novel. Third Concubine, for instance.

Mei: If you're too faithful to the novel, you may lose some end up going deaf to other voices that should be heard. In the sense of the novel, it is not easy for us to see the deeper complexities of Ding WuYuan – she's good at socializing and has excellent relationships with her superior officers as well as her subordinates, so as to effectively protect her standing and give her life stability, and she serves the Lords with a positive disposition and a happy heart. But if I'd just left it at that, there wouldn't have much in the way of dramatic tension. So, I created the characters of a Boss Tong and Boss Xu. Ostensibly the two families they are on intimate terms, totally chummy-chummy and buddy-buddy, even calling each other brother and sister; but when it comes to business, the two have totally separate and conflicting interests. Chinese culture is pretty intriguing. The two men are united on face, divided in heart; but the man's Third Concubine and the other man's daughter are close friends. In their sisterly relationship, some subtly amazing things are sure to happen. For example, in the movie, there is a pretty nifty conversation between the two of them. Third Concubine is worried about Miss Tong's marriage and advises her to marry soon, but boss Tong is really afraid that her daughter would find an unreliable son-in-law to wrest his property away. The script is completely different from the novel. In the novel, the military police catch two students who are squatting on the farm. These two students are taken away by on suspicion of being traitors and have nothing to do with Qin MiaoZhai. But in the script, boss Tong is worried about his property, he's afraid that Qin MiaoZhai would run away with Miss Tong, so he sends the military police to catch Qin MiaoZhai. But in the end the wrong person is caught. Mrs Zhang spills the beans to Third Concubine when she's beaten in a game of Mahjong. Third Concubine is furious and throws a fit to Master Xu, telling him he actually treated Boss Tong as one of his own, but Boss Tong sent people to their farm to accuse them of being traitors. That conversation between Third Concubine and Boss Xu is very important. Based on what Lao She started in the book, the film took what he had already done a step further and brought a different colour and timbre to it. Even the details that have been brought in the novel, such as between the shareholders – the rich, the capitalists, the two-faced double dealing, the angling, the infighting. It was all vitally important to the film. To prepare to write the script, I read a lot of background materials from the Chongqing era of the War of Resistance, and Ding WuYuan's dramatic fate became clear. In the novel, he only faced a crisis, that is, his job was at stake, but in the script, the situation becomes much more delicate – he was standing with Boss Xu but also suspected by Boss Tong. To replace him, Boss Tong promoted Yu Daxing, who had just returned from the West, to the position of the director. Behind the incident is a classic case of infighting. These are some of the biggest changes to the story during adaptation.

Xu: Ding WuYuan is the closest character to the original incarnation. He reminds me of a concept 'round character'. In the jungle of the relationship between the characters, when a person comes into contact with other people, he or she shows a different person, or 'face' to others. The characters themselves are enriched while developing complexities in association with the surrounding characters.

Models and Style

Xu: Visually, although the film is not entirely Bazin style, it is still pretty close to it. Was this a conscious creative decision?

Mei: Yes. When I was doing visual design before shooting, I was in constant communication with the DP. I said, even though there is some dramatic turns of events in Chief Ding that ruffle his feathers a bit, he felt like he was doing Tai Chi the whole time, his character is like a rock. So, the camera needed to be stable on him the whole time, so it was always mounted on a tripod. Qin MiaoZhai is an intruder and destroyer, so we did a lot of handheld mobile photography and Steadicam work. The character of You Daxing needed to be dark, so the scenes between he and Ming Xia were basically shot at dusk, except for the morning scenes. You Daxing's part should have absolutely no tracking or moving shots, so the camera was stationary on him from beginning to end. The audience would have the illusion that the movie was one stationary shot after the other from beginning to end, and the motion shots, tracking shots, dolly shots, handheld shots and so forth, in the middle would seem to disappear from the memory.

Xu: Because in the second part, the main bulk of Chief Ding's scenes were shot with a stationary camera, breaking up the visual impression formed by Qin MiaoZhai's handheld shots. The continuity of the stationary shots would kind of form a visual pattern. The choice of far-off, wide shots brings a certain sense of separation from the film, is that what you were looking for?

Mei: Yes. Do not make moral judgments about the characters. We like Jean Renoir because he does not make any so-called black-and-white, clear moral judgements about people. How did he do it without judgement? This is related to his dramatic method or shaping the character, and also related to the objectivity of his shots. Jean Renoir's visuals and Hollywood's visual and narrative system have a particularly wide aesthetic gap between the two, or perhaps they themselves are two separate systems. Now, our movie tries not to replace it with a positive or negative shot or to disassemble the shots. Once we get emotionally involved, the audience will be distracted from the subjective, panoramic birds-eye view of the characters and the human condition. The most important thing about Lao She's novel is that he did not invest himself emotionally in them. The exaggeration, the inaccuracies, the distortion and irony of the characters in the novel sometimes reaches a mean level, because Lao She did not get involved, and the novel did not show the 'I' of the narrator. The camera lens of the film also needs to be like Lao She's narrator. We can't draw attention to the 'camera'.

Xu: Many people have mentioned that the film plays pretty close to a Japanese film.

Mei: At that time, I didn't choose Japanese movies as a reference for aesthetics and visual design. I chose only to watch those early Chinese movies. I talked more with my cinematographer about Robert Bresson's, *Au hasard Balthazar*, which refers to the way it organizes the natural countryside and indoor spaces. However, the final result is easy to reminiscent of Mizoguchi Kenji's long takes cinematographic method – beautiful tracking shots, and large depth of field, aesthetics-wise they look like a scroll painting. Very similar to Stanley Kubrick. So, you will find that using an aesthetic compass in the history of film is useful, but risky at the same time.

Xu: The *mise-en-scène* in the film borrows a lot of classic film aesthetics. For example, Ozu Yasujiro and Hou Hsiao-hsien. In addition, the way they use the synecdoche to avoid conflicting actions and the method of displaying partial images instead of the whole is somewhat like Robert Bresson. When you gave the scripts you'd written to Lou Ye, you consciously wanted him to use Bresson-esque stylistics in the piece. Now that you are your own director, you definitely take Robert Bresson as your aesthetics reference. How did you go about drafting your storyboards?

Mei: We didn't storyboard the film. But in mind I already had a visual map.

Xu: How long did it take to edit the film?

Mei: A month or two, because we had a total of less than two hundred shots. The individual takes are pretty long. By cutting the film according to the script, the pacing and information in the shots were simple, and it was about the same length as we expected. I even think that the creatively edited scenes are represented by the people working in the field are very interesting.

Xu: What did you add to the film in post-production?

Mei: The post-production process allowed me to understand what the real pacing of the film. The importance of editing isn't just unifying the style, it was also the opportunity to conceptualize a wholly new visual experience for the audience that's unlike anything they've seen before. I couldn't make it a panoramic view or put the audience in the middle of a panorama or a huge panorama from the opening fade in to the ending credit roll. So, the close-up shots placed in the middle of the film allowed for adjustments to the pacing. There are two scenes in particular that will keep the audience from getting bored. One is the scene where Xiao Shaoye's birthday is over. The audience will definitely feel the rhythmic ups and downs. The other is that the scene after Yu Daxing's comes and works in the field where the pacing and tonal shifts give the audience a breath of fresh air just as the air starts growing a bit stale, so to speak.

Xu: What about sound design?

Mei: The sound brings another dimension to the film, giving the audience a sense of realism or illusion. We designed the sound on a Dolby 5.1 Surround Sound System. Zheng JiaQing's sound work is particularly sophisticated and multi-textured. The sound of playing Mahjong in the middle of the night, the sound of bombings off in the distance when the characters are eating and chatting in the house, and the landing of the shells. A cacophony of sounds can be heard in concert, the sound of insects, chickens, barks, cattle and sheep on the farm. These sounds will be especially clear in a surround sound theatre. When Ding WuYuan's name comes up on the screen, the sound of an owl hoot is audible. When You Daxing's name comes up, you can hear the ticking of a clock, emphasizing that he comes to work in a timely and efficient manner. The sound effects are amazing, but they don't stick out at you of course. It's necessary to create sound design with a natural logic. JiaQing took the job real serious and got real creative writing an explanation for all the sound effects.

Xu: And finally, is there anything you'd like to say to the prospective audience of the film?

Mei: This is a slow-paced, black-and-white art film; but it is also a very beautiful movie to look at, with dramatic, well-fleshed out characters and things that happen with a dramatic effect. I believe this film bring the audience a singular experience like no other.

Xu: Ok, we're all looking forward to its release.

15. Interview with Director Lu Yang: What Matters Is What You Do with the Truth

Date: 8 August 2017
Location: VIP Room of Chinese National Academy of Arts
Interviewee: 路阳/Lu Yang (Director of *Brotherhood of Blades II: The Infernal Battlefield*)
Interviewer: 贾磊磊/Jia LeiLei (Researcher, Chinese National Academy of Arts)
Compiled by Wang YuCan and Zhang YiWen

Creative Genesis

Jia LeiLei (hereinafter referred to as Jia): Where did your creative ideas for this film come from?

Lu Yang (Hereinafter referred to as Lu): In the beginning there was a conception, about an encounter between Shen Lian and the artist Bei Zhai in a mountain. And it was good. Shen Lian is a fan of Bei Zhai, but Bei Zhai doesn't know that this person idolizes him, even after their encounter in the mountain. A Ming imperial guard who is part artist, part hit-man and his unexpected encounter with a gorgeous painter, and therein was the life of the idea.

Jia: You mean that the first inklings of the characters began like this?

Lu: I just visualize cool characters, and then visualize a cool meeting. Then look for the connection between the characters and history and put the characters into it. I wanted to take *Brotherhood of Blades II* to another level than part one, and then put our heroes right into the thick of history. Of course, no one can change history. But, sometimes a person may profoundly influence someone who can change history.

Jia: You guys first wrote a literary story. Later, during the filming, a literary story became poetry of image. Did you hit any speedbumps during the process, and is there anything you're unsatisfied with?

Lu: Transforming a literary script to image form is definitely a taxing process. However, our problems weren't that pronounced, since I was involved in writing the script from day one. I wrote the script together with the screenwriter and went through the entire process together with him. So, the whole time we were working on I was visualizing the finished product on the fly; I'd basically internalized it. After the script was finished, we went to look at the shooting locations and after we got back we could storyboard the whole thing. If you aren't there every step of the way through the conception and writing of the script, but then have to go through a process of visualizing it, it makes things hard. So, you'd better just do it from the beginning, then you'll be all up to speed.

Jia: Then from the very beginning you'd begun thinking about the need to visualize a literary story?

Lu: Yes, it was all pretty vivid in my mind the whole time we were writing the script.

Kung Fu and Drama, Both the Stuff of Film

Jia: The martial arts film will inevitably involve conceptualizing a lot of scenes of violence. How did you and action director, Sang Lin, work with each other during the making of the film?

Lu: Director Sang Lin is a very imaginative fight choreographer. He started working with the action directors in Hong Kong and later went to Hollywood to take a lot of movies. But he always gives his action scenes a human touch. He majored in Chinese in college, so he's totally unlike any other action director you'll ever meet. He and I have had some real lively discussions. He knows every historical reference and the origin of every weapon like the back of his hand. Right from the start we decided we wanted a realistic tone to the film. The action had to look real, to have a sense of realism to it. At the same time, I also told him that we needed to keep the drama going in the action scene. The characterizations had to be there, we couldn't lose the character portrayals because of all the action. Because to me, theatre and action are both the stuff of film. The rhythm of the drama absolutely cannot be broken.

Jia: In most movies, it's almost like you can see the demarcation line between drama and action. How do you as an artist see the creative methods employed in drama and martial arts films? Are there any differences?

Lu: The scene where the archive is being burned, which is actually drama crossed with martial arts. It's a parallel narrative. And after the two narrative threads become one, there is another battle. To maintain realism, we really limited the use of wires in the martial arts scenes. I actually shot a lot of footage with wires, but later cut whatever was done with wires to the very bare bones. The action scenes were the same. People can't scale a wall in one jump, fly very high, or fly very far. I don't think that stuff looks good, and I didn't want it in this movie. Especially those parts that I think seem to violate the laws of physics on the screen, I left all that stuff right on the cutting room floor.

Jia: That was the right call I think. Otherwise this film would be too easily confused with some generic martial arts action film.

Lu: I argued with Sang Lin until I was blue in the face on this point, but he finally came around. I don't want to break the tone we'd established from the first film. I hoped to create a real world for my characters to inhabit, one where Shen Lian doesn't have the guts to kill people indiscriminately, because killing is against the law, then he'd be in some serious trouble and be hunted down.

Jia: There are lots of actors working in China today who don't know the martial arts. With that in mind, what were your considerations when casting the film?

Lu: In our criteria, first and foremost, we had to consider the complete performance. It all goes back to that concept I mentioned earlier, both drama and martial arts are the stuff of film. We had to think of whether an actor was right for the part. Because we were planning to shoot a ton of close-ups in the action scenes, what could be read on the face was of prime importance, it wasn't all about the body. I even think that acting ability helps the action, because, it can evoke emotions in the audience, who will then suspend disbelief, and be totally committed to the truth of this action. The resulting action scenes are all the more enjoyable. So, in the early stages of casting, we put a ton of scrutiny on whether this actor could actually act and act well.

Jia: Considering the fact that *Brotherhood of Blades II: The Infernal Battlefield* is a martial arts movie with costumes and sword fights, there are almost no professional martial artists in the film. How did filming go so smoothly in the action scenes?

Lu: There is only one athlete, one true martial artist, and that was the actor who played the eunuch of the East Faction of imperial guards. He is a professional martial artist. He's actually a pretty capable dramatic actor, and he turned in a very intelligent performance. Though the character he plays is pretty boxed in. There's not a lot of room for creativity. That said, he fleshed it out well. The end product was a very Pekinese court eunuch, a middle-level minister of the East Faction, though he didn't play him very evil. The character is loyal and dutiful until his death. And all of our actors did intensive stunt and action training well before we started filming. We had to take into account the fact that these actors were used to starring in dramas. Dialogue movies. Most of them had done very little action work before signing on for this film, so we had to reserve some time for training. While that was going on, the main actors talked about the script, and the rhythms, their parts, and discussed the motivations of their characters. They did some pretty intense preparation before filming began.

Jia: It's not easy for actors to find time in their busy schedules to come together and discuss a script.

Lu: It's definitely not easy. We got together for a week! That's not something that happens very often, and I was very happy about it. Of course, the more time you spend on anything, the better it will be. There are a few scenes that we had to rehearse the day before. We rehearsed the scene of eating vegetarian food in the Yongan Temple was the day before we shot it. We rehearsed for a whole afternoon. The actors really had it down pat, so that made for an easy shoot. They were clear on every single detail. What to do in the scene, where to find the drama and conflict, where to tense and where to relax. If we could've done that for every scene, things definitely wouldn't be better.

Jia: That scene looks great and plays really well.

Lu: But we were limited a little bit, there was no way to rehearse every scene beforehand.

Jia: Was it a scheduling issue?

Lu: Yes. We had no breathing room in the shooting schedule at all, day shoots were difficult to control, and preparation for night shoots took a long time, but was easier to manage. During the day, it was sunny one minute and rainy the next, and the heat gave some of the actors heatstroke. Then the bridge came crashing down filming a suspension bridge scene. It would rain five or six times during the day and all we could do was wait. We didn't know how long the rain would last, so we'd shoot as quickly as we could after the rain stopped. If we couldn't film the scenes that day, the actors contracted on-set hours would run out, so we had to rush to get their scenes while we had the chance. Zhang Zhen really saved our bacon, he gave us nearly ten extra days and didn't charge us a thing. We had to hurry shoot as fast as possible. But we were really under the gun the whole time.

Martial Arts Action Supported by Digital Technology: 10:1

Jia: How many shots does this film have?

Lu: Around 4000 or so.

Jia: Besides final colour correction, how many shots were processed digitally?

Lu: The final print went through digital intermediate colour correction. The current process generally calls for all shots to have at least some correction done. Our colourist is a man of great skill, let me tell you. He has a foundation in pre-shooting and cinematography, he is unbelievable at colour control, and lighting control as well. So, many times he had to restore the effect we got in the pre-shoot. Because the tone of the original footage was kind of grey, and had a big dynamic range, so we had to find a way to restore the tones we saw on the monitor in the pre-shoot. In some spots we had to even out the tones to make them like the environment we had on set.

Jia: How much 3D graphics work was done in the film? What kinds of lenses did you use throughout the shoot?

Lu: There are about five-hundred CGI Effects shots, of which about two-hundred are relatively simple erases, such as wire removal, digital environmental alteration, and more than one-hundred environmental supplements, for example, some environments were shot on a sound stage. Inside, we needed a building-complex, but we could only cover one-half of the building. After finishing the green screen shots, whole CG environments were constructed and dropped into the shots. In fact, there were so many special effects in the film, and some audiences may not even notice them. In the part where the archives are set on fire, that entire large building complex was actually shot on a sound stage, and the small buildings around it were all special effects dropped in.

Jia: How much of the overall budget was dedicated to special effects?

Lu: Less than ten per cent.

Jia: Oh, that's pretty small.

Lu: Yes. More specifically about eight per cent or so.

Jia: Mainly for post-production?

Lu: Yes, it was a little more than we budgeted for in pre-production. The money was mainly spent on wire removals, background CGI and all that stuff. It ended up being more than we had budgeted for initially. Due to the fact that we have a very complete shooting script in pre-production, and we storyboarded everything out, we knew exactly what we wanted in each shot; we could still make a pretty accurate estimate.

Jia: Your script was completely storyboarded right?

Lu: Yes, with individual storyboards.

Jia: After storyboarding was complete, how much did you change on set?

Lu: Not more than ten per cent.

Jia: You basically shot everything exactly according to the storyboards?

Lu: Yes, because we spent fifty days during pre-production storyboarding the film, and we storyboarded each scene. The way we did it was like this: First we complete the script, then afterwards the art department and costume departments did their work copying what was in the storyboards, because when we were writing the script, the art director went out to view the locations. After giving a thumbs up to all the locations, including the interiors and exteriors, the art department made a mock-up of each location, including the size, furnishings and room layout; when that was all done, all we had to do was to make the storyboards according to the models; the purpose of modelling each scene was to embed the *mise-en-scène* right into storyboards. I think we staged each scene about seven or eight different ways, and pick what I thought was the best out of them. I chose whatever design just fit best in the shot. We would reconceptualize the shots according to the models and then go from there.

Jia: There are many martial arts movies that make textual changes in the script when shooting on location.

Lu: We had conceptualized and reconceptualized the thing to death in pre-production, so the chances of any changes on set were slim. But occasionally an actor would make a suggestion we felt fit in well within the context of the scene, the suggestions or maybe some other members of the creative team would have a flash of inspiration, or someone might improvise something within the process of shooting, so there were some minor changes. Also, because once changes are made the entire scene has to be redesigned. When shooting, we normally have everything storyboarded out before we ever roll camera. For example, the night before the shoot, I'd draw the camera placements onto the storyboards and then think over the order of each setup. Because time on set is super tight, how I order things between shot-to-shot is critical, as it directly affects efficiency and rhythm of the shoot.

Jia: Martial arts movies are pretty heavy on action, how many cameras do you have rolling during your important action scenes?

Lu: Up to three. Because when there are too many cameras clicking away at one time, there is no particularly good-looking angle. After you start shooting, some angles may be scrapped. Most of the time it's two cameras, even when shooting action scenes, sometimes even just one camera. Because when you shoot with more than one camera, it limits your ability to optimize lighting and angles. You have to compromise on the number of cameras you use, or the scene won't look very good. Sometimes I start a scene shooting with three cameras, and if it doesn't look good, I remove the extra ones.

Films That Speak to the Current Generation

Jia: King Hu also imbued a lot of his martial arts films with the Ming Dynasty background, such as *The Valiant Ones* and *Dragon Gate Inn*, including *A Touch of Zen*, are stories based on a large historical dynasty. What do you think of King Hu's swordplay films?

Lu: The Hong Kong movies that I was first exposed to when I was a child were all from the early 80s. I actually first saw Director Hu's films when I went to the (Beijing) Film Academy, and it was there that found a bunch of films about the Ming Dynasty imperial guards. Or else they were about the East Faction and West Faction. Their aesthetics and visuals were completely based on director Hu's own creative ideas. I only know that he was really truly amazing. The way he made his films and the structure he created affects filmmakers even today.

Jia: How did he influence your work?

Lu: Back at that time, we were doing martial arts movies and wondering how we could step out from under Hong Kong cinematic conventions and use other techniques to make action pictures. But King Hu, Tsui Hark or Ang Lee's films all had a profound impact on me. I watched action movies from an early age and was a huge fan of the genre. However, due to each generation's different views and perspectives on the world, the angles we see things from are definitely not the same as Hu's. I was raised on a steady diet of classic films. After learning from the great directors of the past, I hope I can make some films that speak to the current generation. So, this is the approach I took in making *Brotherhood of Blades*.

Jia: *Brotherhood of Blades* has some flashes of humanism in it. It speaks of the value of the individual's existence, which was rarely mentioned in the any other martial arts films, and it ended on a social justice standpoint. Then, in the *Brotherhood of Blades II*, out of Lu Wenzhao and Shen Lian, Lu Wenzhao may be more inclined to the side of individual worth, the negative side of pursuing individual worth; and then Shen Lian makes a return to righteousness. However, he not only talks about social justice, but accomplishes his mission at the social and historical levels. His devout personal feelings sometimes even surpass his just mission. This is the continuation of the mindset first established in *Brotherhood of Blades I*.

Lu: When we created the second part, we seemed to be somewhat aware of the awakening and thought processes of the characters themselves. There may be a little bit of philosophical underpinnings here, but that was not our original intention. The character does hope. He thinks about what kind of soul is the soul of freedom. He contemplates the question of faith and belief, thinking about the interests of individual and the group, weighing which is more important, and how to balance this relationship.

Jia: The film doesn't just function on the action level, but also on an ideological level, reflecting on the pursuit of individual value and self-worth. This kind of thinking or expression, in a sense, has philosophical significance.

Lu: Confronted with a choice between power and emotion, the king chose righteousness. He needed the kingdom to be just, and to save the dynasty – a lofty goal for which he is willing to sacrifice many lives. From Shen Lian's point of view, the king's belief may be correct. But is there no value for those individuals who were sacrificed? Isn't the value of these people important compared to another country? This may be a question that our entire generation will contemplate. What I mean is, to sacrifice the one for many, isn't this absolute justice?

Jia: So, what's your opinion?

Lu: I think that from an individualist perspective, he should have had more autonomy, independent thought, and more complete selfhood. And he should have had his own firm beliefs. It is his self-doubt that led directly to having to go out and face the world, and everyone in turn questions his motives. When he sticks to his guns, he has to pay a huge price. Would you still stick to your own beliefs in the same situation? I think that most viewers don't think about this when watching the movie, but some might. After all, it is presented as a genre film, so the subject is still a story, a character, an archetype and so on. However, some viewers have discussed these ideas with me, which made me happy.

Brotherhood of Blades Is the *Type of Film that I Really Want to Make*

Jia: So, let's talk about your current worldview. Do you identify with the idea of the free soul of the person or the individual? Where does this mindset fit in to your life at this stage?

Lu: It fits in some small way. Because reading comic books was a highlight for my generation. The culture of comics and manga and so forth was actually introduced from abroad, but from a young age the culture of comics had already permeated our consciousness. And to tell you the truth, it brought us all something different that the education we had received up to that point. Whether it's comics or games, novels or movies (Xu Xuan also reads comic books), we must have been nourished by it in some way, not only the hot comic of the hour for teens, or the collector's item issues, but also a lot of comics with social commentary, many of them are social, ethical and family-oriented, and they're just as amazing as the superhero or manga for teens. It's great that there is such a wide selection. It means that you're exposed to a wide variety of ideas.

Jia: We went to Fujian and Guangzhou some time ago to get to know the art education over there, at the primary and secondary school levels, as well as at the university level. But at what stage do we discuss with the teachers about the children's worldview? It seems kids' worldview is actually formed in the upper grades of elementary school.

Lu: Yes, that's about right.

Jia: And it's completely formed by about middle school or high school. Like our generation, I also thought about my worldview later, including my understanding of movies. Our 'red memories' from the fourth and fifth grades of primary school. Just look at the films, *Zhang Ga the Soldier Boy*, *Guerrillas on the Plain* and *The White-haired Girl*. Maybe you might read some comics and establish your own value judgements from it.

Lu: Yes.

Jia: Not long ago an American movie called *Sully* was released. I read the book Captain Sully wrote, it's called *Highest Duty*, which I also recommended to my students. When Sully was 13 years old, he heard that a girl was killed in her own home.

It was splashed across the headlines in the States at the time. More than thirty families in the girl's neighbourhood heard her cries for help and her bloodcurdling screams, but no one came to save her. Sully made up his mind in that moment that if anything like that happened in the future, he would definitely come to help. Later, in his fifties he landed a plane safely in a river that had been disabled by a bird strike. Captain Sully's story had a tremendous impact on people, young and old. Those comics, or cartoons you were so fond of when you were young do actually have a big impact on people. You now control the tools of the film narrative, actually telling a story with a boyhood and childhood dreams, giving you the power to impact people. Very interesting.

Lu: Yes it is.

Jia: I've noticed a pattern in cinematic history. There are many directors who got their start making art films, and later enter the world of mainstream film production. For you, how did you make the transition? Can you simply describe it? I'm mainly referring here to the psychological aspects, your value recognition and so forth, how did that transition happen?

Lu: Actually, let it be said that *Brotherhood of Blades* is the type of movie that I really want to make. But in the beginning, I was desperate for the opportunity to make any movie, no matter what kind. So long as it was a movie. I had an investor backing me, and I liked that story very much. Actually, when I was filming *My Spectacular Theater*, I tried to use some genre film techniques to tell the story of that movie.

Jia: Your first movie had genre film stylings like those in *Brotherhood of Blades*?

Lu: Yes. When I was filming *My Spectacular Theater*, we used a lot of handheld photography, which seemed to be subconsciously preparing for the future filming of *Brotherhood of Blades*.

Jia: Roman Polanski said that all of his films were made in preparation for *The Pianist*, the theme of which has been his most enduring. The first films the fifth generation of directors in China wanted to make was the stories they'd carried with them since their teenage years. But years after making *Yellow Earth*, Chen KaiGe went on to make *King of the Children*. Every generation has its own obsessions.

The Point of the Movie Is the Choices the Characters Make After Seeing the Truth

Jia: Let's go back to the subject of martial arts movies. Because there are many entries in the genre that take the word 'sword', in their name like, *The One-Armed Swordsman* and *Blood Sword*, *Brotherhood of Blades* is more like a topic. The film is named after a 'Brotherhood of Blades'. It is not deliberately described as 'knife'. What was going through your mind at the time you named the project?

Lu: At the beginning of the project, I wrote it about a character who was an, 'imperial guardsman', so I wanted to call it 'The Imperial Guardsman'. (Note: the Chinese name of the film is 繡春刀 meaning Imperial Guardsman.)

Jia: Another movie about the 'imperial guardsmen?'

Lu: Well, at that time, director Daniel Lee Yan-kong's film, *14 Blades* had been released, but you can't use duplicate names in the industry. The only thing I could do was choose a different name. That's why I named it, *Brotherhood of Blades*.

Jia: You said before that you wanted to name part one the 'Imperial Guardsman?'

Lu: Yes, I wanted to call it 'Imperial Guardsman' when it was first conceived. But the advantage of calling it *Brotherhood of Blades* is that the blade can actually represent the guards who wear the embroidered uniforms, and the name 'Brotherhood of Blades' has a feeling of great conflict to it. Just the sound of it is romantic, and the blade can be used to kill. It fits right in with what I had in mind right for the character right from the start. He is conflicted between his conscience and his duty. It is surrounded by an air of mystique and romanticism. And to top it all off, it is a noun that is quite unfamiliar to most viewers.

Jia: What I mean is, from the very beginning, you had your heart set on the title, 'Imperial Guardsman'.

Lu: 'Imperial Guardsman' is pretty popular, pretty direct.

Jia: And it has a certain ring to it.

Lu: Yes, but it was already taken, so there was nothing I could do about it.

Jia: *Brotherhood of Blades II* had 20 separate investors. In today's market climate, it is very important for a young director to earn the trust of the market. Based on this trust, what does the future hold for part three? Or will you take your creativity in a different direction?

Lu: It may continue from the same theme, but it is not necessarily possible to make a *Brotherhood of Blades III* right away or even continue down the road of these same kinds of period action movies. It is also possible to take a stab at other genres, but I will most likely continue on exploring things in this same direction. I'm planning to make a modern movie down the road.

Jia: Is it going to be an action movie?

Lu: There's going to be action, suspense and quite a few are fantasy elements. It is not fantasy realism; it is realist fantasy. And there is going to be plenty of magic in it.

Jia: This sounds great, change it up a little bit. So, about the genre mash-up thing, you just said that you wanted to set a new standard, or at least make a really great genre film. If that's the case, then there are a bunch of things you could do with the mash-up. For instance, I started watching the movie and felt that it was really similar to *Nirvana in Fire*, because the movie started with a bloody battle, with 270,000 people of the Red Flame Army meeting their death, it was pretty out-of-this-world. How did you go about writing a martial arts epic like that?

Lu: The initial concept just started with two characters who unwittingly got embroiled in a conspiracy that could cause revolutionary change in the era they are living in. It had to involve a great number of characters and power struggles as well. Actually, the conspiracy in it had to be much larger than the one in *Brotherhood of Blades*; and far more complex. And the stakes had to be huge. Then on top of that *Brotherhood of Blades II* adds a little detective work and logical deduction on top of the action and suspense. This time around, Shen Lian may have taken on more of a detective role. The first half of the story is him doing the detective thing and cutting through the fog of lies to find the truth. But actually, the film itself is not about the truth, but it's about how to make choices after seeing the truth. More of the deduction and reasoning is concentrated in the first two-thirds of the film. In fact, the real focus is on what you do after the truth is revealed.

Jia: The content of the second half.

Lu: Yeah.

Jia: Actually, every movie has to have something the audience can root for. For you, Shen Lian definitely leans more towards the good guy role. But Lu Wenzhao, and this is just my personal take on it, but I think he is actually more able to touch on the hopes and desires of the individual audience members. In the beginning actually, he awakens a value system in one of the characters. He wants to sidestep human fate and find self-worth. This self-worth thing is something everyone can grab on to, but he ultimately goes in another direction, and he no longer cares about things like his mission and faith. He is more concerned about his own existence and way of life. Lu Wenzhao seems to exist in a state where his values are floating, starting in one direction and then meandering over to the other. Maybe the average viewer might really identify with a character like that.

Lu: I wanted to write Lu Wenzhao a little bit like the kind of person you might meet in real life. Shen is fiercely idealistic. Very absolutist. His value system is entirely oriented around chivalry and freedom. Lu Wenzhao on the other hand is very pragmatic. He might be willing to abandon love and integrity to realize his values. He has big goals and aspirations and wants to be the game-changer for the whole universe, which is just him staking his claim to his rights. But that doesn't actually happen when it's all said and done. In general, he has positive value system and a fuzzy value system. Positive values represent an ideal universal value that we need to spread widely, whereas fuzzy values are closer to pragmatic reality.

Rimu Defense has this little boy in it whose parents got divorced and then he gets bullied a lot in school. His mother gets sick and no one takes care of him. He gets very depressed and then summons a huge monster from his mind to accompany him. The monster tells him three stories. Usually the stories we tell children are the prince and princess, good and bad guy, hero and villain variety, but there is no good or evil in the story that the monster tells him. When the story is finished, the child just loses it. He starts bawling. He asks why what the good guys do doesn't sound so good, and why what the bad guys do doesn't sound so bad. The monster tells him that this is the real world. You have to see the real world. There are not many princes and princesses to speak of. Good and evil are not so clear-cut. Human nature is often floating around a grey area somewhere. Everyone is very similar. The key is what choices you make at a certain moment in time.

Jia: Absolutely. At the beginning of the film, there is a character working on a case who gets killed. Why does Pei Lun want to catch Shen Lian? Because the person Shen Lian is in hot pursuit of is his friend. It's the ties of friendship and brotherly love at play. Ultimately Shen Lian admits the man is his friend too. You know, love has always been a particularly important value in Chinese martial arts films.

Not just for martial arts movies, the same holds true for war films actually. Is it that writing a war film about social conscience into a story about a just war is something everyone would want to watch? People these days are not easily satisfied with oversimplified depictions of justice. We are more interested in the self-expression of people who they identify with. For a movie like that to attract so many people make a lot of sense. I don't think our audience are going to watch the movie just for the visuals anymore, they are going to start paying attention to the meaning behind martial arts movies.

Lu: Yes, because this is actually moralism it is rooted in two divergent schools of thought. One moralistic and idealistic, the other practical and pragmatic. Shen Lian sticks to something that exists outside of the moral codes. Shen Lian is just that kind of guy. Thought as a member of the Imperial Guard, there are some lines that he still won't cross. And that line is his honour. We need to look at it in that context.

I Want My Film to Have Oriental Flair

Jia: So, what kind of overall visual style were you going for on this movie?

Lu: Well, I wasn't totally clear on that when I started. I discussed that very question with my D.P. The film features a lot of imagery that's not very commonly seen in movies, like the bamboo forest night scene, few directors have shot imagery like that before.

We all know that, whether you're talking about Ang Lee, Zhang YiMou or King Hu, they've all done bamboo forest scenes before, but they were day scenes, because nighttime bamboo forest scenes are difficult to shoot. Bamboo is really dense, light doesn't get in so easily, making the movie lighting used seem artificial. On this film we wanted the night scenes to seem like natural light, so we tried lots of different ways. The exterior scenes of the Beijing – the streets, alleys and canals were mostly shot in the Tai'er Zhuang ancient town in Shandong, because the place is a fully restored ancient Chinese village, which looks really similar to the feel of Ming Dynasty Beijing, in terms of colour and texture. Greys, browns, reds, crimsons. But filming there was big-time problematic. It is not a film and television backlot. It wasn't designed with filming in mind. It's a park. There are many small bridges connecting one island. The power generator trucks and cranes couldn't get in; they couldn't drive them all the way to the set. Also, the courtyards and buildings we wanted to film in were huge, and the courtyard was completely surrounded on all sides by buildings. Behind it there was a river and in front of it there was a narrow street. We had to come up with a bunch of different possible solutions for the crane issue. In the end, we completely wrapped the building with three huge scaffoldings, and the lights were installed on the scaffolding. It was even taller than the building. The building was more than 20 metres high, making it very difficult to light.

Jia: What were your requirements for lighting?

Lu: In the early stages, we had some initial ideas about the shots. The colour we set up looked nice, even though there was some colour bleed, which was fine. Because it is a costume film, we tried to use fire to illuminate the scene, mainly with fire, candles and moonlight. We couldn't have any non-natural lighting effects from things like incandescent lamps and fluorescent lamps. Many times, my cinematographer went with fire, which looked very bouncy, very lively, very vivid. The end result looked great. The cool colour of the moonlight and the warm colour of the fire set each other off with a beautiful contrast. We actively designed these looks in the early stages. In terms of the colour matching of styling and art, we didn't choose to overdo it on the colour-blocking, but we did want as vivid of colour as possible. For example, the colour of bamboo forest, yellows and greens, with the hues and texture of the character's clothing on top. We found the richness of it all by basing our colour scheme ash grey tones.

Jia: So, you didn't deliberately set out to achieve a certain style, you mainly based everything on the environments on the set.

Lu: I did think about it at the beginning. We didn't want to use a colour scheme that evoked feelings of melancholy and looked too heavy or gloomy. I wanted the shots to have lustre, to have punch; with rich colour, but not so intensely red or blue. I wanted natural tones, but still saturated with colour. I wanted certain scenes to evoke the artistic stylings of classical Chinese paintings. Thought we didn't get it all exactly like I wanted, I trust it looks Oriental enough, and not in that Hong Kong Kung Fu flick kind of way.

Jia: It's the feeling of walking alone in the rain-drenched bamboo forest under an umbrella.

Lu: Right! I wanted this to be super-Oriental, but to have a youthful spirit to it. That's difficult to depict. But what we got on film I do like. I like how it sometimes gives a feeling of being completely saturated, wet from head-to-toe after the rain.

I Love Everything About Making Movies

Jia: The Director is the main guy on set, and each director leads the team differently. But one especially important point is that he wants his team to buy in to his ideas. I mean, when you're leading your team, getting everyone together to make a movie, what do you do to get everyone to buy in?

Lu: Most of my team's major production experience starting about a dozen some-odd years ago when I was in my twenties. We all loved movies, and wanted to make the movies we liked, so we slowly formed a production team. I've known my D.P. for about ten years now. My sound recordist has been a buddy of mine for about thirteen years, and my editors and I have been hooked up for about seven or eight years. We've been working together but have transcended the working relationship. We are like-minded artists. We practically read each-other's minds and finish each-other's sentences. Maybe people don't believe me when I say it, people might think I'm full of it for saying that, but it's really the way it is. We came together because of a mutual love of movies. If you film it, they will come, basically.

Jia: That's pretty rare to say the least. But in that situation, when your team is always together, isn't there a tendency to just fall back on old habits. A certain habitual style becomes prevalent, like a cliché or a pattern that you can't break out of. As a director, have you considered how to avoid letting these habits or patterns take over your work and how to initiate change?

Lu: For me, making a movie with a group of people who are very close to me is one of the greatest pleasures of the movie-making experience. I really enjoy the process. I hope that everyone in the process is happy too. Instead of going straight to the end result, we try to find the enjoyment in the process. For that to happen you have to have a group of like-minded people. Because they are with you, this movie turns out the way it does. It is possible to change to another team, but the movie would be different, and I like the movie just the way it is.

Jia: This is the team that you gradually got together during your university days, right?

Lu: Yes. We grew up together and we move together in stride. Everything we do is for the dream of making movies together. We always feel that we are still far from success and need keep on moving forward. And that's just how I like it.

Jia: You said that working with this team is one of your great pleasures. What part of the filmmaking process do you like most?

Lu: I liked almost every part of the filmmaking process. Of course, making a motion picture is very tough and very tiring. This film took me seven months to finish, including the editing, but the process is so engaging. Constantly coming up with new ideas and trying different edits. The audience may not realize that there is any difference between this cut and that cut, but we know that maybe changing one shot changes the entire logic of the scene, and the feeling changes. We tried lots of different things to arrive at the final cut. After the film was completed, there were the screenings, the meets and greet with the audience, the convention circuit, looking over viewer feedback – but it's all just part of filmmaking. I love everything about making movies.

I Don't Want to Make Movies for Other People

Jia: Could you say a few words about what you or other filmmakers would do to overcome difficulties in a commercial film environment?

Lu: The problems that I frequently run into everyone says can be overcome by trying to be more commercial. And sometimes when I go to film festival, some people might say that you obviously made the movie for the box office. And why did I even enter it into the festival in the first place? It's pretty contradictory if you ask me. I want to make movies that are beautiful to look at, but the way it usually plays out is that I get branded on both sides. I can't figure it out myself. But I don't want to make movies for other people. If you want it to be a blockbuster you have to make it like this; or if you want to get it into a festival, you have to make it like that.

A teacher once asked me why I wanted to make movies. He said that filmmaking should be based on one's own original creative impulses, rather than lots of set qualifications and pragmatic conditions. I think, we should still maintain our creative freedom, a certain creative consciousness or even a certain creative self. If you are not true to yourself, then how could you face your audience truthfully? So, no matter what, no matter how others see my films, I want to make them the way I like.

Jia: Was there ever a time in the making of this movie that you weren't sure about yourself?

Lu: For certain. Sometimes I think, we all worked so hard on the project, but tickets aren't selling very well. What was the point? Yes, we could sit there stewing over that if we wanted to, but it wouldn't help us to make movies in the future. Because people are just hard-headed. And I don't think it would do any good trying to change them anyway.

Jia: What's your summation of the overall environment of the Chinese film industry? Are there any shortcomings?

Lu: There are several. On one hand, it's the industry itself. China could learn the Hollywood approach and level up to a certain degree. The Chinese market holds more promise than any other film market in the world, because of its size. It's definitely determined by supply and demand, and this market will stimulate the development of a whole industry. But with respect to systemizing how we make movies, we are just not scientific or systemized enough yet. The Hollywood film industry got its success from its very scientific approach to film production. There are still a too many amateurish, unprofessional production methods in China. To put it bluntly, most of the time we're just flying by the seat of our pants. Accurate, precision filmmaking methods? What's that? That's something we don't have here.

Jia: And the problems you've run into are...

Lu: Right now, there isn't a producer in China who can accurately say for certain what all the post-production processes are. What's this indicator for? Why do we need to use this codec? They don't have a clue. It takes time to solve these problems. It may be five years, eight years or even ten years. After they're solved, there will be amazing revolutions in our film industry. Of course, there are other defects in our development. It's a problem that would be encountered in any movie market, which goes without saying. In another respect it may be the market, the audience. The power of the audience is huge, but I think the Chinese audience is very similar to the American audience; they have pretty extensive viewing habits. They have an appreciation for the good, the bad and the ugly.

Sometimes we are also considering whether we should make the film more for popular consumption, or maybe let go of some things we want to express, so that the audience will be more willing to receive the film. But, after grappling with it for a while, I still feel, if there are so many people doing this genre, do I have to do it too? Or will I go on my own and do the things I've been carrying around in my head for so long?

China's film market is massive to say the least, but we still have far less film selection than Japan and South Korea. Sure, we have a very artistically oriented audience, we can say that for certain because the *Paths of the Soul* made one-hundred million at the box office, which is particularly gratifying. But we can also see that the audience for that kind of movie is still small, and mainly concentrated in the first-tier or a few second-tier cities, and the population in the third-tier cities is really small. But actually, the current increase in Chinese movies is still in the third- and fourth-tier cities. *Wolf Warriors 2* had tremendous box office returns, but in the first- and second-tier cities...not so much. That's reality folks. If this particular demographic doesn't go to a movie like *Paths of the Soul*, it may not go to *Brotherhood of Blades* either. That's also reality. We have to consider how to adjust the relationship with the audience and how to guide the audience. I think the audience must have an appetite for popular movies, but the question is how to guide the audience to become fans.

Jia: To expand the audience.

Lu: Right.

Jia: That's the daunting part.

Lu: It's very tough, especially after the big-guns from Hollywood come storming into town. Sometimes the audience will thumb their nose at Hollywood movies, but the fact of the matter is that there is a double standard for home-grown Chinese films and Hollywood movies. To call a spade a spade, when Hollywood productions reach a certain scale, the audience just ignores many other problems. But for our home-grown films, if we can't reach that same scale of production, and we can't reach that same level of special effects, it doesn't matter if our movies are excellent in other ways, no one will even take notice.

Jia: That may be the case, but we rarely see the audience complaining about American movies.

Lu: I complain! But, tickets to the *Transformers* have been selling like gangbusters and the film's taken in more than a billion dollars at the box office. *The Mummy's* done over 600 million dollars in business, even amidst all the boos and hisses.

Jia: It may become a question of consumption habits.

Lu: There is even a guiding voice inside the audience that says, 'From January to August, I will keep the money for when I go to the cinema in September'. This voice is particularly biased, and unfair to home-grown films. The moment there is this dichotomy, it really doesn't matter how good the film critics say that the film is, but the audience says that it can always wait and just spend two RMB to see it online, because they will keep their money for imported films.

Jia: Double the promotion gets double the results. Right?

Lu: Right. For our own films, the audience is like eagle-eyes. They don't let you get away with a single thing. If the audience says it's bad, then you know it's really bad. The audience won't give it a second look. But if a filmmaker takes his job really seriously, I think the Chinese audience will still 'take care of their own'. That's the way I see it anyway.

Don't Let What Others Say Get to You

Jia: And finally, let's talk about distribution. Who's your target audience?

Lu: We were going for a summer release for *Brotherhood of Blades II*, we wanted to focus on the summer movie audience and students. But actually, the student demographic was a tough nut to crack, because *Brotherhood of Blades II* just had one week – just a week at the theatres.

Jia: Just one week?

Lu: Yes, the second week at the box office, our screening rate dropped to less than four per cent. The first week of release the film took in nearly 250 million.

Jia: So, what was the overall percentage of screens showing the film country-wide for the first week?

Lu: More than 20 per cent. If we could have hovered around the ten present mark for another week or two, making 350 to 400 million would have been a given. But a very strongly anticipated film was released the second week and our numbers were slashed in half, so our only really bankable week at the box office was the first week. Doing 240 million in a week is not a bad number, but there is a gap between the real figures and the estimates.

Jia: Are you satisfied with the release of the film?

Lu: I had no clue what a press junket was before this film. Because during the making of the *Brotherhood of Blades*, I didn't participate in any kind of promotion. But I really learned a lot from it this time. For one thing, I think that the promotion for this genre should mainly be target at its built-in audience. First of all, it will more thoroughly penetrate the demographic. I mean the audience that likes action films and costume films. And then some profit will come from that. For example, advertising to the female audience should focus on emotion. But, this time, we probably didn't penetrate the most basic demographics. I think we got a little too anxious to start making money. But promotion and collaboration were pretty good. The promotion and distribution teams were complete pros and very efficient. Everyone was really in sync. Our distributer also handled distribution for *Wolf Warriors 2*, so there were some resource allocation issues there. They definitely leaned more on *Wolf Warriors 2* than us in that second week. We understand, but next time we will definitely pay attention to this issue.

Jia: Expectations for *Brotherhood of Blades II* was an issue in its own right.

Lu: But there was that gap between what we thought and reality. It wasn't big, but it was there.

Jia: This stuff isn't easy.

Lu: Yes, because for me, the rock-bottom lowest number I would have willing to accept was 300 million. That's a difference of about 40 million. If, *Brotherhood of Blades II* could have kept playing on a reasonable number of screens through the second week of release, crossing the 300 million line would've been a cinch. And some other films stole our thunder for sure. But at that point, it was out of our hands.

Jia: *Brotherhood of Blades II* has been released abroad. You've got the feedback from foreigners on the film. Can they understand? Do they like it?

Lu: Before the Shanghai International Film Festival, filmmakers from San Sebastian were invited to watch the film. They invited us to participate, but the film festival was in September. They wanted us to premiere the film at the festival, but it's a summer movie, there was no way we could've done it. And yes, they can completely understand it, and there are no barriers to understanding. They didn't need a history lesson to get the film.

The film festival circuit has been quite welcoming for this Chinese film, which is an all-new experience for them. That includes the Shanghai Film Festival, there were some foreign buyers and programmers there. They were pretty excited to find a film like ours where the production team was all Mainlanders and did not need any of Hong Kong's help to make a film of this quality. That made me happy. We can't surpass the Hong Kong directors in making action films as they're at the top of their game. But we can at least give it our all and make the best film we can make, right?

When I started *Brotherhood of Blades*, all the production companies said that you can't shoot movies with costumes. Costumes are dead. The audience won't sign up for that. So, I said, why the heck not? Just because you say they won't? I have the right to make this film (laughs). No one could convince me I couldn't.

Jia: The box office numbers for *Reign of Assassins*, which was produced by the pre-eminent John Woo, weren't very good, and there are many possible reasons for that.

Lu: Yes. There are a whole host of reasons. But I think that the main reason why it didn't put people in seats had nothing to do with the genre, it's likely because there aren't many good movies of the genre.

Jia: A good film is not dependent on genre or theme.

Lu: Yes, sometimes the noise in the industry can steer the audience in the wrong direction. But we still have to try, we can't just give up, we can't listen to what anyone else says. That's the mindset I take with me behind the camera. Every character in the film told Shen Lian he was wrong. But he said, 'I am going to do it anyway'. I think some of my own beliefs and attitudes made it into the film.

Jia: Isn't it funny how that works? Sometimes whatever we're told we can't do we want to do all the more, and whatever we're allowed to do we have no interest in.

Lu: Yes, I'm increasingly convinced that we should always try to do whatever we're really interested in.

Jia: Let's just suppose for a second, and this hypothetical question is a bit on the extreme side, but... let's just say that you can only decide between two alternatives. You can either make a movie you don't like, and you can get a theatrical release, or you can make a movie you like, but can't get a theatrical release. Which one would you choose?

Road: I would always choose to make my kind of movie. Whether it gets into the theatre or not is immaterial. The only difference is money. But I care more about the process. Sure, it's always great to have big box office. Everyone wants to be validated in that way, but the most important thing in the world to me isn't money. It's the process.

Notes on Contributors

ChuanFa, Wan (万传法), Associate Professor, Department of Theater, Shanghai Theater Academy
Feng, Xu (徐枫), Professor and Producer, Department of Film and Television, Central Academy of Drama
Hong, Yin (尹鸿), Professor, School of Journalism and Communication, Tsinghua University
Hong, Zhang (张宏), Professor, School of Advertising, Communication University of China
HongYun, Sun (孙红云), Associate Professor, Department of Film Studies, Beijing Film Academy
Hui, Hu (胡慧), Master of Film Science, Grade 2014, Art Research Institute, Art Department, Communication University of China
Junjian, Liang (梁君健), Assistant Professor, School of Journalism and Communication, Tsinghua University
LeiLei, Jia (贾磊磊), Researcher, Chinese National Academy of Arts
Lihong, Hu (胡黎红), Associate Research Fellow, Art Research Institute, Art Department, Communication University of China
ShuGuang, Rao (饶曙光), Researcher, China Film Association
Weifang, Zhao (赵卫防), Researcher, Institute of Film and Television Arts, Chinese National Academy of Arts
XiaoLi, Zhang (张小丽), Engineer, China Distribution and Exhibition Association
Xiaoyun, Chen (陈晓云), Professor, School of Art and Media, Beijing Normal University
XiQing, Qin (秦喜清), Researcher, Chinese National Academy of Arts
Yan, An (安燕), Professor, School of Humanities, Southwest University of Communication
Yichuan, Huangfu (皇甫宜川), Researcher, China Film Art Research Center
Ying, Yue (岳莹), Lecturer, College of Communication Science and Art, Chengdu University of Technology